Advance Praise for *The 9 Steps to Keep the Doctor Away*

"In his new book, *The 9 Steps to Keep the Doctor Away*, Dr. Buttar lays out an effective system for ridding the body of toxicity and reestablishing a healthy internal environment. In a world where good health is now the exception rather than the norm, following Dr. Buttar's wellness plan will save lives."
—Jordan S. Rubin, *New York Times* bestselling author of *The Maker's Diet*

"You might be thinking, 'Oh, great, another "CAN DO" book that I can't do!' But you would be wrong and amazed to later learn that you had turned your back on one of the finest guidebooks ever written on how to *really* live. You can do it! And this remarkable book will show you exactly how."
—John Parks Trowbridge MD, FACAM, bestselling author of *The Yeast Syndrome*

"If you value your health and the autonomy to control your own physical future, this is an absolute MUST read. Filled with heartwarming true stories which illustrate practical steps anyone can master, this book is the light at the end of a dark and confusing medical tunnel."
—Greg S. Reid, *Wall Street Journal* bestselling author of *Three Feet from Gold*

"Dr. Buttar understands and acts to solve the fundamental problem of our time: You were not born to live in this world. Your environment has changed, and the toxic burden of modern life threatens your vitality. As an overfed yet undernourished nation, we struggle to find the roots of our native diet and to remove the buildup of modern toxins to live a vibrant and disease-free life. Dr. Buttar offers a clear and practical way to do just that: Eliminate the causes of chronic disease and find a true balance in mind, body and spirit. *The 9 Steps to Keep the Doctor Away* is desperately needed and highly recommended."
—Al Sears, MD, author of *The Doctor's Heart Cure* and *PACE: The 12-Minute Revolution*

"Due to his revolutionary innovations, Dr. Rashid A. Buttar is perhaps the most impressive health practitioner of the modern era. In this brilliant book, he 'spills the beans' on how to get healthy and stay healthy, based on his personal experience with literally thousands of patients from all over the world. In light of the abysmal health of many doctors, you might be inclined to follow the maxim, 'Never accept health advice from an unhealthy doctor.' But Dr. Buttar not only talks the talk, he walks the walk. He is a picture of health because he *lives* his own advice. This book is essential and will be life-changing. When I began to read it, I honestly couldn't put it down. It should be in everyone's library! Read this book! You won't be sorry."
—Ty Bollinger, author of *Cancer: Step Outside the Box*

"Dr. Buttar is awake! He brings 'Consciousness' to medicine, healing and health. That is who he is and why he does what he does. His role in helping all of us awaken to a new understanding of disease, of toxicity and of the possibility for our health has been assigned by the highest source. It is this preordained quantum convergence of old and new knowledge that has allowed him to help so many from all over the world. Dr. Buttar's favorite slogan, "Making the Change the World Is Waiting For," has already begun. And the possibility of a new, healthier and better world about to be born as a result is now becoming a reality."

—John Malherbe, founder, Harvard Medical School affiliate MSP Telemedicine SA

"Dr Buttar's new book, *The 9 Steps*, is a breath of fresh air. From his correct implication of vaccines as the principle driver of the multibillion-dollar health care system, he lays out a no-nonsense approach for getting and staying well. We have lost our ability to think for ourselves and have been incrementally enslaved with media brainwashing and medical misdirection on a global scale. His challenge to each person—take on self-education and implement self-responsibility—hits the bull's-eye for restoring health and reforming healthcare. Take the '9 Step' 30-day challenge. You'll be glad you did; your life and your future, literally, depend upon it."

—Sherri Tenpenny, DO, AOBNMM, author of *Saying No to Vaccines* and *Fowl! Bird Flu: It's Not What You Think*

"We face awful challenges from the toxic world we live in. Dr. Buttar's *The 9 Steps to Keep the Doctor Away* demonstrates clearly the power of healthy lifestyle choices and the tremendous need we have for optimal nutrition and multiphasic detoxification in order to thrive in today's environment. It can be done, and Dr. Buttar shows us how using these 9 simple steps. I really appreciate this wonderful guide to optimal survival and good health."

—L. Terry Chappell, MD, author of *Questions from the Heart* and past president of the American College for Advancement in Medicine and the International College of Integrative Medicine

"*The 9 Steps to Keep the Doctor Away* does in 352 pages what thousands of pages in the federal 'health care' takeover can't do. This book empowers you to restore yourself to health instead of government foisting 'disease maintenance' upon you while robbing you by taxation. Until we address the fundamental causes of disease, we will pay more, get less and remain ill with bodies that cannot heal. With these 9 Steps, you can avoid the 'disease maintenance' paradigm and reclaim your own body. If America were to awaken to these nine simple truths, there would be no 'health' crisis, and no need for government takeover to prop up a failed system."

—Robert Jay Rowen, MD, editor-in-chief of *Second Opinion* newsletter, www. SecondOpinionNewsletter.com

"As a seasoned and bold physician who has fully recovered his own son and thousands of other patients from poor prognostic conditions, Dr. Buttar is uniquely qualified to shed light on what will eventually become common 21st-century health care. America spends well over $2 trillion per year on a rich mixture of high-tech medicine, including useless diagnostics, defensive medicine, palliating symptoms with expensive and dangerous drugs and hopeless therapeutics for many cancers and autoimmune diseases. By implementing the simple but powerful advice in this book, individuals can prevent and reverse common ailments, while this country may well save itself from bankruptcy over our unmanageable health care costs. Highly recommended!"

—Patrick Quillin, PhD, RD, CNS, author of *Beating Cancer with Nutrition* and 16 others books that have combined sales of over 1.2 million copies

"Dr. Buttar's extensive knowledge and intuitive understanding of effectively healing disease by clearing the body of toxic burdens and regeneration of tissue by optimizing physiology has been compressed into a book that makes 'feeling better' simple to achieve and easy to follow. This book is an incredible gift and an effective tool for people who are not only looking to improve their physical health but also want to understand what the journey is all about. I loved *The 9 Steps to Keep the Doctor Away* and can't recommend it enough. Absolutely a must read!"

—Victor A. Marcial-Vega, MD, author of *Rejuvenation Protocol: A Nutritional Medicine Guide for Effective Healing* and ranked among the top 10 oncologists in the world in the *Alternative Medicine Definitive Guide to Cancer*

"Dr. Rashid Buttar has done it once again, this time in his book, *The 9 Steps to Keep the Doctor Away*. He has clearly demonstrated in his unique way how each one of us can take simple yet effective actions in our everyday lives that will cause a positive shift in body, mind and spirit, leading to optimal health and longevity. A wonderful book that I highly recommend!

—John Cline MD, author of *Detoxify for Life* and adjunct faculty member, Institute for Functional Medicine

"Dr. Rashid Buttar understands what is going on in the world of medicine. His eye is on the real medical basics (like mercury and other heavy metal toxicity) and what to do about them to bring a person back to health. He is a tough and forceful physician who does not run away from confronting the establishment and medical consensus when it is wrong, which it usually is. When others say nothing can be done about your condition, it's time to consult with Dr. Buttar. Read this book, for he will take you through some inner territory which most others will not be able to—or are incapable of doing so."

—Mark Sircus, Ac., OMD, author of eleven books on natural healing including *Sodium Bicarbonate: Rich Man's Poor Man's Cancer Treatment* and *Winning the War on Cancer*

A Few Words from Some of Dr. Buttar's Patients

"In 2001, I was diagnosed with stomach cancer. I was told that the best doctor in the United States who addresses the needs of individuals with cancer was Dr. Rashid A. Buttar. I immediately... flew directly to North Carolina to see Dr. Buttar. The rest, as they say, is history. I trust this man implicitly and have even put my own life in his hands. And I would do it again, without any hesitation. With this, his first book, Dr. Buttar has hit a Grand Slam! And believe me, I know books! This fantastic book is an owner's manual showing how the body really works while providing a game plan to achieve and maintain excellent health for you and your family. It is an absolute 'must read'!"

—Burton Goldberg, author of 18 books and 5 films on natural health and alternative medicine, including the worldwide distributed *Alternative Medicine: The Definitive Guide*

"As a patient of Dr. Buttar for more than seven years, I know firsthand the life-changing impact of his work, and I'm proud to call myself one of his many successes.... he is someone I have bestowed with the highest possible honor I could give—intrusting him with the care of my family. For the first time ever, Dr. Buttar is sharing his breakthrough findings through *The 9 Steps to Keep the Doctor Away*. This is a truly priceless opportunity—a glimpse inside the genius mind of Dr. Buttar. If you care at all about yourself, your family, and your future make this book, and the concepts included in it, a part of your daily routine. Don't wait for a health crisis in your own life to start preparing. Allow yourself to challenge traditional medical thinking and, most importantly, make the most of this precious gift. After all, the life you may be saving by adopting these principles might just be your own."

—Greg Provenzano, president and cofounder of ACN Inc., the world's largest direct selling telecommunications company providing services in 21 different countries

"Anyone who has any concerns about their health needs to read this book. It tells the truth in plain language so you and I can understand it, and does so candidly, without any concern or... fear of the FDA, mainstream medicine, and big drug companies. I became a patient of Dr. Buttar in March of 2003 after having four heart catheterizations (which didn't help) for blocked arteries that were causing chest pains and shortness of breath. I was seventy years old at the time. After tests, Dr. Buttar started me on a specific chelation program, changed my diet, and set me up on an exercise program. It didn't take long for my strength to start coming back, and the angina and shortness of breath became a memory of the past. I resumed a work schedule tailored to my own desires and meeting my needs. As I write this, I am approaching my seventy-eighth birthday, and play golf three to five times per week. I take no medications at all anymore and firmly believe I would not be living today if I had not found Dr. Buttar and started on his very sensible program. You can be helped too by reading this book and applying the principles outlined [in it]. Thank God for Dr. Buttar's research, beliefs, talents, and dedication to help others."

—Ned Jarrett, two-time NASCAR National Champion, inducted into 15 Halls of Fame and the only person in history to retire from NASCAR while still a National Champion

THE 9 STEPS TO KEEP THE DOCTOR AWAY

Simple Actions *to* Shift Your Body
and Mind *to* Optimum Health
for Greater Longevity

RASHID A. BUTTAR, DO
FAAPM, FACAM, FAAIM

Published by GMEC Publishing LLC
Lake Tahoe, NV

Distributed by Greenleaf Book Group LLC

For ordering information or special discounts for bulk purchases, please contact Greenleaf Book Group LLC at PO Box 91869, Austin, TX 78709, 512.891.6100.

Design and composition by Greenleaf Book Group LLC
Cover design by Greenleaf Book Group LLC

Publisher's Cataloging-In-Publication Data
(Prepared by The Donohue Group, Inc.)
Buttar, Rashid A.
    The 9 steps to keep the doctor away : simple actions to shift your body and mind to optimum health for greater longevity / Rashid A. Buttar. -- 1st ed.

    p. ; cm.

    Includes bibliographical references and index.
    ISBN: 978-0-9794302-4-4

1. Self-care, Health--Popular works. 2. Mind and body--Popular works. 3. Longevity--Popular works. I. Title. II. Title: Nine steps to keep the doctor away

RA776.95 .B87 2010
613   2010924092

Part of the Tree Neutral™ program, which offsets the number of trees consumed in the production and printing of this book by taking proactive steps, such as planting trees in direct proportion to the number of trees used: www.treeneutral.com

TreeNeutral™

Printed in the United States of America on acid-free paper

10 11 12 13 14 15   10 9 8 7 6 5 4 3 2 1

First Edition

Disclaimer and Implied Promise to Hold Harmless

All contents of this book, all educational materials referenced in this book, and all other material mentioned or referred to in this book (including DVD/video programs, audio programs, websites and any additional written material)—collectively known as "Dr. Buttar's educational materials"—are provided strictly for educational and informational purposes only. None of the aforementioned information is intended to give medical advice, nor can it be construed as medical advice, and it is not intended to diagnose, treat, cure or prevent any disease process.

The information and opinions expressed in this book are the author's and are based upon his education and experience only. Steps discussed in this book or shown in any accompanying material may not apply or suit every reader or viewer as a result of biological individuality and genetic uniqueness along with the variance of each individual's personal circumstances and health status. All these and other factors must be taken into consideration under the appropriate medical supervision of a physician with whom the reader has established a formal patient-doctor relationship.

Contents of this book and accompanying material must not, under any circumstances, be construed to have intended to replace, modify or effect in any manner whatsoever the treatment prescribed by your own attending physician. Any implementation of any ideas, information or suggestions provided in this book or from accompanying or referenced material must be undertaken only under direct advice, control and supervision of a competent, experienced, trained and licensed integrative physician (DO or MD).

By reading this book or using any contents from this book or any of the accompanying material, all readers thereby EXPRESSLY agree and warrant that all actions taken pursuant to and results arising from the reading or use of any of this book's contents or viewing of associated videos or accompanying material are their own acts and they bear the sole responsibility and accept the full consequences of their own actions, holding the author totally harmless and free of any liability. Furthermore, by reading this book, the reader agrees that the contents of this book and accompanying material do not provide advice, diagnosis, treatment or cure for any disease process.

In addition, by reading this book or accompanying material, all readers also wholeheartedly agree to hold the author, clinic, publisher, copyright owner, distributor, talent or any other party directly or indirectly involved with the creation or dissemination of this material harmless and not responsible for any direct or indirect consequences of actions taken pursuant to and results arising from the material (that is, the contents of this book and any of the accompanying materials, including video, audio or any other additional reference material), whether that material was read, heard, viewed and/or used in any way.

To my father, Abid,
who taught me that all things are possible

and

to my son, Abid (Abie),
who proved it!

Contents

Be careful of reading health books, you might die of a misprint.
—MARK TWAIN

FOREWORD

The purpose of a foreword can be many things; it can be a voice of authority or an endorsement of the pages and words that follow. It can be an attempt to explain the author's reason for writing at all. It can be a vote of confidence for the author or reassurance for the reader. It can calm the critic, and in some cases even attempt to explain the author's intention and aim. It can serve as a warning to be avoided by anyone with a rigid and scientific mind. It can open a door and invite the reader to take a closer look, beyond just the reading of words and the introduction of concepts. But when a subject is this important, it can be an invitation from the spirit that inspired it, to enter the spaces between words beyond the knowledge it transports and join the reader to the understanding . . . and change everything.

—JOHN MALHERBE

Life has key moments. Moments that come down to when you truly experience life fully, to a few pivotal people you meet, to a few profound books you read—all that will change your life forever.

This is one such moment. It is a moment where you can't deny the absolute truth anymore: the most important thing in your physical being and existence on this planet is your health. Scholars can argue all day about the most important thing in life, but without good health, you can't enjoy any of life's incredible blessings—not even silent and peaceful prayer.

This is one such moment where I have the huge honor—burden, role, duty, privilege, obligation—to share with you one of the most significant things that has impacted my personal life and that has awakened my awareness about my own health.

This is one of those books that while reading it you'll begin to wonder which isolated island you've been stranded on all this time. You'll find yourself asking why the lights of truth have been turned off for so long.

This is a book that embodies the spirit of one of those men that when you meet him, your life can't help but change, a change that is for the better.

This is a moment about change. YOUR change! A moment where you decide the terms about how you will carry forward whatever mission you have in this life, in this borrowed body.

Do you want to be an "average" human being and just let life pass you by, praying that you get unnoticed, living a life of mere existence, one mediocre day at a time?

If you answered yes, please do not waste your time any further. Stop reading this book now! But if you're honest with yourself, I would seriously doubt anyone would want to have such a life. And if you are really honest, you'll have to admit that nothing, and I mean *nothing*, is worth as much as your health.

If you are willing to improve your life and the life of those who you love dearly, if you seek optimal health, then this book will be your wake-up call. It will be your tool, your guide and your blueprint toward unlocking the secrets of "peak performance."

Why should you listen to this man, Dr. Rashid A. Buttar? Perhaps the best way to answer this question is by asking you a question.

When was the last time you met a doctor who repeats his creed so many times every day that you'd think he's obsessed? Who insists each of his staff take an oath to this creed after every single staff meeting?

His creed: "To Make the Change the World Is Waiting For." And the oath his staff take: "I vow to do more than my share in making the change the world is waiting for." Even his children take this oath!

I could go on and on about this man. However, I'll let you read his actions, his footprints, his adventures; let you experience the juice of his experience. You are about to embark on a rare adventure with a man unusually obsessed with enhancing and enriching the lives of others. A great man who strives to live his principles of optimal positive change so as to impact as many people as possible before he leaves this planet. A man whose obsession I can assure you I feel every time I talk with him. A man who you will experience firsthand yourself as you read this book.

It is my sacred duty, my obligation, to insist on the urgency and importance of this matter of your health.

Regardless of the state of your life now, whether you are in good health today or suffer from some terrible medical crisis, you deserve to know how good health is achieved, and once acquired, what you must do to maintain it.

Above all, you deserve to know what true health and longevity really mean. It is your God-given right to learn how you can attain it, but even more important, to experience the taste of it for yourself.

Ultimately, this book is about YOU for one reason. Because YOU truly matter: You are the center of your universe. Everything orbits around you. So, the question now is, how do you choose to live your life?

You owe it to yourself to embrace change, to share the concepts you'll be learning with the ones you love and those you care about most. Even if you don't believe in Karma, good deeds or just simply doing good, it's clear that our actions—and the consequences of those actions—have an impact and will make a difference in the lives of others.

Even if you read this book and do just one thing differently because of it, you will have implemented a change. This change will impact your environment. And by making your environment and entourage better, you will ultimately have made your own life better and the world a better place.

This is an invitation for you to open your mind and begin reading this amazing book. It's an invitation to ponder your life and ask yourself how satisfied you are with your current state of health. And then ACT. Act for change. Act to be the change! Strive for better. And spread the word.

How surprised will you be when people around you ask you how you did it? You will be able to tell them that somebody cared to dedicate his life and to sacrifice so much so that you could have a better one and that you are honored to share with them these 9 Steps of optimal health, just as I am honored to be able to now introduce them to you.

So make time for yourself. And may you be blessed with great health all your life.

Aymen
Vancouver

PRAYER FOR THE PHYSICIAN

*Before I begin the Holy work of healing the creations
of your hands, I place my eternity before the throne
of Your glory that you grant me strength of spirit and
fortitude to faithfully execute my work. Let not desire for
wealth or benefit blind me from seeing truth. Deem me
worthy of seeing in the sufferer who seeks my advice—a
person—neither rich nor poor, friend or foe, good man
or bad, or a man in need. Show me only the man.*

*If doctors wiser than I seek to help me understand, grant
me the desire to learn from them for the knowledge of
healing is boundless. But when fools deride me, give me
fortitude. Let my love for my profession strengthen my
resolve to withstand the derision even of men of high
station. Illuminate the way for me, for any lapse in my
knowledge can bring illness and death upon your creations.
I beseech You, merciful and gracious God, strengthen me
in body and soul, and instill within me a perfect spirit.*

—MAIMONIDES 1135–1204 A.D.

How Best to Use This Book

I've concluded each of the 9 Steps chapters with what I call a "Fast Wrap." In these summaries I address a series of questions that you yourself will likely ask after reading about each of the principles set forth in this book. These questions are variations on the following four themes: What is different about this principle? Why is this principle important to my health? How can I use this principle to improve my health? If I make this change, what can I expect? Each Fast Wrap is a summary to help you remind yourself about the essence behind each of the 9 Steps.

While reading this book, you will also notice at times that you may be directed to a "members-only, book owners' website." Access to this exclusive area is provided to all book owners absolutely free by simply answering a specific question that anyone with a copy of the book will be able to answer. This members-only area was specifically designed to provide you with additional information and further resources.

Those resources include audio lectures, video programs, and even substantial savings on items or services that I may have mentioned in the book, which will be made available exclusively to you as a book owner. All of the components on this website are designed to build upon the information provided to you in *The 9 Steps to Keep the Doctor Away*.

The book concludes with a section called resources. In it I provide brief details on additional resources that you may find of benefit. Many of these resources will be general in nature; more specific information continues in the exclusive members-only area of the book owners' website, accessible by visiting the www. The9Steps.com.

INTRODUCTION

One of the greatest pains to human
nature is the pain of a new idea.
—WALTER BAGEHOT

There are key moments in life when you're faced with a huge decision—one that will dramatically impact your future and the lives and futures of those around you. In rare instances, your decision could impact the entire world. Some refer to such moments as "crossroads," and the intensity and challenge we feel at these moments can be a wake-up call for radical change.

This is especially true in the sense that these metaphorical "crossroads" may present us with more than two distinct choices: We can accept the conventional paths, which are quite often the "easy" solutions. Or we can challenge the norm and take the road "less traveled by" so eloquently described in Robert Frost's poem.

In my case, I had the greatest of all possible motivations for taking the road less traveled. Ten months after I stopped seeing autistic children in my practice, my beautiful son Abie was born. He was a healthy, vibrant baby, but by the time he was a little over a year old, and shortly after having been vaccinated, he had lost his vocabulary of fifteen or so words and become "developmentally delayed."

Mainstream medicine said that there was simply nothing that could be done about his condition and that he would "grow out of it." By the age of three, there were no words and only a repetitive "dey, dey, dey." In the limited world of conventional medicine, this was a genetic problem and "defect"—something that could never, ever be cured, only treated with medicines to calm the child and keep them manageable. The solution they offered was nothing more than a chemical restraint. To this day, ask virtually any medical doctor about autism spectrum disorder (ASD) and you will get the same story—it's a genetic condition for which nothing can be done.

For most of you, it's easy to see the crossroads scenario I faced. I could either accept what the medical establishment told me about my son's condition—including its cause and treatment—or I could go the road less traveled and search for a real solution that could possibly return my son to me. In a sense, it was *impossible* for me to look into his bright little eyes and not choose the latter, more challenging path. In reality, however, there was no choosing. I only saw one path. A path that has often brought me criticism, ridicule and harsh treatment from others in my profession—no matter how extraordinary the results have been. And yet, I would make the same choice a million times over. Even if my life lay in the balance. Without even a moment's hesitation!

Even now there is nothing that brings me more peace than knowing I chose this direction—for I get to actually *see* and *experience* the incredible joy resulting from my choice every single day. For one, my son is now 100 percent free of any symptoms of toxicity, ASD or developmental delay—something the medical establishment said was impossible. And not only is Abie entirely free of symptoms, he's actually the picture of health—happy, energetic, a leader in his academic class and a world-ranked Black Belt martial arts triple crown state champion in his age group.

I cringe when I think what his life would have been like had I just accepted what the so-called experts and authorities had told me. And I can't imagine what life would be like for others—like the hundreds of children with vaccine injuries we've treated, some who nearly died from this common medical "treatment"—had God not blessed me with the faith, wisdom and conviction that *anyone* and any *condition* can be healed, as long as you're willing to take the road less traveled. The sad thing is that there are literally hundreds of thousands if not millions of people still out there who could regain their lives, if only they chose to take the path less traveled.

So what about you? What brings you here at this point in your life?

No Accidents

I personally believe it's no accident you're reading this book right now! Chances are, you've found this book because you're at a crossroads with your own health—perhaps even your life. Maybe you've received a frightening diagnosis or perhaps you just feel awful and don't know why. Or maybe it's your loved one who is facing these challenges.

Whatever your reasons, please know that you, too, stand at a critical juncture in the road, and what you do now, including how you use this book, can and will impact your life forever. You can choose to take the route most people take, which is to sit idle, blindly hoping that nothing bad happens and then potentially succumbing to the pressure of drugs, surgery and other standard medical treatments.

Or . . .

You can journey on a road far less traveled and take your health into your own hands—which is what this book is truly all about. I cannot promise you it will be easy every step of the way. Like me, you may need to endure doubt, ridicule and even attack. In addition, you will need to cultivate a great deal of patience, especially as your body takes the time it needs to reawaken its natural, God-given healing powers and abilities.

But I assure you that it's well worth it! There is absolutely no substitute for good health, and once you experience the awareness that your health is in *your own hands* (not "their" hands!) and realize the power of being in control of your own body, no person, institution or force on Earth can take that realization away from you. Your life will never be the same, and you can never be taken advantage of—or be manipulated by—any authority, no matter how great their station.

This will be new and uncharted territory for you, which is a good thing! However, please understand that taking this more challenging and infinitely more rewarding path is not without pitfalls and traps. One such pitfall is simply the tendency to think that you've "heard all this before" or that you "already know" the material, just because you've skimmed the table of contents and recognized the information within the 9 Steps.

The risk is that by concluding you already "know" something in the pages that follow, you could block yourself from opening your mind to another field of possibility. Maybe it's a new way to use one of the healing foods you hear about or another form of treatment that you hadn't fully considered previously. Don't make the mistake of assuming you already know (even if you really do) and fail to approach everything with a completely open mind. I've personally experienced this unexpected result when approaching a subject I thought I knew like the back of my hand and embracing this correct mind-set. Nearly all patients who have succeeded with my teachings and approach share this "open minded" philosophy, and I'm confident you'll have the same experience and learn more than you thought possible if you try it for yourself.

Speaking of avoiding assumptions and keeping an open mind, let's quickly address the subject of "experts." Claiming the title of expert implies that you know everything there is to know about a particular subject, that you have all the answers. It's an arrogance that immediately shuts you off from ideas that aren't your own. It's a nearsighted approach that keeps us locked up in our own little self-centered world, with no ability to see the bigger picture. When this happens, you stop asking questions. Without questions, there is no learning. Without learning, there is no growth.

This unfortunately characterizes much of my chosen profession despite so much new evidence to contradict their conventional beliefs and practices. Their assumptions about autism are just one example, but there are many others. In fact, I believe that we as a society have reached the point where our entire perspective on the subject of disease and healing needs to be questioned—because the current medical model is simply not working. To be quite blunt, the best results will be seen by those who release the limitations of their dying model.

Unfortunately, you will encounter resistance. Experts are afraid of leaving questions unanswered. Without providing answers, they risk losing their self-proclaimed authority. So, they stay where it's safe, in the familiar world they know. As a result, most "experts" I know aren't very courageous. Very few have the absolute fearlessness to jump into the unknown to further progress and to create advancement. I know. I've been blessed to have met such rare people, some of whom became my mentors.

Such fearlessness means trusting in something bigger than yourself, taking risks and despite not having all the answers, believing they will come. I've always felt that trouble begins when human beings claim to know more than the One who created us. That's why I've learned to prefer providing guidance over giving instructions and believe in advocacy before authority.

As a result, I've had to deal with tremendous ignorance in the form of authority that has really been the only cause of any trials and tribulations I've experienced in my professional life. But it was all worth it if it made a difference and saved even one person's life. I don't claim to be the ultimate medical guru. My work and results speak for themselves and yet, my ideas about medicine, my proven ideas, have been attacked numerous times by the medical establishment. Despite my being recognized by and having testified before the U.S. Congress, the medical hierarchy ignores the documented truth. Despite hundreds of people, including congressional staff members, having witnessed firsthand the indisputable truth with their own eyes, the facts are ignored, buried or ridiculed and the bearer ostracized, demonized and even persecuted. The good news is that if history is an accurate indicator, I'm keeping with good company.

It hasn't been easy but then, doing the right thing is rarely the easiest thing to do. However, my clinical success, which threatens the paradigm of the medical hierarchy or my conflicts with the medical establishment, is not what this book is about. History is full of stories where authority is threatened by evolution of new thought. It's no different in the medical profession, perhaps even more pervasive in medicine than any other profession. I've often said if advances in technology were measured by the decreasing size of a microchip, our current state of medicine would be like having a laptop computer the size of a small house.

The primary purpose of this book is to eliminate the misinformation you've been fed and to arm you with the real, practical, proven tools you need to achieve genuine change in your health. For more than eleven years, patients and professional colleagues alike have asked me to write my experiences down. Honestly, I've never had the desire, interest or time to write a book. I was always too busy trying to figure out a better and more efficient method of treating one toxicity or another or coming up with a newer, more effective therapy than what I already have had available in my arsenal.

But now, after years of seeing patients suffer from being caught in the same patterns of misinformation over and over again—and participating in the remarkable healing stories of hundreds of people whom all the "experts" had simply written off—I feel more compelled than ever to share this truth with all who desire to learn it. I have come to know these truths both professionally and personally to be fundamental to any discussion about health and wellness. If I accomplish anything through this book, it would be the hope to "deprogram" all the wrong information that you and thousands upon millions of others just like you have been indoctrinated with. I don't want anyone on this planet to ever have to suffer due to ignorance and the lack of this crucial information. Sure, some may not believe this truth but this book wasn't written for them. It was written for you, to provide real knowledge that can help you live a healthier, longer and more fulfilled life.

Handwriting on the Wall

The "old" way of practicing medicine is dying. Most of the misinformation that continues to be propagated in the name of medicine and science is actually harmful to your health over the long term. The flood of medical advice and nutritional information that inundates print, radio, TV and other media is more than just silly and untrue. It can be downright dangerous. Yet the more these standard conventions come into question, the greater the medical hierarchy and those who profit from it will try to defend them. And, unfortunately, the harder they will try to force them upon innocent people.

One example is the current issue of vaccines. The more information and evidence that surfaces to question the safety or effectiveness of vaccines, the harder the vaccine advocates try to eliminate your choice or freedom with regard to the issue. The Washington Redskins cheerleader we treated who received international coverage and nearly died after receiving a flu shot is just one such example. Yet there are millions of other lower-profile cases each year that go unnoticed.

That's a big reason why this book was written—to arm you with truths you won't find anywhere else. You see, the keys to true health you'll be learning in this book weren't taught to me in medical school. I didn't read them in a book, nor am I repeating something I heard on a video or during some radio show.

These truths, which we'll refer to as "the 9 Steps," arose from years of taking care of some of the sickest patients in the world, the "throwaways" of modern medicine, the ones who were told that nothing could be done for them or even worse, that it was "in their head." Can you imagine what it must feel like being in pain and misery and then being told by the people who are supposed to help you that it's all in your head? Unfortunately, many of you reading this book *can* imagine this because you've personally experienced this embarrassment we commonly refer to as "modern medicine" and its "standard of care."

I've been instituting the principles underlying these 9 Steps into a healing system in my clinic since 1997 when I opened my own practice after exiting the military. I have not only seen astounding recoveries from heart disease, autism, stroke, Alzheimer's, cancer and all the other chronic diseases that modern medicine says are incurable, but I've documented these recoveries with video and audio, in the patient's own voice and with clinical evidence and laboratory data to further objectively support the patient's own personal experience.

I'm here to tell you this one truth . . .

You Can Return to a Better State of Functioning and You Can Return to Vibrant Health

The contents of this book will lay the foundation for you to begin moving in the right direction to achieve this better state of wellness. For some, the steps we detail in this book will be all you'll need. For others, it will be the first step you'll take in regaining control of your health and your life.

At first, these essential principles won't be easy for you to incorporate into your daily life because they're most certainly *not* based on what you want to hear. But please know that I've observed these principles in clinical practice, and they have been taught to me by my most valued teachers: my patients. I'm talking about direct, tangible experience with thousands of patient cases since 1989 when I started my clinical rotations as a medical student.

However, having said that, I encourage you *not* to take what I've said as truth just because I said it. Rather, challenge me! Don't just simply take my word for it. I could be lying to you, just like most doctors are lying to you—perhaps not intentionally, but nonetheless, the effects are the same. Look up the information yourself. Learn all the different points of view. Understand the issues. Then, and only then, use the brain that God gave you to reach your own informed conclusion.

Doctors often expect patients to simply believe whatever they are told. Herein lies your first lesson. If a doctor becomes upset because you ask for more information or becomes nervous when you don't believe them simply because he or she "said so," you need to find yourself a new doctor. Run, don't walk. Remember that doctors are just human beings with a license to make life-and-death mistakes as long as they are using an approved method within the "standard of care."

For the skeptics reading this (God bless you all), I can only say that the vast majority of this information and all the clinical stories you'll read in this book have been documented by video, most often in the patient's own voice. In some cases, I may have blended two different patient stories in order to bring the salient point home as succinctly as possible. These are all real people with real health issues who triumphed against the "medical odds" by incorporating these 9 Steps you are about to learn. And behind every story lies a real truth from which you can benefit, if you take the necessary action.

Keep an Open Mind

I've had the privilege of hearing people tell me that I've either saved their lives or changed their lives forever well over a thousand times now during my nineteen years of practicing medicine. I've even been called the "best doctor in the world," the "most passionate speaker" and even a troublemaker, at times. Of course, I've been called other things that are not as complimentary as well. However, now it's only being called an "expert" that bothers me. I prefer to be known as "excellent" in what I do.

Before I turned thirty-five I realized that there was more to learn than could be learned during the limited time we have on this planet. It was a very humbling experience, especially because what I thought I knew, I didn't really know. So this book becomes my challenge to you—to your body and your mind. It will challenge you to open yourself up to a much greater understanding of things you thought you already knew.

It will challenge your body as you watch it pass limits that you thought were unreachable. You can achieve a level of health beyond anything you've imagined, but you have to first believe that it *is* possible. And you must also actively choose to engage. Don't worry about having the answers for everything. Just step into the unknown with me and accept the challenge.

After reading this book, and especially after you choose to take action on what you've learned, you'll understand why I do what I do and you'll learn what fuels me. For now, all you need is the *desire* to keep an open mind and the *ability* to take action.

Final Words Before Starting

Make a commitment right now to follow this program for the next thirty days. I am absolutely confident that the changes you'll experience and level of health you'll come to enjoy will astound you. I know. I live these 9 Steps daily. And I've seen it many, many times make the necessary difference in the lives of my patients. In fact, these 9 Steps often are the difference between success and failure in treatment of people who are severely ill. For you, chronic conditions you may have been dealing with for years will significantly decrease and, with *appropriate* medical intervention, sometimes even cease to exist. The result is you'll enjoy a quality of life and a level of functioning you never thought was possible.

Start with an open mind. Forget everything you thought you knew. Begin with a clean slate. Bernie Siegel, MD, once said, "There is no such thing as an incurable disease, only incurable people." Choose to become "curable" and make this investment in yourself, because your health is the most valuable asset you can possess. Get excited! Get committed! Get ready to experience the change of your life!

For those who understand, no explanation is needed;
for those who don't understand, no explanation is possible.
—DAVID R. KAMERSCHEN, PHD, PROFESSOR OF ECONOMICS,
UNIVERSITY OF GEORGIA

JUST ANOTHER SELF-HELP
HEALTH BOOK?

The possession of facts is knowledge, the use of them is wisdom.
—AUTHOR UNKNOWN

The words didn't quite register. "I'd rather die than let you bastards touch me again."

She was a cancer patient with intense bitterness about her experience with the medical establishment, and she had somehow found herself in my emergency room. In addition to anger, there was palpable fear and frustration in her eyes. I was turning to leave the ER bay after giving her the devastating news that her cancer had recurred and she needed to revisit her oncologist when she almost spat the words out. I didn't know what to do or say. I was in shock. I sat down next to her, something I had a reputation for never doing when working in the ER. I was looking down at the floor, staring at my shoes trying to think what I could do or say to make things different, and at the same time thinking why her words had cut me so deeply. When I did finally look up at her again, her eyes had softened. I suppose she could see that I was trying. And then I suddenly remembered a television report I'd seen a few weeks earlier.

The show was a segment on *20/20* called "Sharks Don't Get Cancer." It came to me in an overwhelming rush. The story focused on the work of Bill Lane, PhD, a biochemist who had been successful in treating a number of patients with solid tumors using shark cartilage. Dr. Lane had expanded upon a theory first put forth by Harvard researcher Dr. Karl Folkers, who discovered that certain types of cartilage were effective in cutting off the blood supply to tumors—in effect, starving them to death—a process known as antiangiogenesis. Eleven years later, I would tell Dr. Lane this story and watch him beam with pride, knowing that he had helped in some way to influence me, an event that eventually led to a change in my course in medicine.

Prefacing my statements with a disclaimer and a request for the patient not to say anything to the other doctors (after all, I had a reputation of being a "good" doctor), I shared what I'd learned about shark cartilage on *20/20*. I made no promises. Although in my mind I questioned if what I was doing was right, there was no doubt that it definitely *felt* right. Was there anything else I could offer her?

What I'd done really felt right. And as if in confirmation, her eyes showed that she was very grateful. Was it the information? Or was it the simple fact that I had sat down with her? Perhaps, for the first time, I gave her some genuine *hope*. Or maybe, just maybe, it was merely the reflection of myself I saw in her eyes, grateful because she had rescued me from the close-minded abyss into which I had been unknowingly sliding.

In my heart I knew I wasn't "one of those bastards," but, looking back, I couldn't help feeling that I may have acted like one many times. But now, suddenly I didn't feel like "one of those bastards" anymore. At that moment, I realized I was feeling a familiar but almost forgotten emotion, one that I had rarely experienced for a patient. I had felt it for one of my goats that had died on my farm, as well as all four times I had lost my dogs. But it had been a long time since I'd felt that for a patient—maybe not since I had originally been drawn to the medical profession when I was a Medical Explorer in high school.

It was strange, as if I had accidentally run into a long-lost friend I hadn't seen in years. I felt hope for her and an overwhelming amount of emotion, which almost seemed out of place. I had nothing else personally to offer this woman and really wanted this shark cartilage to work for her.

I discharged her with instructions to follow up with her oncologist, with whom I talked before discharging her. He didn't seem impressed with the shark cartilage idea but was okay with it "if it made her feel better." She left the ER giving me a warm pat on my shoulder, looking at me now with smiling eyes, which made me feel better about myself. I remember thinking it was strange that although she was the patient, I was the one who felt better after the encounter—almost as if I was the sick one and she was trying to make me feel better! That little bit of information was all I could offer her, and I told her to get a copy of the show from *20/20*. I never expected to see her again.

Unexpected Inspiration

About three months later, a smiling, elderly lady walked into the back entrance of the ED, carrying a fruit basket. For a moment, she looked remotely familiar as she hurried toward me waving a paper. And then I recognized her. It was the elderly cancer patient I'd had such a powerful interaction with just a few months earlier. She looked stronger and had obviously gained some weight. She handed me the basket and then held up a CT scan report for me to see. It was a report dictated the day before showing that her tumor had shrunk by more than 75 percent!

She had not undergone any further surgery, chemo or radiation that had been recommended. She had only started taking the specific type of shark cartilage that had been described by Dr. Bill Lane. The fact that her condition involved a recurrent, very aggressive tumor made her outcome even more astounding. Word spread, and from that day on, people came to me in the ER asking questions about their medical conditions when they wanted a "more natural" approach. Even doctors from the departments of internal medicine, family practice and orthopedics sent patients to me in the ER when patients requested information other than the routine pharmaceutical interventions. That was early spring of 1995.

I ran into that little lady only once more in the following months. After that, I never saw her again, but the power of her words still permeates my life and practice. They were the words that led me down the path that eventually allowed me to seek to become a true healing conduit of the Creator's power. It was those words that eventually led me to open my clinic a few years later just north of Charlotte, North Carolina, in the Lake

Norman area. In many ways, it is because of those words that you hold this book in your hands today.

On a side note, please don't go out and get shark cartilage, expecting to treat tumors. This lady was fortunate, but by no means is this indicative of the general response most people have. There are many specific components necessary to address the needs of an individual with cancer. For example, cancer is a symptom of a deeper underlying issue, related to some form of toxicity which has by definition, caused some type of damage to the immune system. This toxicity and resulting damage to the immune system must be addressed or the cancer will come back. There are many other additional issues. You will be directed to this information, if you have an interest, via the members-only area that has been set up for book owners, which you get access to at no additional cost.

A Nation Spinning Out of Control

The rate of disease in the United States has risen dramatically over the years. In fact, a report from the Milken Institute released in 2007, titled "An Unhealthy America: The Economic Burden of Chronic Disease"[1] showed that despite the significant improvements in therapies and treatments, more than half of all Americans now suffer from one or more chronic diseases, creating a huge, invisible and growing burden on health-care costs. According to the authors, these conditions cost the United States, alone,

---

1 Ross DeVol and Armen Bedroussian, with Anita Charuworn, Anusuya Chatterjee, In Kyu Kim, Soojung Kim, and Kevin Klowden. October 2007. *An Unhealthy America: The Economic Burden of Chronic Disease—Charting a New Course to Save Lives and Increase Productivity and Economic Growth.* Available: http://www.milkeninstitute.org/publications/publications.taf?function=detail&ID=38801018&cat=ResR. Last accessed December 4, 2009.

$1.3 trillion per year in lost productivity and treatment. By 2023, the report projects a 42 percent increase in the rate of chronic disease, raising overall costs to a staggering $4.2 trillion! Yet there is a silver lining in these eye-opening numbers. For instance, if we are able to reverse even a portion of the projected numbers simply by empowering people with effective preventive measures, health information that actually works and "good medicine," we could avoid 42 million new cases of chronic disease. On top of that, we could increase the gross domestic product (GDP) by $905 billion just from the renewed productivity.[2] It all sounds overwhelming, but it can happen, and it will happen, one person at a time. However, as with everything in life, it will only happen if we believe it's possible and if we take the action necessary to make it happen.

No matter how advanced medical technology becomes, I've always believed in the divine intelligence of the human body and the body's innate ability to heal itself. I sincerely believe that each and every one of us, regardless of whether we have cancer or heart disease or any other serious chronic medical condition, has the ability to return to a natural, disease-free state of optimum health and vitality.

If you do have a life-threatening condition, you must do two things immediately. First, find a competent and experienced doctor. Then, make these 9 Steps a part of your life, immediately and permanently, in order to get better. Even if you don't have a serious health problem, there's no reason to wait. Now is the time to make these lifestyle modifications so that you exponentially decrease the chances of ever having to deal with a life-threatening chronic illness. By the way, you will also be provided with

---

2 Ibid.

a network of highly skilled and incredibly talented physicians whom I've personally worked with and trained and whom I can recommend without any hesitation, available in the members-only area of the book owners' website.

Beware of This Dangerous "Answer"

One of the most prevalent and most dangerous perspectives in modern medicine has been to simply attribute diseases like cancer, heart disease, stroke, diabetes and arthritis, plus a host of other medical problems, to the aging process. You either get it or you don't, and other than following some very basic food recommendations, we're essentially told we have no control over our bodies from a disease prevention standpoint.

How do I know? Well, I've seen patients in my clinic from thirty-seven different countries representing every continent in the world, express to me how other doctors have told them not to worry about their ailments because they're "just part of getting old." Sweeping these conditions under the all-inclusive rug of "aging," just because doctors can't provide an adequate answer, is one of the greatest untruths and blatant cop-outs in medicine. It's NOT because you're getting older! It's because your doctor doesn't have a drug to cover up the symptoms of increasing oxidative stress.

Virtually all of these so-called aging issues result because you haven't been correctly told what you need to do on a daily basis to prevent these conditions from developing. To attribute these conditions to the aging process is an admission of how ignorant we doctors are about the causes of chronic disease, as well as a pathetic excuse to placate the patient and appease our own sense of inadequacy. It's proof of our inexcusable ignorance and blatant arrogance that just because we don't understand, therefore it *cannot* exist.

When you're driving on the highway, notice the other cars on the road. Most are new or relatively new. However, a large group of the cars are anywhere from seven to fifteen years old . . . and they look like they're old. The paint job isn't as good anymore and they've got their share of rust spots and dents. Of course, there are also the junkers that have no business being on the road.

But on a rare occasion, you'll also see a car that may be thirty or forty years old and yet it doesn't have a scratch on it. The paint is perfect and the chrome is gleaming. The owner is driving with his head held high, and people are craning their necks trying to get a glimpse of that "gorgeous car." The price? Well, the price of the car is ten or more times higher than when it was brand new. It's now considered a "classic."

What's the difference between that classic automobile and the junker or the car that's seven to fifteen years old? After all, the junkers are less than half the age of the vintage model, and the technology in the seven-to-fifteen-year-old cars is far more advanced than that in the vintage. Is it the quality of the workmanship of the classic car? No; otherwise, all the cars of that model and year would still be around. Is it the technology? No: the technology in the seven-to-fifteen-year-old cars far surpasses the vintage roadster.

Obviously, the answer is how well the car was taken care of. It's what the owner of the car did every single day, on a consistent basis, to ensure that the car would last a lifetime and not become a junker. Do you see the point?

If you do all the right things on a regular basis, get your oil changed, use the best type of gasoline, get your paint waxed, belts tightened, filters cleaned, fluids drained and refilled, take care of the upholstery and maintain your "vehicle" with care and love, you too can look every bit as amazing as you did during your thirties—maybe even better!

Inflammation—The Good and the Bad

Even though most doctors and scientists see disease and aging as unavoidable, there is a growing exception, which gives hope to a new thought process. This good news on the horizon comes from a small but ever-growing group of scientists who believe that the ultimate cause of all the chronic diseases is oxidative damage due to free radicals. Notice I didn't say "virtually all" or "almost all." I said "all!" Yes, genetics does play a role in predisposition, but it is toxicity-induced oxidative injury that causes the disease process to start in the first place.

We'll talk in more detail about the nature of "oxidative injury" and "free radicals" later. But for now, just keep in mind that any substance that accelerates the process of oxidative damage or oxidative stress is considered a "free radical." Thus, a heavy metal or a persistent organic pollutant (POP) would be considered a "free radical," as would any atom that has lost an electron, for example, as a result of having been exposed to that heavy metal or that persistent organic pollutant.

The overall process is sometimes referred to as oxidative stress or the "reduction reaction." This process results in oxidation, or the free radical reaction commonly known as the "rusting process." The cell membrane is one of the most susceptible areas of the body to this oxidative injury. Damage to cell membranes from free radicals causes lipid peroxidation, or oxidative injury to the lipids that comprise the cell wall. This oxidative reaction causing injury lasts merely a fraction of a nanosecond, but the resulting inflammatory response may last for hours or even days.

Science has been aware of this fact for quite a long time, but it was not until the turn of the century that this concept became popular as an important contributor to aging. Today, inflammation is widely accepted as a leading cause of aging. Although overly simplified, this concept has huge implications.

Before going on, let's define some terms first. Free radical damage or the reduction reaction, also known as oxidative injury, is the simple process you see happening when a banana turns brown after having been peeled and allowed to sit in open air for a few minutes or what happens a few minutes after cutting an apple. It's the same process that happens to a nail that slowly rusts while sitting out in the rain. Oxidative stress in fact can be simply thought of as the rusting processes in a system that is alive. It's this same process that is also responsible for the slow but steady onslaught of aging.

Therefore, it would be a forgone conclusion to assume that if oxidative damage was the cause of accelerated aging, then slowing down oxidative injury would theoretically slow down the aging process. In actuality, that is exactly what happens. By reducing the source of oxidation and the resulting inflammation in the body, you can essentially slow the aging process down. We may not be able to stop oxidative damage completely, but we can significantly reduce the extent of oxidative damage by removing any source of oxidation (removal of toxic substances acting as and creating more free radicals) and thereby reduce inflammation.

We can also reduce this inflammatory cascade by changing our habits and making specific lifestyle choices.

Even as you continue to grow in chronological years, this process can be slowed. In one of the later chapters, we'll discuss an incredible advance in science, which occurred more than ten years ago, that reduces this cascade of inflammation from occurring. Although this advance in science has relatively gone unnoticed, it is the secret of many of the rich and famous and those who make it a point to remain informed and stay young.

Crucial Organs of Detoxification

It's essential for you to have a basic understanding of how your body works. This knowledge is the most powerful tool you can have to preserve or rebuild your health, particularly because it will prevent you from being misled by others. It begins with understanding that there are certain organ systems that play a much greater role when it comes to regulating the amount of toxins that enter and leave our bodies, which eventually determines how you attain and maintain a state of good health.

Each organ has a vital role, but the simple truth is, the four most important organ systems in the body related to detoxification are among the four primary organs of elimination. These four are the hepatic system (liver); the gastrointestinal system (stomach and intestines, also known as the GI system); the renal system (the kidneys); and the integumentary system (skin), which is the largest organ of elimination. The liver and the GI system are arguably the most important for detoxification and nourishment—*the two major components of healing and rebuilding.*

If the liver or the GI system is not functioning properly, your body becomes highly vulnerable, and when they stop functioning, death will soon follow in a slow and agonizing manner. Disease establishes itself and stays when these four organs of detoxification are not properly functioning, resulting in what we call a "chronic" condition. And as you'll learn later, disease will stay as long as these key systems are not functioning optimally.

Progress at a Price

According to the World Health Organization (WHO), 80 percent of all deaths in the industrialized world are from heart disease or cancer.[3,4] Think about this for a second. The combined total of all the human deaths that result from every single cause of death—including all natural disasters, all wars, trauma, suicide, crime, car accidents and dozens of other causes in every industrialized country, including every other single disease processes besides cancer or heart disease—represents just two out of ten deaths in the modern world. Cancer and heart disease represent the remaining eight out of every ten deaths in the industrialized world!

No other cause of death comes anywhere near the number of lives taken by cancer and heart disease! That's stunning to me, but if you spend ten minutes in any public area, you begin to see the reason why. Far too many people are overweight, out

3 Dr. E. Krug. 1998. *Leading Cause of the Global Burden of Disease.* Available: http://whqlibdoc.who.int/hq/1999/WHO_HSC_PVI_99.11. pdf. Last accessed March 21, 2004.
4 World Health Organization. 2004. "Annex Table 2: Deaths by cause, sex and mortality stratum in WHO regions, estimates for 2002" (pdf). *The world health report 2004—changing history.* http://www.who.int/whr/2004/ annex/topic/en/annex_2_en.pdf. Last accessed November 11, 2009.

of shape, engaging in terrible habits and unable to maintain a healthy diet.

In the last ten years, the human population has seen a significant increase in the diagnosis of various chronic diseases. Those who wish to hide the truth and placate society attribute this increase in diagnoses to better technology and testing. But that simply is not the case and once again, completely opposes the truth.

Any ethical biostatistician or epidemiologist would confirm this just by glancing at the data. Remember, the secret is simple observation and a little common sense. For example, since the 1920s, millions of new chemicals have been developed, and as a result, many of these synthetic substances have since been introduced into our environment. There are now well over 32 million synthetic chemicals that have been developed and are being used within the global economy, and that number is increasing by more than 1 million per year.

According to the World Watch Institute (www.worldwatch. org) in a report released in 2000, a new chemical was being synthesized every twenty-seven seconds. That of course has now increased. Although 99.5 percent of these substances will remain academic curiosities, well over a 1,000 of these substances enter the global economy in enormous quantities every single year. More than 110,000 synthetic substances are now in international commerce, but the number is far greater in our environment due to byproducts (example: dioxins) that are generated during the production of these substances. Such chemical innovation creates an astronomical biological risk beyond our ability to fathom. The implications on the environment and within our systems are beyond our comprehension. The physiological burden is so phenomenal that we're just beginning to scratch the surface of the consequences.

I believe that the reason we have greater chronic disease today is because of this chemical innovation, which inadvertently increases the toxic burden within our systems. Along with a consistent departure from the specific things the ultimate biological engineer wanted in our bodies, chronic disease has now become inevitable. As we take more toxic substances into our bodies, we hasten the oxidative injury and the resulting inflammation and aging process. And unless we take action to counter these trends, we will experience a continued increase and further progression of human suffering on an unimaginable scale.

Through my direct experience with thousands of patients during nearly twenty years, I have witnessed a specific set of choices that, when acted upon, consistently activate the body's innate healing system and dramatically arrest the aging process. What I've come to refer to as the 9 Steps to Optimum Health, most recently now described in this book as *The 9 Steps to Keep the Doctor Away*, will help you improve your overall quality of life and state of health. These 9 Steps will show you exactly what you need to do to stay ahead of the ever-increasing train of oxidative injury that is always nipping at our heels.

The Way Out

Cleaning up a toxic world is a monumental task. Cleaning up our individual lives is equally monumental, but it is simpler in the sense that we have greater direct control. The goal of this book is to give you the important "take home" practical steps with the most important life-preserving information available at your fingertips. Some of this information will help you reduce the toxic substances in your body that contribute to poor health and early aging while helping you overcome much of the damage you can't avoid simply because we live in a toxic world.

These 9 Steps are absolutely essential to any healing process. Without them, it's like trying to put a puzzle together with more than a third of the pieces missing. You'll never get the full picture, and you'll certainly never reap the full benefits of enjoying the completed puzzle. Can you make a full recovery without these 9 Steps? Yes. But it will be far more difficult to get better, and the little recovery that is achieved without the 9 Steps will be short-lived at best.

Also, pay special attention to the Three Foundations I will describe before we get into the 9 Steps. Understanding these Three Foundations is essential and will provide you with the target for which the 9 Steps will serve as the arrows. Just as a highrise building with nine floors needs a strong foundation, these Three Foundations provide the necessary strength, support and environment in which the 9 Steps can really begin working and your health can, in turn, truly flourish.

Are you ready? I challenge you to take the first step in regaining control of your own health. The time for all excuses is over. This isn't a softball approach. If you can come up with even one excuse why it's too difficult to apply these 9 Steps to your life, no matter how logical your reason, then this book is NOT for you. It's a waste of your time. Why? Because excuses tend to multiply like an untreated infection—you must stop them at the source. No exceptions.

If, on the other hand, you're finally fed up with your state of health or how you feel and you're willing to do the work it takes to lead a life of vitality, regardless of what that work entails, whatever the price is, then this is the right book for you. Don't look to this book for the feel-good material that's going to placate you, justify why you feel like a victim so you can get sympathy or insist that your current state of health is someone else's fault. This book does not have the fluff that fills the pages of most of the best sellers in this genre. The goal is not to become a best seller (although that would be nice) but rather to elicit the best change in your health, which will impact the rest of your life in a positive manner.

As already stated, we know that knowledge is power and once you have that power, you get to choose what you allow into your life. You become a creator in the deepest sense and your own innate wisdom will help you to choose how to use this increasing power. And the power is what gives you the ability to make the changes necessary to reap the rewards of having acquired that knowledge in the first place.

Remember: Every choice you've made in your life up to this point has led to your current state of health. In fact, this is true with everything in your life, not just in the arena of your personal health! It's a tough pill to swallow, but it's the truth. You've chosen what to do with your body. You've chosen what to put inside your body. And you've chosen what to put inside your mind.

Claiming full responsibility is painful, but it's also the beginning of the miracle because if you had the power to get yourself into this situation, then you most certainly have all the power you need to get yourself out. That's why anyone who opts to be a victim is doomed, simply because you give up the power when you're a victim. You also can't attain the power if you don't claim the responsibility for using it. It's time to accept the responsibility and claim the power and begin your journey back to optimal health! By doing so, you'll be able to keep most doctors away and, let's face it, that in itself will help you stay healthier longer.

By applying the principles in this book, you will begin to construct and activate a "medical matrix" in your life where science and spirituality can't help but come together. You will consciously begin to create your health through universal laws that are as certain as the law of gravity. What goes up MUST come down. For every action there is an equal and opposite reaction.

Positive change is a foregone conclusion. It's not a question of IF health returns or improves but, rather, *when*. You will become the guide in a God-given process that restores and maintains vibrant health that's exponentially superior to any pill, device or surgical procedure. So begin by assuming responsibility for your own health, take back your power and begin the journey to a place of health and healing that, up until now . . . you've only imagined.

The Correct Mind-Set

During this journey, I also want you to think about rebuilding your health as if you were building a house. The first eight steps are the wood, windows, doors, roofing supplies, tools, nails, electric wire and so on. The ninth step is the "finishing material"—such as the paint, crown molding, window treatments, etc.—that makes the "house" beautiful and all "your own."

But make no mistake. The ninth step is also acting as the general contractor, making sure things you are not aware of are being addressed, enhancing the processes and optimizing everything to reach perfect balance.

Before you begin your journey, just as in building a new house, we need to ensure that you begin to build your new dream home of health on a sound, solid and secure foundation. You obviously don't want to build a house on sand, right? The Three Foundations we are going to discuss next are the concrete, cinder blocks and steel pilings you'll need to have in place before creating a house that is strong and unshakable.

I cannot stress enough the importance of building your house from the bottom up by starting with these Three Foundations first. The reason why most people attempt to change their diet, add a little exercise and perhaps do one or two other things only to see limited improvements, if any, is because they have no foundation for what they are doing.

Their entire structure is built on sand or mud, and upon the opening of the door, everything begins to slide and collapse. It's the difference between being one of those huge, stately, 100-year-old Colonial homes you see in the middle of small town America compared to a house trailer that will deteriorate and collapse during a strong storm. Which would you rather be living in? So let's get started and begin building.

Real knowledge is to know the extent of one's ignorance.

—CONFUCIUS

THE THREE FOUNDATIONS

The human body has been designed to resist an infinite number of changes and attacks brought about by its environment. The secret of good health lies in successful adjustment to changing stresses on the body.
—HARRY J. JOHNSON

Karen's Story and the U.S. Congress

When Karen came to me, she was at the end of the line, literally. I was the sixteenth doctor she'd seen in five years, with most of them having told her she was depressed and needed to be on antidepressant medication. She was just thirty-four years old but was suffering terribly from a list of seventeen odd and different symptoms, which included problems with facial hair, lactating breasts, loss of libido, joint pain, muscle aches, balance issues, articulation difficulties, heart palpitations, gait problems, chest pain, headaches, blurry vision, anxiety, depression, confusion, memory loss and hearing disturbances.

At the end of describing the odyssey she'd been through, she said to me, "Dr. Buttar, if you can't help me, I'm going to *help* myself." As she made that statement, Karen patted her purse. To this day, I don't know if she had a gun or drugs in there or what her intentions were, but I knew that I was dealing with a very desperate woman.

After making her promise me that she would NOT hurt herself (I would have had to admit her for suicide precautions had she not promised), I reassured her that I felt confident I could help her. Judging from all the symptoms with which she was presenting and my experience with heavy metals, I knew it could be just one thing—mercury poisoning.

"But I've already been tested for mercury," Karen said. "There's nothing there."

I told her that blood tests for mercury are useless. Many of the metals are so toxic that the body ushers them right out of the blood stream and isolates them in the deeper tissues. For instance, lead is preferentially stored in bones and mercury in fat and the myocardium (striated muscle that makes up the heart). A challenge test needed to be done, followed by a timed urine collection.

"But that's what I had done, Dr. Buttar," Karen answered. I was a bit confused so I requested her previous medical records from the doctor who had reportedly done this challenge test.

When I received Karen's heavy metal challenge test from the doctor in a city about five hours away, I was stunned. Her mercury registered a level of just 2.5 ug/g creatinine. Anything less than 3 ug/g was considered "normal." I didn't know her former doctor, but he knew who I was and was in fact using my testing protocol. Apparently he had heard me lecture at a medical conference, and the challenge test records I received were on a form titled "Buttar Challenge Protocol."

This doctor had done exactly what I would have done. Still, the results just didn't make any sense. No amount of mercury is safe in the body, but this was well below the elevated range where symptoms should be manifesting. I would have bet a full year's salary that there was a lot more mercury in her body. Thinking that it was a lab error, I asked her to retest.

The second test came back at 2.8 ug/g creatinine. Now I was really confused. I had no explanation. For the first time in my medical career, I felt that I couldn't help someone because I didn't know what was happening with this woman. The one thing I was certain about was that it was not "in her head" as she had been told by most of her previous physicians, one who even went so far as trying to put her on antipsychotic drugs.

"Can you still help me, Dr. Buttar?" Karen asked. There was almost a pleading in her voice, a sound that you usually hear when someone is truly holding on by just a string. I didn't want to say "no," and yet I couldn't say "yes" because I didn't know what was wrong with her.

She changed the question. "What would you do if I were your sister?" she asked.

Little did I know that this simple question would eventually change the future of my own life, both personally and professionally, as well as the future of tens of thousands of children and hundreds of other doctors all over the world. It was one of those rare pivotal moments, imprinted exactly in your mind—only realized when looking back from the future—when everything would have turned out different if another course of action had been chosen.

I've always regarded my patients with the highest esteem and deepest respect because they are often moving into the unknown with me and have entrusted me with their lives. It's a responsibility that I don't take lightly, and I would like to think I treat them no differently than I would treat a close family member. But Karen's response to me changed forever the way I look at a patient now.

I was sitting there with two different tests that said Karen had virtually no mercury in her body. She had just one amalgam filling and no prior exposure incidents. Yet, there were all these unrelated symptoms. Why had this woman been prescribed numerous antidepressants and even an antipsychotic drug by her previous doctors when she had all these issues going on? There was only one thing that could cause multisystem organ failure, and that was trauma. And in a situation like that, the patient is in intensive care, usually on life support. Yet, here was this woman, walking and talking, and she was in nothing less than multisystem organ failure.

By asking me what I would do if she were my sister, it changed my perspective. I would do anything, whatever it took, to help my sister, without regard for the restrictions by the medical boards, without regard to conformation with the medical hierarchy. Without hesitation, I looked at Karen and answered: "If you were my sister, I would *not* rely on these tests. I'd treat you empirically for metal toxicity."

"I want to start today," she insisted.

I started Karen on our IV detoxification program. After twenty weeks, her mercury level jumped from 2.8 ug/g creatinine to 9.4 ug/g creatinine, going from well within the normal reference range to more than 300 percent above the normal reference range. Her arsenic shot up from 13 ug/g creatinine to 260 ug/g creatinine! It's important to mention here that these tests are only measuring what we are able to effectively *pull* out of the individual. They are *not* accurate from a quantitative standpoint (the amount in the body), but they are highly accurate from a qualitative standpoint (the type of metal in the body). *Now* we were getting somewhere. We were succeeding in drawing the metals out from the deeper stored layers and removing them from her system. And many of her symptoms, with the grace of God, had quickly begun to improve.

Each week like clockwork, Karen came into the clinic and we continued to pull mercury out of her system. Within the first twenty weeks, her heart palpitations were 90 percent improved and the breast lactation stopped. At the one-year mark, Karen's mercury level doubled again, registering at 19 ug/g creatinine, showing that more and more mercury was being pulled out. Meanwhile, she continued to feel better and better. At eighteen months, her mercury continued to increase, registering at 27ug/g creatinine, more than nine times what she had shown on the initial testing. That's almost a 1,000 percent increase in her mercury levels and nine times what's considered to be safe! By this time, she was virtually symptom free.

The last test we did was almost two years from the day she walked into my office. The mercury reading: 1.7ug/g creatinine.

I began to realize that heavy metal challenge tests are good for qualitative analysis—just to see what heavy metals exist in the body. They are not reliable from a quantitative standpoint, however, to determine *how much* of these metals are actually present.

The only quantitatively definitive test would be multiple site biopsies, which obviously would not be conducive to life. Most patients wouldn't like that—at least while they're still alive.

I've seen this counterintuitive pattern of excretion with many patients since treating Karen. These patients don't seem to have the ability to efficiently detoxify their own systems. I refer to them as "nonexcretors" because they have difficulty excreting heavy metals because they have a genetic predisposition for the inability to excrete metals. As a result, they experience the related symptoms of metal poisoning but without the standard method of testing showing the presence of metals (my standard, not the conventional standard). This patient population includes children with autism and patients suffering with Alzheimer's disease. We also observe similar findings with cancer patients.

Sometimes, all it takes is a slow coaxing of the body's own detoxification pathways to open up and release the toxic heavy-metal burden. In Karen's case and in the case of many chronically ill patients, it's takes more than a slow coaxing. Karen's full story and her test records, showing the results as well as the principles behind this foundation, are documented and part of a comprehensive DVD available in the appendix of this book.

The rest of the story is a matter of historical precedence and documented in the Library of Congress. I presented Karen's case before the U.S. Congressional Subcommittee on Human Rights and Wellness on May 6, 2004. I was accompanied by my son Abie, who on that day became the youngest formal witness ever to have testified before Congress. (You will learn more about my oldest son's history later on in chapter 12.)

Karen obviously wasn't my sister, but I have her to thank for helping guide me in understanding this nonexcretion phenomenon and reframe how I view my patients, not just in words, but in action. Taking care of Karen later showed me what I had to do to help regain my own son's health and what eventually impacted tens of thousands of families and hundreds if not thousands of doctors all over the world.

I trust my instincts more now and firmly believe it was the higher source, once again, that led me in the right direction. I do for my patients exactly what I would do for myself and my own family, regardless of the consequences from the medical hierarchy. Before someone thinks this is heroic or gives me some undeserved accolade, I have to tell you I have no choice but to act in this manner. I am simply honoring the process that led to my son's full and unprecedented recovery and keeping the promise I made to the Creator.

The First Foundation—
Systemic Detoxification

As I mentioned in the preceding chapter, it's a toxic world. I don't think anyone would argue with that statement, at least not an honest person. All you have to do is look at the "Do Not Swim" signs posted everywhere along beaches from the East Coast in the USA to the exotic Mediterranean beaches of Malta. Or how about the smog in Los Angeles, so thick on some days that you can't even see a thirty-story building just two hundred yards from you? The mistake most people make is thinking that just because they don't live in a big city like New York or Los Angeles, they're free from pollution of all kinds. In fact, some of the worst offend-ers are the coal-burning plants throughout the Midwest.

Health problems arise when these toxins find their way into our bodies—and we have created many ways for them to do so, sometimes actually facilitating their entry. Because of over industrialization, it's virtually impossible to escape the effects of our toxic world, no matter where you live. Through the air we breathe, water we drink, food we grow and eat, livestock we consume and even social structures we've created, toxicity has permeated every facet of our lives.

When these toxins enter our bodies they immediately begin causing damage. It doesn't matter if the toxin is a heavy metal, a pesticide or a food additive. Every toxin uses the same method of creating physiological damage—oxidative stress. I have already introduced the concept of oxidation. Now it's time to explore this destructive process in more detail.

Why Oxidation Kills

Let's go back to high school biology class. Luckily, there's no quiz, so you can actually relax and learn. Every atom in your body has a specific number of protons (positively charged), electrons (negatively charged) and neutrons (no charge). Because there is a perfect balance of positive and negative charges in each atom, the net charge is zero or neutral.

Now enters a toxin. A toxin is made up of free radicals, or atoms that have a net + charge. They are missing an electron and are desperately seeking to pull an electron from another atom. When toxins (free radicals) enter your body, they steal electrons from the atoms that make up the cells in your body. The atoms that lost an electron now have a net + charge, just like the toxin/ free radical.

So a free radical has a net + charge and is an electron "stealer." When the free radical steals an electron from a surrounding atom, the atom becomes highly unstable. In an effort to rebalance itself, the unstable atom begins bombarding healthy atoms, trying to steal one of *their* electrons. As a result, a chain reaction begins by which the surrounding atoms begin to change from stable structures to free radicals, eventually causing a change in the cell structure and becoming an abnormal cell.

This domino effect continues, with normal healthy atoms having electrons stolen from them by a free radical, in turn becoming a free radical themselves and then looking to steal an electron from *another* surrounding atom. The unstable atoms being driven by this process and in turn driving this process, are called free radicals, and the resulting damage they inflict upon the healthy cells (remember that atoms make up everything, including cells) is known as oxidative stress, oxidation or free radical damage.

This is the process that occurs when you've just peeled a banana or cut an apple as mentioned earlier. In just a matter of minutes, the fruit turns brown. Free radicals also create the exact same situation, which is essentially the rusting process, inside your body. The good news is that we do have countermeasures, commonly known as *antioxidants*, which are substances that reverse this process by donating electrons. Our bodies produce our own antioxidants, which prevent the oxidation process to a certain extent. Examples of the antioxidants we produce ourselves include superoxide dismutase, catalase and glutathione. We can also consume additional antioxidants such as Vitamin C in our diet to create a bigger buffer of protection, which I will explain later.

In a world so overcome with organic and inorganic pollutants, our bodies simply cannot keep up with this free-radical onslaught of epic proportions. Additional toxicities within our bodies that we aren't even aware of also add to the oxidative burden in our systems, further requiring us not only to increase the antioxidant buffers but also, more importantly, to reduce the oxidative damage by reducing the toxicities.

Increasing antioxidants has become very popular in the last ten years. By just increasing antioxidants, however, a false sense of security is generated. You may even see an improvement in certain symptoms, but the toxicity leading to the oxidative stress that caused the symptoms in the first place has not been removed. In time, this toxicity will further accumulate and you'll need a higher quantity of antioxidants to achieve the same benefit, until eventually, so much damage has been done that no amount of antioxidants will yield a benefit any longer. This is the point, essentially, when the chronic diseases appear. Therefore, the removal of the offending toxic substance becomes paramount, ideally well before the disease develops. Simply stated, consumption of antioxidants along with the removal of the source of toxicity distances you from the possibility of acquiring a chronic disease.

The Toxins and Disease Connection

All chronic disease, whether it's heart disease, cancer, a neurological disorder or any other chronic condition for that matter, results from damaged cells as a consequence of oxidative damage. Damaged cells come from free-radical damage, and free radicals are created and generated by toxins. Where the damage takes place in your body from the free radical together with your particular genetic predisposition, will determine the disease your body will manifest. So it may seem unbelievable or downright crazy to say that cancer and heart disease have the exact same cause. However, the fact remains—cancer and heart disease and many other chronic diseases do have the same cause, and it doesn't take a Mensa scholar to realize that this common cause is oxidative stress from free-radical damage, despite what the medical hierarchy may wish you to believe.

The most significant as well as crucial misunderstanding in medical science that has occurred in the last 100 years is the lack of connection between the cause (toxin-induced oxidative stress from free-radical damage) and the problem (steadily increasing incidence of chronic disease). This lack of correlation has even more serious implications for advancement in the health sciences and medical interventions today and will have a tremendous impact on our future generations tomorrow.

Despite literally hundreds of billions of dollars put into cancer research, until toxicity is effectively addressed, no significant advance in cancer survival will ever happen. The same goes for all the antiaging and longevity research being conducted. To discuss longevity and increased life span without first considering and adequately addressing toxicity is like planning on running a marathon without even having learned how to crawl, let alone walk or run.

Even though we're inundated by all the media garbage about longevity and antiaging, few (very few) "incredible advances" have actually shown substantial evidence of increasing life span . . . literally! We'll discuss the most prominent of these later in this book, but it's going to be up to you to first open your mind and see the possibilities, followed by choosing to experience the results for yourself.

An Error in Perspective

Eliminate the phrase "all of a sudden" from your medical vocabulary. Nothing happens "all of a sudden" in the body, unless you're talking about being shot or stabbed. Every effect has its cause and that cause usually has the opportunity to build itself up over time, long before we see the end result.

That's why the missing link of toxicity, the cause of the worst epidemic of chronic diseases in the history of man, has all but been ignored by the medical establishment. They are trying to work on the disease itself, the end of the pathological chain of events—the effect of the toxicity, the symptom of the problem— not the cause. In order to heal any disease or correct any chronic disorder, you *must* go back to the original cause. Failing to address the cause will absolutely guarantee certain defeat in this war against chronic disease, which should be correctly labeled as a war against toxicity.

Imagine you just got back from a month-long tour of Europe. You've had a terrific time. As you open your front door to walk into your house, you're almost knocked back by the foulest stench you can possibly imagine. It smells like a sweaty gym locker stuffed full of old rotting food. It's July, and all your windows have been closed for thirty days straight. You follow your nose, go to the kitchen and discover that you forgot to empty your trash before you left. It's been sitting there, putrefying for over a month, with no ventilation. Flies are swarming around, feasting on the goopy mess.

What does common sense tell you to do at this point? Open a window? Perhaps. Spray air freshener or disinfectant? It may help. Start swatting the flies? Sort of useless at this point. None of these things will solve the problem. They may make it a little tolerable for a short period of time, but the problem still remains and will continue to be there. What is both the most definitive and the smartest thing to do? Immediately take the trash out of the house! The smell will now eventually leave and the flies will buzz off to find another feast.

Unfortunately, however, modern medicine has spent the last fifty years swatting at the flies and opening up the windows to address the rotting garbage of chronic disease. This rotting garbage is *really* the toxicities that we have been talking about. Doling out pills for secondary problems and symptoms provides just a temporary relief while the internal oxidative damage rages on and patients just continue to get worse, requiring higher dosages of medications and the addition of even more drugs.

By the same token, "alternative" medicine actually makes the same mistake, albeit the doling out of vitamins and herbs may not be nearly as damaging as the dispensing of one drug upon another. However, the fundamental approach is just as flawed because the primary etiology, the *cause* of the problem, is not being addressed. It makes no difference if a Chinese herb or a homeopathic extract is replacing the drug and covering up the symptom in question. Okay, it may be less damaging to give an herb as compared to a drug but the point is that it essentially amounts to the same ineffective pill-for-a-problem solution to cover up the symptom.

Since all chronic disease stems from some type of toxicity, it follows that detoxification of whatever makes up the toxic substance must first occur if chronic disease is to ever be effectively addressed and/or reversed. Systemic Detoxification must be undertaken. And it's this Systemic Detoxification that comprises the First Foundation.

Of course, what that actually means for you depends on the junk you've been carrying around and how long you've been carrying it. The good news is that no matter what you're dealing with, toxicity can be effectively removed from the body. It may not happen "all of a sudden"; in fact, chances are it will take some time. This especially is true if you already are suffering from some type of chronic disease. You didn't get sick overnight, right? If you think you did, you're mistaken. Even a sudden heart attack took years in the making. It was a slow progression and steady accumulation of the atheroma (clot) that resulted from the body trying to heal micro-vascular damage caused by the increased oxidative stress (lipid peroxidation caused by metals and other free radials) on the vascular wall where the clot accumulated.

Well, just as you didn't get sick overnight, health isn't regained overnight either. It usually does not return fast, but it does return. The question is not *if* it will occur, but rather *when* will it occur.

The Second Foundation— Immune Modulation

Ellen arrived at my clinic supporting herself with a walker. As she made her way down the hall, I could tell every step was a significant struggle for her. She, like Karen, was just thirty-four years old but was trapped in the body of an old woman. She was forced to sell her house after becoming incapable of climbing the stairs. She had to leave her job in computer programming because the pain in her hands from typing was excruciating. Her passions for playing piano and for classical dance were distant memories.

By the time she arrived at our clinic, Ellen had already seen more than ten different specialists, most recently at the Mayo Clinic, and she was scheduled to be seen at Johns Hopkins University. The doctors were confounded by her condition and ventured her condition was caused by some sort of neuropathy along with a degenerative joint condition. Although each of the hospitals had varying opinions regarding Ellen's diagnosis, they were all certain and in agreement that her condition would continue to degenerate, ultimately leaving her in a wheelchair in less than six months. There was nothing they could offer.

After our evaluation and testing, it was clear that Ellen had high levels of a number of heavy metals as well as persistent organic pollutants within her body. Her immune system had been highly compromised as a result, and the joint pain with tingling was just a symptom of the inflammation caused by the toxic burden and a secondary autoimmune response. We immediately started her on a detoxification program specifically to remove the heavy metals and persistent organic pollutants from her system.

Once her toxic burden was reduced and her immune system remodulated, I fully expected the symptom of her joint pain to resolve. By simply getting the roadblocks out of the way and eliminating the trash within her body, we would be able to get her system back on line and start functioning properly again.

Six months after beginning treatment, Ellen wasn't confined to a wheelchair as Mayo Clinic had predicted. Instead, she'd experienced significant improvement in her mobility and was able to walk unassisted. After one year, the only painful joint that remained was her left wrist. At eighteen months, Ellen was completely pain free with just her left thumb causing some discomfort when the weather was cold or damp. She was climbing stairs again and even returned to work in a programming management position. The best part was that Ellen was playing the piano again and was able to perform classical dance without any pain or discomfort.

Regardless of what the experts had told Ellen, her apparently degenerating joints were not the problem. The pain and tingling was only a sign to simply look deeper. As with a number of similar patients, beyond the complex diagnosis with the long, confusing name of "chronic, idiopathic demyelinating polyneuropathy," the situation was really a much simpler issue waiting to be solved. Health is a simple matter. We complicate it. When we get out of our own way and allow God's design to function, everything falls into place and the music comes back into life.

War, Gut and Impaired Immune System

Any time heavy metals or persistent organic pollutants enter the body, the immune system by definition will become compromised. The level of compromise depends upon many things, including the specific type of metal/pollutant, the actual amount of toxin, the duration of exposure and the individual's constitutional ability to handle physiological stress, as well as his or her genetic predisposition to process the toxin out of the body. In fact, when the body is exposed to *any* type of toxicity, the immune system becomes compromised to some degree. And once the immune system isn't functioning at an optimum level, the body becomes vulnerable to all sorts of disorders and disease.

This explains why many patients often visit doctor after doctor, trying to find the answer the experts keep missing because they're looking under the wrong rocks. They eventually affix a diagnosis with a name half the doctors themselves can't pronounce let alone explain, but the game continues with the focus on covering up the symptoms.

What they've chosen to ignore or have missed is that the disease itself is just the symptom of a deeper underlying problem, one resulting from some form of toxicity, an inner pollution. Once the body is properly detoxified and the burden of pollution is removed, the immune system will naturally remodulate. It has no choice but to revert to the state of normal function. The result of remodulation after detoxification is that the symptoms usually begin to disappear, indicating that the disease itself is beginning to resolve.

When most people think of their immune system, they think of white blood cells. That's what we're taught in biology class, and for most of us, that's where the story of the immune system ends. But there's a lot more to the immune system than most of us realize. Whether you recognize it or not, a significant portion of your immune system exists in your gastrointestinal tract. Billions of "good bacteria" or probiotics flourish in aiding proper digestion, assimilation of nutrients and the elimination of waste, all designed to maintain the essential ecological balance of the gastrointestinal tract.

They also act to balance against disease-causing microbes and parasites, which try to invade the body. An example is when a woman takes an antibiotic for a throat infection and ends up getting a vaginal yeast infection. Essentially, the antibiotics are not selective and kill the bad, disease-causing bacteria in the throat but also end up killing much of the good bacteria normally residing in the gut and vagina. This leaves the "opportunity" for the yeast (fungus) to flourish without having to compete against the healthy bacteria that normally keep the growth of the yeast in check. When nothing is holding it back, the yeast takes over, creating the vaginal yeast infection.

Think of this as a war. When toxins enter your body, the first casualty is your immune system. Since a substantial amount of your immune system lives in your gastrointestinal tract, the gut is usually affected in some significant manner. But among the most widely purchased group of over-the-counter medications that Americans continue to buy are so-called digestive aids such as antacids, laxatives and gas relievers. And of course, these substances simply serve to further aggravate the overall situation.

As a culture, we're conditioned to accept digestive upset as almost a rite of passage as we age. Digestive problems are the first chink in the armor of your immune system and your body is sounding the alarm. It's crucial that you listen to the message your body is sending you to improve the quality of nutrition, reduce the burden of toxicity and pay attention to the signals being provided (symptoms) so that the major catastrophes of chronic disease can be prevented. Show me a patient who is chronically ill with virtually any condition and I'll show you a person who is toxic with a major imbalance in their GI tract.

Watch Out for Friendly Fire

Medicine has hardly been a friend to the immune system in the past five decades. In fact, medicine has done more to harm the immune system than help it. We've all heard about how the massive use of unnecessary antibiotics has resulted in the mutation of pathogens, creating the "super bugs" or microbes that are now resistant to nearly all antibiotics. Just as important, however, is the damage inside your body caused by antibiotics. Don't get me wrong. Antibiotics are a valuable and lifesaving tool in medicine, but only when used appropriately and with great discretion. Regrettably, that simply is not what happens in medicine today.

When antibiotics are prescribed for a patient unnecessarily (which occurs far more often than we realize), the prescribing doctor has inadvertently contributed to weakening the immune system. As mentioned, antibiotics kill bacteria. But they can't rationalize and distinguish good bacteria from the bad; they kill the good bacteria living in your GI tract and other areas along with the bacteria causing the infection. The good bacteria actually provide a crucial role in protecting you against the infection in the first place, but the antibiotic takes that natural protection away by indiscriminately wiping out most, if not all, microbes that are present. This is why probiotics are so popular as a supplement. Remember that probiotic means "for life" and antibiotic means "against life."

Your body is a walking miracle. Under the proper conditions and with the right tools, it can heal itself from practically anything. Name one machine where the more you use it, the better it gets. We measure engine life in tractors by the number of hours the engine has been run or in cars by the number of miles traveled or in planes by the number of flight hours. But in a human, the more you use your body, the better it functions, the longer it lasts, the more efficiently it performs, the better it looks, and the less likely it is to have problems.

Imagine how compromised most people's immune systems have become after decades of using various drugs (over-the-counter, prescription and illegal), lack of exercise, drinking toxic tap water or, worse, drinking sodas and eating nutrient-deficient, synthetic-filled imitation food. It's a wonder anyone is standing upright! The fact that most of us can still function is a testament to the power and strength of our bodies and the design of the ultimate engineer, the Creator. The ability to carry around such burdens, with immune systems functioning at just a fraction of capacity, begs the question, "What would our bodies be capable of if we were to actually take care of ourselves by eliminating toxicity and maintaining the strength of our immune system?"

The Secret to Getting Back on Track

The masses, however, are finally beginning to wake up to the importance of the immune system. The formerly unrecognized but significant role the GI (gastrointestinal) tract plays in our overall health is becoming more widely accepted among health enthusiasts despite the lack of embracement of this key principal by the mainstream medical community. An example of this increasing awareness can be seen in the increasing popularity of probiotic products, which seem to be available everywhere now, even in the average grocery store.

While I'm happy to see this paradigm shift, you can't take a squirt gun to put out a five-alarm fire and expect to be successful. Only when the body is properly detoxified will the probiotics and other interventions become consistently effective. The great news is that the lining of your intestinal tract, where the good bacteria (probiotics) live, is one of the fastest-regenerating tissues in your body. In fact, the rate of regeneration becomes faster in people who have been sick recently. The GI tract is just an example of *one* of the major areas that must be addressed in systemic detoxification. Once effective detoxification has been completed with a reduction of the toxic burden in the entire system, the immune system will remodulate itself and you'll be well on your way to getting back on track to good health.

The Geek, the Tree and 13 Women

This story is not as exotic as you might be expecting from the title! I was in the middle of a divorce that made war look like a mild disagreement. I couldn't see my way very clearly during that time of my life, and I was in a dark and confusing place spiritually and emotionally. It was one of the toughest things I've ever experienced in my life, especially because my children were involved.

But one issue that was especially frustrating during this difficult time was that I wasn't able to successfully help a specific handful of patients who had sought my help. I suppose we'd become spoiled at my clinic because we were used to routinely helping patients no one else was previously able to help.

This handful of patients all shared two characteristics in common: they were all women, and they were all dealing with severe hormonal imbalances for which I had not been able to find the underlying trigger causing the problem.

Sometimes when I don't know what to do in the case of a particular patient, I'll pull that person's chart, lay it on my desk, just stare at it and go back to the basics. It's kind of like a meditation, I suppose. Eventually, something always comes to me.

It was a beautiful Saturday spring morning, and I was in my clinic, with the charts of these thirteen women spread out on the floor in front of my desk, hoping that some inspiration would hit me. I'd already learned the difficult lesson a few years earlier that when dealing with a hormonal imbalance in a woman, you must address the GI tract. In some of my physician conferences where I teach other doctors what we do, I've stated that if you ignore the gut in these types of cases, you will most certainly fail in helping the patient improve. However, in all thirteen women, I had addressed their GI tract and there had been little if any improvement.

As I sat there, nothing was coming to me. My back phone line rang and my good friend, Dr. Craft, was on the line, inviting me to go out on his boat on the lake. He was clearly trying to distract me from my divorce situation. Using the charts as an excuse, I explained that I needed to work on them, to which he responded that I was a geek and hung up.

I turned to the charts again, now getting angry and more frustrated—not at the charts, but at myself, wondering if I really was a geek. As I swiveled my chair slightly so that I wouldn't have to stare at the stupid charts, the huge oak tree outside the office window caught my eye. Its heavily laden branches were dancing ever so slowly in the breeze, back and forth, framed by the gorgeous clear blue sky, waving at me, almost inviting me to participate in its hypnotic dance. The more I stared at it, the more it put me into a kind of soothing trance. It was mesmerizing and the charts were forgotten.

I don't recall how much time went by, but when I realized what was happening, I got even angrier. In my mind, I was wasting time. That tree had broken my concentration, which should have been focused on the charts. I looked down at the thirteen charts spread out on the floor like a big deck of cards before me, and for the first time, noticed the fourth chart from the left had a sheet sticking out of it that had not been properly filed.

As my staff will quickly tell you, I absolutely HATE it when sheets are not properly aligned in a chart. The more I tried to ignore the misaligned sheet, the more it aggravated me. Finally giving in to all my frustrations of the morning, I grabbed the chart and flipped it open to the misaligned sheet, fully prepared to rip it out and have my staff re-file the document properly. And suddenly there it was, the answer, staring back at me.

On the misaligned sheet was the result of a heavy-metal challenge test. I could clearly see this woman had elevated mercury levels. My anger suddenly forgotten, I quickly moved clockwise to the next chart. Sure enough, there was a heavy-metal challenge test that showed elevated mercury. I went to the next chart. No challenge test on this chart. Next one, yes, there it was! By the time I had come full circle, I realized that more than half the women had undergone the challenge test I'd ordered. The rest of the women had not been evaluated for metals.

Over the next few weeks, we did a challenge test on the remaining women. When all was said and done, twelve of those thirteen women ended up having elevated mercury levels. There was only *one* woman who did not have elevated mercury on challenge testing: Karen, the woman whose clinical story began this chapter. Karen's case was eventually presented before the U.S. Congress because it was her case that first demonstrated to me what I later termed the "non-excretor" phenomenon. This woman, the only one who did not show elevated mercury of the thirteen, would eventually show mercury levels increase by more than 1,000 percent after two years of treatment!

Most doctors realize the essential role hormones play in our health and quality of life. But most people in my profession don't know the crucial lesson I learned that day, which showed me that toxicity can have a serious dampening effect on hormonal balance. In fact, all toxicity can and does have a tremendous impact on the endocrine system, the system responsible for all hormones in the body, from the sex hormones to the stress hormones and everything in between.

Needless to say, we immediately got each of these women appropriately treated for mercury toxicity. The length of treatment varied for each of the thirteen women, with the exception of one—Karen's treatment being the longest—but they all resolved. ALL of them!

The Third Foundation— Hormonal Optimization

Most people think of hormones simply in a sexual context. The fact is that every function within your body is controlled by hormones, from your libido to your sleep cycle to your hunger response to your body temperature. All of these signals come down from a complex cascade of originating hormones you may never have even heard of, from the pituitary-hypothalamic axis in your brain. You may have thought it was just about testosterone and estrogen. Most people do.

But this incredibly intricate, interconnected hormonal network we so often take for granted is related like a set of domino chains. When our bodies need to perform a specific function, this domino chain is triggered with pinpoint precision and each domino causes the next one to trigger. It's like a finely tuned orchestra where the success of every step depends on the one before it. If even one note is out of tune, the entire orchestra sounds "off."

Imbalanced or low hormone levels can create many problems in the body, the least of which is making you feel lousy with no energy. The problems begin when a doctor runs a blood test and finds a patient's testosterone level is low. Since the patient is, for example purposes, a fifty-year-old, the dip is attributed to "normal aging," testosterone gel is usually prescribed, and the patient is moved down the "conveyor belt" out the door. This is a perfect example of "symptom management." The symptom is feeling lousy attributed to low testosterone, so the patient is treated and sent home. On the surface, this seems perfectly appropriate. But there is a problem. A big problem. No one asked *why* the testosterone level was low in the first place.

Testosterone is produced in the testicles in males. Every physiological part of your body needs to be exercised or "worked" to stay healthy, and the testicles are no exception to this rule. If you don't work out, what happens to your muscles? They lose their form and begin to slowly waste away. Ever notice what a broken arm or leg looks like after being taken out of a cast? It looks ridiculously smaller compared to the opposite limb because the muscles atrophied from not being used. The same type of thing happens to the organs that produce hormones in our body, including the testicles.

When supplying testosterone, in this example say to a body builder, the body slows down its own supply of testosterone because there is "too much" testosterone coming into the body. The constant supply of "extra" testosterone the body builder is introducing into his body causes the normal organ that produces testosterone (the testicles) to shut down to keep from having too much testosterone in the body. This is why many bodybuilders who use testosterone and other performance-enhancing drugs experience extreme, irreversible testicular shrinkage, which occurs because the testicles are no longer being exercised as they normally would be when they are producing testosterone.

What happens is the protective physiological mechanism known as the negative inhibitory feedback loop (NIFBL), designed to keep the hormones in balance, gets initiated to prevent overproduction of hormones. This NIFBL is the messenger system that makes sure the balance is being achieved and hormones are not being overproduced, which can cause many medical conditions and contribute to the cancer process. The result of artificially meddling with this process by giving "outside" hormones causes the NIFBL to further shut down and inhibit the very gland designed to produce the hormone in the first place.

The crucial point to understand is that it doesn't matter whether you're using synthetic hormones or bioidentical hormones. By giving the end hormone, whether it's bioidentical or synthetic, you're short-circuiting the process and shooting the messenger. The real question that should be asked is, *why* is the hormone level low in the first place?

The controversy over bioidentical and synthetic hormones and the media hype surrounding it is so foolish, it's no wonder chronic disease continues to increase. The issues that are really important are being ignored because of the illusion that's created surrounding this controversy. In reality, those understanding physiology know that the argument between bioidentical versus synthetic hormones is really irrelevant. The question is, what caused the body to fail to produce its own necessary hormones in the first place?

During the process of treating the group of thirteen women mentioned earlier, and without my conscious realization, I was addressing all three of the foundations we've discussed. These women underwent systemic detoxification (for mercury and other toxins); they had their immune systems modulated (simply by removing substances that are known immunosuppressive agents, such as mercury); and they finally achieved hormonal optimization with minimal, if any, direct intervention.

Separating Hormone Facts from Fears

In recent years, several therapeutic options in the arena of hormonal manipulation have been made available to reportedly help people live not just better lives but to actually become physiologically younger and have the promise of a longer life span. The goal behind all these therapeutics is to increase one primary hormone, known as human growth hormone (hGH or GH). GH steadily begins to drop off after we reach our early to mid-twenties. By the time we're in our forties, our GH levels have significantly dropped compared to what they once were. According to one study, 35 percent of men over the age of sixty were found to be GH deficient.[5,6]

---

5 D. Rudman, A.G. Feller, H.S. Nagraj, G.A. Gergans, P.Y. Lalitha, A.F. Goldberg, R.A. Schlenker, L. Cohn, I.W. Rudman, D.E. Mattson. 1990. Effects of Human Growth Hormone in Men Over 60 Years Old. *New England Journal of Medicine.* 323 (1):1–6.
6 Ian Chapman, Mark Hartman, Suzan Pezzoli, Farnk Harrell, Raymond Hintz, K. Alberti, Michael Thorner. 1997. Effect of Aging on the Sensitivity of Growth Hormone Secretion to Insulin-Like Growth Factor-I Negative Feedback. *Journal of Clinical Endocrinology and Metabolism.* 82 (9): 2996–3004.

In another study, GH production rate in all adults was determined to fall by 14 percent with every advancing decade, with some that don't produce any growth hormone at all.[6,7]

GH is essential to health and vitality for several reasons. Not only does it promote the creation of lean muscle mass, eliminate unnecessary fat and give you a more youthful appearance, it's also essential for every cell in your body to regenerate and grow. Whatever the need for regeneration in your body, GH allows those cells to rebuild. It's because of all these reasons that there has been an enormous rush by health-care practitioners to take so-called longevity medicine to the next level. As a result, several therapies to increase GH levels have been heavily promoted in recent years.

However, the problem is that in the rush to "cash in" on the mass market of people who are interested in looking younger and lured by the promise of living longer, the science has gotten lost along the way. This has led to several therapies that aren't just ineffective, but are highly dangerous for patients to be taking. As an example, the use of injectible GH has been directly correlated with increasing Insulin-like Growth Factor—Type 1 (IGF-1). This is definitely not a desired outcome because IGF-1 is directly related to oncogenesis (process of cancer formation), not to mention the fact that cancer makes its own IGF-1 as well.[8]

---

7 A. Iranmanesh, G. Lizarralde, J.D. Veldhuis. 1991. Age And Relative Adiposity Are Specific Negative Determinants of the Frequency and Amplitude of Growth Hormone (GH) Secretory Bursts and the Half-Life of Endogenous GH in Healthy Men. *Journal of Clinical Endocrinology and Metabolism*. 73 (7): 1081–1088.
8 Jing Ma, Michael Pollak, Edward Giovannucci, June Chang, Yuzhen Tao, Charles Hennekens, Meir Stampfer. 1999. Prospective Study of Colorectal Cancer Risk in Men and Plasma Levels of Insulin-Like Growth Factor (IGF)-1 and IGF-Binding Protein-3. *Journal of the National Cancer Institute*. 91 (7): 620–625.

The first response in the hormonal rush (pardon the pun) was GH injection therapy, which involves receiving self-administered daily injections of synthetic GH at a cost ranging between $600 and $2,400 per month. It was soon discovered that putting something completely synthetic into your body may not be a good idea for many reasons. Big surprise! Within six months to a year, patients reportedly ended up with many complaints, including heart problems such as cardiomyopathies and joint issues such as carpal tunnel syndrome, joint effusions and even acromegaly.

Again, the physiological safety valve consisting of the NIFBL, which also serves as a messaging system for the hypothalamus, comes into play. Injecting GH violates this safety feedback loop, just as in the testosterone example given earlier. Plus, the use of injectible GH has been directly correlated with increasing IGF-1, which in turn has been associated with increased risk of multiple cancers, as was previously mentioned.

> Laboratory studies have shown that IGFs exert strong mitogenic and antiapoptotic actions on various cancer cells. . . . IGFs also act synergistically with other mitogenic growth factors and steroids and antagonize the effect of anti-proliferative molecules on cancer growth. The role of IGFs in cancer is supported by epidemiologic studies, which have found that high levels of circulating IGF-1 and low levels of IGFBP-3 are associated with increased risk of [many] cancers. IGFs are related to increased cell proliferation, suppression of apoptosis and increased cancer risk.[9]

9 Herbert Yu, Thomas Rohan. September 20, 2000. Role of Insulin-Like Growth Factor Family in Cancer Development and Progression. *Journal of the National Cancer Institute*. 92 (18): 1472–1489.

Next came the wave of secretagogues (vitamin, herb and amino acid combinations marketed as precursors of GH and IGF-1). Advertisements for them have been clogging up your e-mail with spam for years. These are the supplements you take orally or sublingually (under the tongue) or you spray into your mouth. They're sold at most health food stores, gyms and even some doctors' offices. Some of them even go far as saying they contain actual GH in homeopathic doses. The simple truth is that these products don't work. If they did work, they would have already put the more expensive and far more popular GH injection therapy out of business.

If there is any difference temporarily experienced by the user of these substances, it's due to the high dextrose (sugar) content within the product that may make an individual feel like they have more energy. But the same can be achieved with a cup of coffee. Most of these products also claim to increase IGF-1, attempting to ride on the marketing "coattails" of what appears to have become the misguided goal of GH injection therapy. The question is, why in the world would anyone actually *want to increase* the very substance that cancer itself produces to maintain itself and has been correlated with in numerous studies?

But the GH industry has created an illusion that defies logic and common sense. Of the 180 or so products on the market that fall into the GH-promoting category, none has ever been shown to actually increase GH levels based on any current testing methodologies, and virtually *all* tout the increase of IGF-1 as a desired benefit. Try these products yourself, but the only place you'll see a change is in your wallet.

We will discuss hormonal optimization in more detail later. For now, remember that any hormonal manipulation you attempt should meet the following key standards:

1. The treatment should never violate the Negative Inhibitory Feedback Loop (NIFBL), that is, the treatment should address the issue at the regulatory point, not at the end hormone point.

2. The treatment should never exceed physiological parameters, that is, it should never drive the hormonal cascade into an extreme range. If you adhere to standard No. 1, No. 2 will never be an issue.

3. The treatment should always respect the innate balance of *all* the hormones and their relative interdependence, while eliciting an optimization of not one but all the various hormones.

4. The treatment should elicit the natural endogenous (your body's own) hormones to come into play without introducing any end hormone into the system (see standard No. 1).

5. The end result of treatment should mimic the body's natural response and respect the body's endogenous rhythms of the hormonal cycles.

Relationship of the Three Foundations

As I've said previously, the 9 Steps are the steel beams, bricks, wood and mortar you'll be using to literally build your new self. The Three Foundations we've just reviewed are the bedrock and foundation of this new building. Think of this building as a nine-floor high-rise that also has three parking levels that are underground. This underground parking area not only serves the functional aspect by providing parking spaces but also serves the greater purpose of the foundation of the high-rise giving the structure its strength and support. You've now hopefully realized how the first foundation of Systemic Detoxification lays the basis upon which everything else will be built. The second foundation of Immune Modulation rests upon this first foundation. And the third foundation of Hormonal Optimization lies upon the second foundation.

As we now begin to review each of the 9 Steps in detail, it's important to remember that each of these steps corresponds to the higher floors of the high-rise. The first eight steps are instrumental in increasing longevity and achieving optimum health. If you are currently ill, these steps are mandatory and become essential if you wish to get well. It's that simple.

Your work in the first eight of these 9 Steps must be built on top of a sound structure that is strong and able to support the weight. The ideas you'll get from these 9 Steps alone are all you need to transform your body and mind into a fortress of health and will provide you with this strong and sound structure.

In the ninth step, you'll find the tools you need to construct your new building three times as fast, ten times as high and with a glorious penthouse on top. So when it comes to your health, it's your choice to build a skyscraper instead of a ranch.

It may be important to mention that the last principle, although optional, is one that can exponentially increase the benefits you experience from the first eight steps. The ninth step actually revolves around the subject of the third foundation, optimizing hormonal response. In the ninth step you'll be presented with a comparison to learn about the safest and most effective way to effectively increase the human growth hormone your own body produces without interrupting the NIFBL and without raising IGF-1 levels. In fact, this particular technique drops IGF-1 consistently and is the *only* method known to increase GH while decreasing IGF-1. Furthermore, it positively affects not only all the hormones in your body but does so in a manner where most people can feel the difference within the first week or two of usage—sometimes even as fast as within the first night or two.

The physician is only nature's assistant.

—GALEN (A.D. 129–199)

STEP 1: THE PRINCIPLE OF NUTRITION

*Our food should be our medicine and our
medicine should be our food.*

—Hippocrates, Greek Physician

A Five-Year-Old's Pain

Morgan was five years old when her father first approached me about getting treatment for her worsening condition. By the time I saw her, she'd already been seen by three orthopedic surgeons and five different rheumatologists for her very severe case of juvenile rheumatoid arthritis. She had already been through one operation on her left knee, and the range of motion in the left leg was now less than thirty degrees. But it was her worsening condition that her parents justifiably feared.

At her young age, she was already on Plaquenil, Methotrexate, double the dose of Naprosyn and double the dose of Tylenol 3. Yet, she was still in pain. She was being considered to receive gold injections next, to control her arthritic pain. Her parents had most recently taken her to Duke University, where the medical staff notified them they could do nothing more for Morgan other than to continue to provide her with her medications.

When Morgan's father originally asked me to see her, I declined. I was thirty-one, just out of the military and very new to my private practice. Although I had been a physician for six years at that point, I knew very little about pediatrics and even less about arthritis. My training had all been in trauma, surgery and emergency medicine.

Although I didn't share it with Morgan's father at the time, my biggest concern was the arsenal of medication this little child was on. With such heavy doses of powerful medications, I knew she would be going into renal failure by the time she was in her teen years, just from the effects the medicine would have on her still immature young kidneys. Her problems were so compounded I just didn't feel I had the necessary expertise to treat her. It was clear this child would simply go from her current bad condition to only a worse situation. Already Duke University, with all their resources and hundreds of "expert" specialists on staff, had done everything they could. Surely I didn't have anything that Duke had not considered or could not provide. At least, so I thought then.

One morning I arrived at my clinic very early and was surprised to see a car waiting in the parking lot at that hour. There was a man inside, half slumped over the steering wheel. Strange as that was, I assumed someone was sleeping in their car and paid no further attention. As I unlocked the door to the clinic, I heard someone call my name. As I turned around, I saw Morgan's father standing there, appearing exhausted and holding out a picture of his daughter.

With tears in his eyes, he said, "Please help us. We have no place else left to go." I glanced down at the photograph and was instantly taken aback, seeing the resemblance to my own daughter. They could easily have passed for sisters. I resisted but couldn't keep myself from envisioning myself standing in this man's place. In another world, our roles could have been reversed. It was a powerful moment as I fought back my own emotional response to this father's plea for help. I heard myself saying, "I can't guarantee anything."

I had little more than a remote idea of where to start. I tore through mountains of research on juvenile rheumatoid arthritis, reading late into the night after seeing my patients during the day. The more I researched, the more vested I became and the more useless the information I found appeared to be. It was all the same stuff that had already been done to Morgan. There simply *had* to be *something* else.

It was in some research from Australia that I found a connection between the GI tract and juvenile rheumatoid arthritis and ankylosing spondylitis. The gastrointestinal imbalances the study described made me wonder if addressing these issues could possibly benefit Morgan. I didn't know if rebuilding her GI tract would make any difference at all, but it was certainly worth a try, especially since it couldn't hurt her, unlike the medications she was still taking.

Within six months after testing Morgan and initiating her treatment, she was completely off all four of the prescription anti-inflammatory, immunosuppressive, analgesic medications she had been taking. Her father was overjoyed! I was simply stunned, relieved and even a bit proud of myself. The treatments

I prescribed had enabled her to get off the medications, which I knew in my heart had saved her kidneys and kept her from eventually ending up on dialysis. But I didn't fully appreciate the most important part until one office visit when I asked Morgan how she was doing. She had a big smile on her shy face as she answered, "I don't have pain anymore."

Morgan was now pain free, and her range of motion in her left leg had increased to 45 degrees. Within another year, Morgan's range of motion would reach 90 degrees and she would be developing normally like any other child. With physical therapy, we were hopeful that she would be able to play sports and do everything that other children her age did.

Near the end of her treatment, Morgan's parents got in an argument with each other during an office visit. Morgan's mom wanted to return to all the experts they'd seen in the last few years at Duke University and tell them off because they believed nothing else could have been done for their daughter. Morgan's father countered that it would be a waste of time, believing the experts would never learn and would only end up charging them for an office visit.

Even back then, I had experienced being remarkably successful with a patient when the traditional approach had failed. Instead of wanting to know what we had done, my conventional colleagues just wrote it off, saying their original diagnosis must have been wrong or that, at best, it was a "spontaneous remission." I wonder how many spontaneous remissions have to take place before conventional medicine starts looking at the common denominators in all these improvements.

I never asked what Morgan's parents decided to do or if the Duke medical staff did learn anything from Morgan's case—but I know I did. Taking care of this child, I learned that fear becomes meaningless in the presence of passion and purpose. Morgan's case was also a reeducation for me on the immense power that nutrition and gastrointestinal health carry in our overall well-being. Today, Morgan is a beautiful young woman of eighteen, getting ready to start college, who played all the sports she wanted to play while growing up. Her father Rob and I became good friends and have remained close over the years.

Hidden Gateway to Health

Our bodies are essentially a closed environment. Our skin encases us, protecting us from all the potentially harmful things outside of us that we're exposed to on a daily basis. Our nails protect the tips of our fingers and toes. Skin and nails combined are a protective suit that actually works very well.

On a side note, some substances—liquids in particular—can enter the body through the skin. It's very important therefore to have a filter on your shower, since the tap water in many areas may contain substances you don't want in your body such as chlorine and fluoride and heavy metals such as lead, mercury and even arsenic. These and other substances can directly move into your body through the skin and into your internal environment. This is also why certain therapeutic agents are best applied topically via the skin. (I'll discuss this in more detail later).

For the purposes of this chapter, I'm going to focus on the *primary* means by which most substances that we have control over enter our bodies, which is through our digestive system. Yes, things do enter our bodies through inhalation (lungs) and absorption (skin), but primarily, it is just the substances we take in through our mouths that we can control. From the mouth, down the esophagus to the stomach, through the intestines and out the anus, the entire digestive system is an open tube to the outside world. It's a continuance of the external environment that runs right through us. It's the primary way into the fortress or out of the fortress, and that makes it probably the most important system in your body.

It was Dr. C. Everett Koop, former U.S. Surgeon General, who said that virtually all human ills would eventually be traced back to something we put into our own bodies. The gastrointestinal system is the gateway to health because it's in charge of assimilating our nutrients and eliminating the waste. If one or both of these processes are hindered, the opportunity for chronic disease to become established significantly increases. That's why it's essential that you treat your body like a temple, making sure to put the purest, most nutritious and cleanest elements inside into your body, beginning with the food you eat.

Silent Starvation

When you think of the word *organic*, you might get images of rich people browsing around an exclusive grocery store with overpriced products or, perhaps, hippies with dreadlocks selling homemade granola from a tent. Neither could be further from the truth. The public at large is already beginning to wake up to what it *really* costs them to save seventeen cents on a pound of bananas or a dollar on a pint of conventionally grown blueberries. Fruits and vegetables considered "organic" have been grown without the use of synthetic fertilizers, herbicides and pesticides, in much the same way all farmers used to do before the dawn of the twentieth century. They've also been farmed sustainably, from soil that hasn't been denatured. Sustainable? Denatured? Don't worry. You don't need a degree in horticulture to understand healthy food.

Organic produce not only has never been touched by chemicals but also has been grown using practices that produce little if any lingering impact on the environment. The crops of these fruits and vegetables have been rotated during the various growing seasons throughout the years so that vital nutrients are not depleted from the soil. Let's look at tomatoes, for example. All fruits and vegetables get their minerals from the soil, and these minerals are passed on to us when we eat the produce. Tomatoes require a specific number and amount of different minerals to grow healthy. If tomatoes are planted too often on the same plot of earth without a different vegetable like lettuce being grown between tomato crops—or even better, letting the land rest with *no* growth—that specific set of minerals will eventually get depleted from the soil.

Yes, tomatoes will still grow on the same land every year, at least physically. But they will be devoid of the essential minerals and other nutrient factors that are present in organic produce grown with sustainable practices. The difference between organic and conventionally grown produce is obvious in a basic taste test. Ever notice how a homegrown tomato tastes so much better than a regular store-bought tomato? Minerals and proper growing practices are what give organic fruits and vegetables their luscious flavor.

In fact, organically grown produce has been shown to have a significantly higher mineral and nutrient content when compared to the regular grocery store version of the same fruit or vegetable. It is this rich mineral content, found in healthy produce, that is essential to the nutrient profile and overall healing power of the foods we eat. When we look at it from a scientific standpoint, we can easily see that America is truly starving to death when it comes to minerals.

Weston A. Price, DDS, a nutritionist and dentist, served as chairman of the Research Section of the American Dental Association in the early twentieth century. His research, published in 1939 in *Nutrition and Physical Degeneration*, is an overview of the nutritional habits of many diverse, indigenous cultures from remote areas around the world.[10] These included, among many others, the Aborigines of Australia, the Wakamba tribe of Kenya, the Lotschental inhabitants of Switzerland, the Eskimos of Alaska, the Wanande of the Congo and the indigenous jungle Indians of Peru.

On his personal journeys to all these remote places, Price found that the inhabitants, unaffected by modern society, suffered no impacted molars, cavities or tooth crowding of any kind. He found their bone structure to be sturdy and strong, faces broad and eyes clear. Most amazingly, he never found a single case of cancer, heart disease or chronic disease of any kind in any location he visited in which the inhabitants consumed pure, whole foods from their natural surroundings. Price linked the poor state of the health of Americans to the poor quality of their diet, which in turn was linked to the impoverished quality of the soil where produce was grown.

Shortly after publishing his findings, in a review of the American agricultural climate, Price wrote: "In correspondence with government officials in practically every state in the U.S., I find that during the last 50 years, there has been a reduction in the capacity of the soil productivity in many districts amounting from 25% to 50%." Keep in mind . . . this was over seventy years ago.

---

10 Weston A. Price. 8th edition. 2008. *Nutrition and Physical Degeneration*. La Mesa, California: Price Pottenger. Nutrition. p. 527.

According to data presented in 2001 in Nashville, Tennessee, at the American College for the Advancement of Medicine Symposium by Gerald M. Lemole, MD, Medical Director of the Preventive Medicine and Rehabilitation Center at Wilmington Hospital in Delaware, the rapid decline of nutrient value in the modern food supply is a definite cause for alarm. Over the seventy-eight-year period between 1914 and 1992, one medium-sized raw apple with the skin intact showed a significant decline in mineral content, with a 48 percent decrease in calcium, a 96 percent decrease in iron and an 83 percent decrease in magnesium.

When tested in food analysis laboratories, organically grown food has been shown to have a nutrient content two-and-a-half to three times higher than that of conventionally grown produce from major grocery stores. Fresh vegetables, when compared to canned vegetables, show similar differences in nutritional value, with fresh vegetables containing a significantly higher amount of vitamins and minerals. For example, Dr. Lemole's data showed fresh peas have 76 percent more calcium, 55 percent more iron, 41 percent more magnesium, 65 percent more potassium, 38 percent more zinc and 31 percent more copper than do canned peas. Fresh peas were also found to have higher vitamin content than do canned peas, with 76 percent more vitamin C, 55 percent more thiamine, 40 percent more riboflavin, 64 percent more niacin, 38 percent more Vitamin B6, 62 percent more folic acid, 32 percent more vitamin A and 20 percent more fiber.

Invest in Your Health

We could go through virtually every existing fruit and vegetable making these comparisons, but the results would be very much the same and equally dramatic. The bottom line is that the foundation of all healing begins with what you put in your mouth. It's not enough to stop eating the pastries and candy bars. It's vital that you now begin to give your body the building blocks it needs for repair and regeneration. As you've just seen, an apple is not "just" an apple. You must begin consuming more organic fruits and vegetables every day. Yes, organic produce can cost more, but consider this an investment in your own health that will pay dividends FAR beyond the few extra pennies you will spend.

As you begin to increase your consumption of organic produce, you'll want to focus on getting the biggest bang for your buck. That means eating those fruits and vegetables that are the all-stars for mineral and antioxidant content. To find the most beneficial fruits and vegetables, visit www.The9Steps.com, where you will find my select list of the Top 21 Fruits and Top 21 Vegetables, with a write-up on each, in the members-only section. Even if you don't refer to my list, remember that eating more fruits and vegetables, particularly raw fruits and vegetables, is the first major step toward good nutrition.

If you walk into a grocery store today and look at the labels on food products, particularly animal products such as meat, eggs and milk, you get a very specific impression of healthy, clean products. You usually see a picture of cattle grazing in an open field, with a bright red barn in the background and a rooster perched on a fence post, crowing as the morning sun rises. Above this idyllic scenario the label usually reads, "Such and Such Farms." It gives you a sense of quality and comfort knowing the food you've just bought for your family was personally grown and raised by "Farmer Such and Such." But we all know this is deceptive marketing and is far from the truth.

The family farm as we knew it is basically extinct, especially here in the United States. What we have today are factory farms that act like huge assembly lines, pushing hundreds of thousands of pounds of meat and dairy into the market every year. Through government incentives that literally pay farmers NOT to farm and through corporate collusion, the majority of beef, poultry and dairy products are produced by just a handful of companies. How do fewer farms produce so much more product? Actually, it's not possible without cutting some very important health-related, nutritionally based, and, of course, financial corners.

Let's use beef cattle as an example. When cattle are raised on a factory farm, the goal is to raise an animal that reaches maximum size in less time and has softer, more tender meat. To force cattle to grow beyond their normal size and at an unnaturally accelerated pace they're fed large doses of steroids and hormones. They're kept in small pens to limit movement, crowded next to each other and never allowed to graze naturally. Roaming openly in a field would provide too much exercise that would increase muscle mass, leading to tougher meat. They're also fed antibiotics to prevent disease, an inevitable result of their overcrowded living conditions.

But remember, all these steroids, hormones and antibiotics get into our systems via the meat. The antibiotics sterilize our GI tracts by killing all the good probiotic bacteria and end up depressing our immune system while allowing for unrestricted growth of disease-causing dysbiotic bacteria, viruses and yeast. The steroids and hormones start affecting all our systems, causing massive havoc leading to disruptions in all hormones and eventually contributing to chronic diseases such as cancer, diabetes and heart disease.

The adage "You are what you eat" is *literally* true. Whether a pesticide is spread over the soil, sprayed onto foliage or added to irrigation water, it is taken up by the leaf and root structure of the plant. Whatever a plant "eats," you eat when you consume it. The same holds true for meat and dairy products. If it's injected into livestock, added to their feed or found in the plants they consume or in the soil where they graze, you're eating it as well. That's why it's absolutely essential to begin consuming more organic produce and organic animal products. In order for the body to begin healing—and especially if you're interested in keeping the doctor away—you must first stop putting toxins into your body. We'll deal in a later chapter with the toxins that are already there.

More Dietary Dilemmas

So, now we understand the importance of eating organic foods, but we're left with the question of *how much* of *which products* to eat and *when*. Even if you've never battled weight or health issues and are just interested in staying healthy, the issue of diet can be very complicated. It's no wonder that thousands of books are written on diet alone.

Everyone has a different opinion. There are diets for body type, blood type, gender, cultural groups, high blood pressure, diabetes, anti-aging, vegetarians and macrobiotics, as well as celebrity-endorsed programs. The list is endless. It's no wonder that everyone is confused, especially those who are working on improving their health. Remember, no matter how big or complex the question might be, the answer is always simpler than we think. The simplicity of nature makes it easy for us, but we as humans tend to find ways to complicate issues.

Let me make nutrition simple for you. The first crucial thing to remember is to avoid any food that contains preservatives. Get in the habit of reading labels. If you don't recognize two or more ingredients, do NOT eat the food. The more chemicals in the food, the more you should abstain from it.

The second crucial thing to remember is that the most natural way to eat is to choose a higher-protein, lower-carbohydrate diet. I know what you're thinking. Don't protest about those famous high-protein fad diets that were so famous a decade ago. Remember, we're keeping this simple, so I'm going to appeal to your common sense.

God designed our bodies to do certain things and gave us resources to allow us to do these things. These resources were divided into three parts: specifically, fuel, building blocks and storage or reserves. What is the fuel of life? Carbohydrates. What are the building blocks of life? Proteins. What is the storage form of the energy of life? Fat. Today, we eat many more carbohydrates than our bodies need because food manufacturers can deliver carbohydrates cheaply and easily. It's exactly that increase in carbohydrate consumption that causes many of our health problems.

Whether carbohydrates are complex and unrefined (raw vegetables), simple and unrefined (whole grain bread or spinach pasta) or simple and refined (cakes and candy), they all break down into one substance inside the body: fuel, or sugar. Since we don't have to race across the African savanna to catch our lunch, like our ancestors did, we end up consuming far more fuel than we need. When we don't expend or utilize the "fuel" we're consuming, it leads to excess "fuel" accumulation. This requires more insulin, which causes a whole host of other problems, and eventually converts the "fuel" to "reserves," or fat.

Sugar Dangers

It should be getting clearer in your mind where the problem lies. In a word, sugar is "evil." Okay, maybe I'm exaggerating a bit, but the point is science has known for some time the significant role that sugar plays in all chronic diseases. Once inside the body, sugar causes an insulinogenic response. Chronic insulinogenic response triggers hyperinsulinogenic reactions, eventually leading to diabetes. But this same cascade leading to higher insulin levels also results in cardiovascular disease and cancer. Since all carbohydrates get converted to sugar in the body, it's important to eliminate or limit those that turn into sugar very quickly inside the body. This rapid conversion, which may be experienced as a "sugar rush," creates a chaotic chemical imbalance in the body that takes a huge amount of energy and resources to neutralize.

The worst offenders in this group are the simple refined carbohydrates that turn to sugar most rapidly. This includes all varieties of baked goods, such as cakes, pies and cookies, as well as fruit juice and other processed items containing sugar, of which corn syrup is probably the worst offender. Instead of drinking a can of soda (or even a glass of orange juice) or diving into a pile of icing surrounding some cake, you might as well pick up a baseball bat and slap yourself in the pancreas because that's what happens inside your body when you consume large amounts of simple sugars.

The amount of insulin and energy it takes to neutralize even one teaspoon of sugar is astounding. The goal, then, is to keep sugar levels as low as possible and to maintain a slow and constant rate of glucose release to prevent high surges of insulin from occurring. One of the easiest ways to do this is to start meals off by eating proteins first. Proteins are metabolized at a slower rate, creating a buffer that keeps the carbohydrates you'll eat later from being absorbed too quickly into your system.

Feel free to enjoy fruit liberally, but watch the higher glycemic index fruits such as strawberries and bananas. That's not to say you shouldn't consume them. Bananas, for instance, are a tremendous source of natural potassium, and I personally eat them all the time. In fact, I would much rather my patients consume a ton of these higher glycemic fruits than candy bars and cake any day. The point is that some fruits such as strawberries and bananas do have a higher glycemic index and you should be aware of this fact, especially if you're faced with a critical condition such as cancer or brittle diabetes.

Remember to consume the whole fruit, or if you're going to juice fruits and vegetables, use as much of the pulp as possible. When it comes to processed sugar and simple, refined carbohydrates of any kind, absolutely stay away from them as much as possible. An occasional breaking of the rules, as in once a month, is not an issue, but daily consumption is absolutely not conducive to achieving optimum health.

Protein Priorities

We now know we need fewer carbohydrates because we require less fuel in our modern lives, but why *more* protein? We need more protein because protein makes up the building blocks of the body. If organs, tissue and blood are to regenerate, they need the tools and raw material to build themselves back up again. That's where protein comes in. There's a huge amount of misinformation regarding protein, particularly the myth that humans need only twenty to thirty grams of it per day. That's just nonsense! Our bodies can certainly benefit from more protein than that, as long as it's the right type of protein and from a clean source.

When looking at nutrition in regard to protein, we want to make sure we get the best quality possible. Not all proteins are created equal. A lot has to do with the source of the protein. Contrary to a huge negative press campaign that lasted the better part of fifteen years, red meat is actually good for you, in moderation. Specifically, the iron supply and blood-building properties of beef are very valuable, but you'll want to limit consumption to a few times per week due to the high level of arachidonic acid found in red meat. Arachidonic acid is a type of fatty acid essential for health, but too much arachidonic acid in the diet will worsen the inflammatory cascade.

If you're a red meat lover, lamb and venison are also great choices so you don't overload on beef. Chicken, turkey and other poultry, as well as fish, are all great choices. In every case, make sure the meat is organic and free range or range fed—in other words, from grazing animals. Cheese and organic eggs are also good sources of protein, but again, make sure these foods are obtained from free-range animals.

Selectively consume fish that has been "wild caught," not farm raised. Fish farming, or aquaculture, has exploded over the last fifteen years and has basically become "factory farming" on the water. Thousands of fish are corralled together in small, netted areas where they are left to swim in and absorb their own waste, while at the same time being treated with pesticides and antibiotics. Fish should be bought fresh. The reason you want to be selective with fish is because some wild fish can be dangerous. Be careful of game fish, such as tuna, mahi mahi, grouper, etc., due to the potentially high mercury content that can be found within these fish. Smaller deep-sea fish, like Atlantic cod, that reside far away from the coastal shelves are far safer to eat.

When consuming protein, remember the key is moderation. Overconsumption of protein can create a condition causing a nitrogen imbalance that can potentially damage the kidneys. The vast majority of people will never need to worry about this because they're consuming far too little protein as it is!

How much protein should you consume? With regard to the vast majority of the population in standard occupations and living everyday lives, 25 percent to 30 percent of their daily food intake as protein is a good benchmark. Athletes or those recovering from an injury or surgery may have increased protein requirements up to 40 percent of their daily nutritional intake.

As we discussed earlier, beans are also a great source of protein. When occasionally combined with brown (not white) rice, this combination serves to provide all the correct amino acids needed to maintain good health. Soy is not a good option to supplement protein because a vast percentage of it is derived from genetically modified organisms (GMOs). Men, especially, should avoid soy-based products because of the plant-based estrogens contained in soy, which can create significant hormonal issues in males. We already live in an estrogen-dominant society: xenoestrogens are found in plastics, synthetic estrogens are used in pharmaceuticals, phytoestrogens exist in plants and estrogenic effects result from use of insecticides—all spilling into the environment and causing feminization of males in virtually all species. The incidence of many cancers has also clearly been associated with estrogen dominance.

Milk Matters

There are many arguments about how humans are the only species that drinks milk *after* the age of weaning and that if humans were meant to drink milk, women would continue to lactate throughout their lives. The simple truth is that humans have been nourished by milk throughout life for literally thousands of years. It's a fantastic source of B vitamins, protein and good saturated fats. The problem isn't milk. The problem is what we *do* to milk.

Aside from the steroids, hormones and antibiotics that leach into milk from the drugs we're giving livestock, pasteurization creates an additional problem. Pasteurization is good because it kills all the *germs*, right? Yes and no. Raw milk, as it comes straight from the cow or goat, is full of beneficial bacteria. These act as a natural preservative and go to battle should any bad bacteria try to proliferate. Raw milk is a complete food with everything needed to nourish us.

However, when milk is pasteurized, it is passed through pipes that have been heated up to 161 degrees. Ultra-high-temperature pasteurization heats milk up to 280 degrees. Pasteurization in milk has the same effect as antibiotics used in humans. Like antibiotics, pasteurization doesn't discriminate between the good bacteria and the bad bacteria. It kills everything. Once that happens, it's much easier for spoilage to occur because there aren't any "good guys" left to keep the "bad guys" in check anymore. That's why whole, raw milk curdles at room temperature and commercial milk spoils. These ultra-high temperatures also threaten the integrity and viability of the highly beneficial vitamins and proteins contained within milk.

Milk, like all raw or uncooked foods, contains all the necessary enzymes within it for your body to properly digest and assimilate its nutrients. When any food is heated above 110 degrees, the digestive enzymes within it are destroyed. Ever wonder why there are so many lactose intolerant people who can't digest milk?

Beginning in the 1930s, Francis M. Pottenger Jr., MD, conducted a famous research project that lasted for ten years. The study examined the effects of raw versus cooked food on cats. A predominate portion of their diet was milk. The group being nourished by whole, raw milk grew strong and had healthy kittens. The group consuming the pasteurized milk was thin and prone to disease and each subsequent generation was increasingly sickly and less vital. It's an eye-opening study that you can learn more about through the Price-Pottenger Foundation, a terrific resource for nutritional information.

Pasteurization is a form of processing, and any time we process food, it tends to become denatured. As I've said before, if it's in the form God created it, it's good. If it's not, leave it alone. To help you remember, here is the formula again: God given = Good. Man-made = Madness.

Unfortunately, finding raw milk today is like finding the Holy Grail. The milk industry and its lobbyists are as powerful as the pharmaceutical corporations in spreading their misinformation. Unless you actually own the cow or goat the milk comes from, it's tough to get your hands on raw milk. You may be lucky enough to find a local cooperative that provides it, or if you live in a rural area ask your neighboring farmer if he's willing to sell you some. A lot of Amish communities also drink their own raw milk. Just remember to inquire about any hormone usage first.

There are also arrangements known as "goat shares" by which you can purchase a portion of a goat for as little as $20. The farmer then allows you a certain number of dairy products from that animal, based on the number of shares you've bought in it. It might sound silly, but a lot of people are doing this because, in most states, it's legal to consume raw dairy products only from an animal that you own. If all else fails, buy organic milk, which is now readily available at any quality grocery store. Simply taste organic milk and compare it to regular milk, and you'll experience the difference firsthand. You'll never go back to regular milk again.

Cow Confusion

One last word on dairy. Most of the milk consumed by humans throughout history has always come from goats or sheep, and it still does. The United States is one of the rare few countries where the milk consumption is almost entirely from cow's milk. In his book, *The Devil in the Milk*, Keith Woodford, PhD, professor of farm management and agribusiness at Lincoln University in New Zealand, presents compelling research on the consumption of modern cow's milk and the state of chronic disease.

The simplest way to explain Woodford's research is that milk consists of three parts: cream/fat, whey and milk solids. The solids are composed of many kinds of proteins, which are made up of long chains of amino acids. One of these proteins is known as the beta-casein. Approximately five thousand years ago, a mutation occurred in the amino acids of this protein, causing it to produce a peptide called BCM7. The mutation occurred predominantly in cows from Europe but not those from Asia and Africa. Almost all Holsteins, commonly known as dairy cows (the famous black-and-white cows seen in milk commercials), carry this peptide.[11]

Cows that carry the BCM7 peptide are known as A1 cows. Those that do not are referred to as A2 cows. What's important to know is that BCM7 has proinflammatory, opiate-like properties and has been shown to contribute largely to a wide variety of chronic diseases, including autoimmune conditions, heart disease, autism, schizophrenia and various neurological disorders. Injecting BCM7 into animals caused Type 1 diabetes to occur. (Interestingly, the French in their culinary arrogance have always

---

11 Keith Woodford, PhD. 2007. *Devil in the Milk: Illness, Health and the Politics of A1 and A2 Milk*. Nelson, New Zealand: Craig Potton Publishing. p. 242.

refused to use A1 milk in their cooking because they regard it as inferior. Some say the French have terrible manners, but no one disagrees that they make terrific cheese.) As ominous as it sounds, there's no reason for too much of an alarm here. BCM7 is not absorbed to any great extent into the human bloodstream of people with healthy GI tracts. However, as in the case of children with autism or those with poor GI function, BCM7 may indeed have a significant contributory role in worsening the disease process.

Interestingly enough, BCM7 is not found in goat's milk or sheep's milk. Raw or not, goat's milk has been shown to be much easier to digest than cow's milk. The protein molecules are also much smaller, allowing for better absorption of the nutrients. If you can get goat's milk, make the switch.

The best products of all are those that come from raw cultured dairy such as yogurt, kefir, cultured butter and sour cream. Not only do these have all the necessary vitamins, good fats, proteins and enzymes, they're also filled with beneficial probiotics excellent for your immune system and digestive tract. When you consume dairy of this quality, it really does do the body good.

And Fat?

As with most things, there is a tremendous amount of misinformation about fats as well. For instance, saturated fats such as butter and coconut oil have gotten an incredibly bad rap over the last fifteen years. We have just recently begun to see how important fat really is in our diets. All fats are fatty acids made up of chains of carbon atoms, with hydrogen atoms attached to these chains. There are three main types of fatty acids: saturated, monounsaturated and polyunsaturated. The terms *saturated, monounsaturated* and *polyunsaturated* refer to the degree of "saturation" of these carbon chains with hydrogen atoms.

A saturated fatty acid has the maximum possible number of hydrogen atoms attached to each carbon atom in the chain making up the fat. Therefore, it's said to be "saturated." Think of it as saturated fats being maximally "saturated" with hydrogen. Monounsaturated fats would have one double bond, or one carbon site *not* saturated. Polyunsaturated fats would have multiple double bonds, or two or more carbon sites *not* saturated with hydrogen.

Saturated fats are mostly derived from animal sources and, in some cases, plants. These include beef fat, butter, cream, milk, cheeses and other dairy products made from whole milk. And yes, they do contain dietary cholesterol. Do yourself a favor and eliminate all concern you may have about cholesterol. Instead, concentrate on the *types* of fats you're consuming.

Plant sources of saturated fats include coconut oil, palm oil and cocoa butter. Saturated fats are usually solid at room temperature. Monounsaturated fats include canola, olive and peanut oils, as well as oil from avocados. These fats remain liquid at room temperature but are solid in the fridge. Polyunsaturated fats include safflower, sesame, sunflower, corn and soybean oils, as well as the oil in many nuts and seeds. These fats are usually liquid at room temperature and in the refrigerator.

Many people recognize the need for saturated fats because this kind of fat is quickly assimilated into the body and utilized for energy, leaving little if any to be stored as fat. That's why bodybuilders and athletes prefer it. But what many people don't realize is, in reality, many foods contain both saturated and unsaturated fats, yet are described as one or the other depending on which fat makes up the majority. So, a healthier fat such as olive oil contains both unsaturated and saturated fats. Another generally unrecognized fact is that the specific saturated and unsaturated fats, such as those found in fish, olive oil, egg yolks and flaxseed, are vital to cell membrane integrity, organ function and hormonal production. And it doesn't just stop there.

You may be surprised to learn that certain saturated fatty acids are also needed for important cellular signaling and stabilization processes in the body. Saturated fat such as coconut oil is rich in vitamin E and loaded with lauric acid and caprylic acid, known for their antimicrobial, antifungal, antibacterial and antioxidant properties. Another advantage of coconut oil or coconut butter is that it can be stored without refrigeration for months without going rancid. Because it remains solid at room temperature, it can easily transform to a liquid in higher temperatures. Real butter and cream are also terrific sources for good saturated fats.

Preferred sources of monounsaturated fats include olive oil, nuts and the fat in avocados. Generally speaking, avoid poly-unsaturated fats as found in the oils from corn, safflower seed, cottonseed and soybeans. They're far less stable, go rancid quite easily and are simply not tolerated well by the body. However, there are two polyunsaturated fats that are essential for the biological system, specifically linoleic and alpha-linolenic acid, which are found in high quantities in flaxseed oil. More on them in a moment. Steer clear of any hydrogenated fats and trans-fatty acids. These include the fat in any commercially fried food and vegetable shortenings.

The best types of fat to consume from a true health perspective, and which I recommend to all my patients, are the following: extra virgin olive oil; organic butter (preferably raw); ghee (also known as clarified butter); organic coconut oil; and flaxseed oil.

Do your own research and learn the truth about these five ideal fats. If you consume these fats and stay away from the other types as much as possible, you'll have given your body and yourself one of the greatest gifts you could ever give. The attacks against butter and the anti-saturated fat campaigns, along with promotion of the polyunsaturated fats and oils and their partially hydrogenated cousin known as margarine—of the "I can't believe it's not butter" fame—have probably contributed as much to chronic disease as all junk "food" on the planet combined.

I will say more about margarine in a moment, but first let's briefly discuss the supposed link between saturated fats and high cholesterol/heart disease, along with other chronic diseases.

Fats, Cholesterol and Heart Disease

This supposed link is simply propaganda designed to confuse us and keep us in the dark about facts that would allow us to regain control of our own health. You see, nearly all commercial foods will typically contain either all polyunsaturated or partially hydrogenated fats containing some combination of margarine and unsaturated fat mixed together. These include all the chips, crackers, pastries, breads, cakes, cookies, candies, dips, condiments such as salad dressings and mayonnaise, snacks, cereals and bars, as well as all foods promoted as "cholesterol free," "fat free," "diabetic healthy," "weight loss" food and "all vegan" prepared foods.

These foods are advertised and promoted as being the "health-conscious" options for consumers, whereas, in truth, these are among the worst foods you can consume. Even the supposed "saturated fats" found commercially, as in grocery-bought meat and poultry, are partly unsaturated because most cows and chickens are fed corn- and soybean-based feeds that contain unsaturated fats. But as mentioned earlier, there is a caveat. Flaxseed oil is the exception to this general rule and is highly beneficial because of its high concentration of linoleic and alpha-linolenic acids.

Probably one of the most important reasons to consume flaxseed oil has to do with the work of Dr. Johanna Budwig. Dr. Budwig was a German biochemist who was nominated for the Nobel Prize seven different times. Her research on fats and oils has been considered by the world's leading authorities as among the finest, even as far back as 1952 when she served as the German central government's senior expert for fats and pharmaceuticals.

Dr. Budwig's research demonstrated the tremendous destructive effects and severe damage to the cell membranes resulting from lipid peroxidation occurring from the commercial processing of fats and oils that we consume in our diets. She was able to show that the consequences of this damage caused a reduction in the intracellular voltage, eventually resulting in chronic and sometimes terminal diseases.[12]

Remember that the physiological system is electrically based. All animal cells have a nucleus in the center that is positively charged, and an outer lining of the cell, known as the cell membrane, that is negatively charged. For example, when we obtain an EKG, we are obtaining an electrocardiogram that actually is measuring the electrical conduction of the heart tissue. Similarly, an EEG, or electroencephalogram, assesses the electrical activity of the brain.

Dr. Budwig discovered that when unsaturated fats are chemically treated, their beneficial unsaturated qualities are destroyed and the natural electrical field is disrupted, resulting in a loss of electrons. The commercial processing of fats facilitates

---

12 Johanna Budwig. 3rd ed. 1994. *Flax Oil As a True Aid Against Arthritis, Heart Infarction Cancer, and Other Diseases.* United States of America: Apple Publishing. p. 64.

destruction of this electron field, which must be present within the cell membranes of the 75 trillion cells that make up our bodies. Without a healthy and functional cell membrane, there is absolutely no possibility for the cell to function properly.[13]

As an example, the common understanding of why heart attacks occur is due to the "fat clogging" of the vessels that feed the heart muscle. But as we've already learned, the process is always dependent on oxidative stress and the resulting lipid peroxidation, or what actually occurs to the fats as a result of oxidation. We never look beyond the "fat clogging" idea to see how these highly dangerous fats and oils are affecting the overall health of our system on the cellular level.

Without the proper metabolism of fats in our bodies, every vital function and organ system becomes affected. This includes everything from the generation of new life to the production, on average, of 500 million new cells daily. One of the key components of this proper metabolism that Dr. Budwig noted was the essential ability of fats to associate and mix with protein to achieve a state of water solubility within the functional body.[14] With the commercial processing of fats, however, it is this critical component that is completely destroyed and characteristic of the mechanism leading to chronic disease postulated by Dr. Budwig.

The resulting cascade eventually leads the fats that are no longer active and unable to flow through the single cell capillary networks to begin causing circulation issues to arise. These problems additionally compromise the process of cellular division and

---

13 Johanna Budwig. 2008. *Cancer—The Problem and the Solution*. United States of America: Nexus Gmbh. p. 127.
14 Johanna Budwig. 2010. *The Budwig Cancer & Coronary Heart Disease Prevention Diet: The Revolutionary Diet*. United States of America: Freedom Press. p. 176.

regeneration, which is responsible for all growth and repair. The entire process of healing is thus inhibited because it is critically dependent on these rich fatty acids, which are no longer active. As a result, when this normal process of fat metabolism is interrupted, the body essentially begins to die. It is these commercially processed fats and oils, in essence, that cause the shutting down of the electrical field, which in turn leads to the various chronic and sometimes terminal diseases to manifest.

Thus the final word on fat: Don't worry about the amount of fat, just the *type* of fat you consume. It's that simple.

Deadly Duo

There are two things that you should *never eat* in your entire lifetime. My belief is that simply by abstaining from these two you'll significantly reduce your chances of getting a chronic disease. The first thing to never eat is margarine. It's great to use as a substitute for axle grease in your car, but do NOT put it in your body. Think of margarine as liquid plastic. By consuming margarine, you displace essential components of the cell membrane crucial for the functioning of every cell in your body. The cell membrane is made up of a lipid bi-layer that allows cells to essentially "breathe," but consuming margarine replaces these essential lipids (fats) causing your cells to suffocate.

A good visual would be to imagine yourself taking a plastic bag, putting it over your head and then trying to breathe. That's what consuming margarine does because you're changing the permeability of your cell membranes and preventing the cells from functioning the way they were designed to function. Butter, however, is fine. It's one of the good guys. Patients say, "My doctor said I shouldn't eat butter because of cholesterol." Butter is *natural*. Margarine is *not*! The general rule for fats is no different from what's already been discussed: God given = Good. Man-made = Madness.

The second thing you should avoid consuming is the flesh of a pig. Why? Is it because the Muslim and Jewish religions say not to consume it? Is it because Christ never ate pork? Is it because it's a "dirty" animal that carries the trichinosis worm? Well, all these things are true, but there's a more important reason why the meat from a pig should not be consumed even if you're not religious and don't mind eating a few trichinosis worms.

The reason not to eat meat from these animals is that pigs are 84 percent genetically identical to humans. Where do we get insulin? We get it from porcine sources. Where do we go to harvest heart valves for transplant patients? We get them from pigs. Pig-to-human kidney and lung transplants have already been successfully performed. When I was training in general surgery, we learned how to do esophago-gastro-duodenoscopies and colonoscopies on pigs because the anatomy of a pig's GI tract is almost indistinguishable from that of a human's GI tract. Would you eat another human? How about a gorilla, with whom we share 96 percent of our genetic code?

We're now beginning to witness autoimmune problems related to pork consumption.[15] Luckily, you've probably never run into a cannibal, but if you did you would see that, after consuming human flesh for so long, a cannibal's body begins to deteriorate.[16] The body begins to reject the meat because it's too

---

15 H.R. Dalton, C. Pritchard, R.P. Bendall. 2008. Pig Meat Consumption and Mortality from Chronic Liver Disease. *Journal of Hepatology*. 48 (2): S100.

16 Michael Day. May 23, 1998. Warning: Cannibalism Is Bad for Your Health. *NewScientist*. 2135 (1).

similar to self-digestion. I believe that's what happens in our own bodies when we consume pork or pork products. It would be interesting to see a study comparing the level of autoimmune and chronic disease within a culture that primarily consumes pork and one that abstains.

Regardless, it should be intuitively obvious that consuming the flesh of an organism that is 84 percent genetically identical to ourselves is *not* a good thing. Even as far back as 1897, Dr. J. H. Kellogg wrote a book called *The Dangers of Pork Eating Exposed*. It might explain why many of the monotheistic religions of the world, including Islam and Judaism, have always prohibited their followers from consuming the flesh of a pig. What does your intuition tell you?

Appetite and Attitude

There's a reason why the first three letters in the word *diet* spell DIE. Eating in a healthy manner doesn't have to be painful, although it may *feel* painful at first. You're not going to die by passing up that cheese Danish tomorrow morning and replacing it with a bowl of grapes. By the way, if you make your own cheese Danish with real organic cheese and butter from raw milk, healthy fats, eggs from range-fed chickens and natural organic ingredients, then go for it (and send me some). No, you won't die by making a better choice right now . . . but you *will* die sooner rather than later if you don't start making the right choices in life. You've got a lot of healthy choices in front of you now for your next meal. Just remember, the healthiest item to include in all your meals is a big helping of positive attitude!

Attitude plays a tremendous role in how you respond to the changes you make—and also how well you're able to stay on track with those changes. One way to really change your attitude and appreciate the food you are consuming is to say a prayer of gratitude over the food. Your positive mind-set and thoughts will change the energetic resonance of the food you're consuming and the food will actually *taste better*. I know what you're thinking, so rather than try and explain this to you, let's just experience it.

Remember what we said in the beginning. Open your mind and recognize that you don't know everything there is to know about everything. The beauty is that as soon as you accept this, the reward in itself is the new knowledge you begin to acquire virtually immediately. So here's the experiment. Get something healthy and delicious to eat. Some fresh fruit, like a juicy pear or a delicious apple, will work for this example. Then, sitting quietly, stare at this food for a few seconds. Think about where it came from. Think about how it was grown or how it was produced. Think how it came to be on your plate in front of you. And then bless it. This is not a religious denominational prayer. Simply thank the universe for this sustenance you've been given. Bless it because it's about to become a part of you. Bless it for sustaining you and giving you the fuel needed for life. Then slowly taste the food and chew it. Savor it. If you're honest and take the time to experience this, you'll have proven to yourself what I stated.

Those who think they have no time for healthy eating will sooner or later have to find time for illness.
—EDWARD STANLEY

FAST WRAP
Step 1: The Principle of Nutrition

What's different about nutrition today?

In order to turn out huge amounts of produce, meat and diary, the "family farm" has been replaced by agricultural assembly lines. Steroids, pesticides, herbicides, caustic fertilizers and antibiotics are used to artificially increase yield and drastically decrease growing time. The focus is quantity, NOT quality.

Why is this important to my health?

Fruits and vegetables grown from "denatured" soil have drastically reduced the amounts of vitamins and minerals in food, all of which serve specific functions in healing and regeneration. Produce and animal products from "factory farms" contain powerful toxins that can prevent healing and even make physical conditions worse. Nutrient-dense foods support and speed the healing process. This is important to you because it can be the difference between staying healthy or succumbing to a chronic disease.

How can I use nutrition to maximize my health?

Begin to increase the amount of organic produce you consume, aiming to eat exclusively organic as your budget permits. Make sure you're getting healthy fats from items like eggs, real butter, olive oil, flaxseed oil and coconut oil. Selectively consume range-fed or free-range eggs, dairy and meat products. Stay away from foods containing preservative and chemicals. *Never* consume margarine or pork. And always remember to bless your food before consuming it.

If I make this change, what can I expect?

Your body will begin to celebrate. You may experience more energy, better sleep, clearer skin, a renewed sense of well-being and possibly the waning of some symptoms that have bothered you for some time. Nutrition provides the building blocks of healing. Every little change is a step back toward health. Get ready to make the shift.

STEP 2: THE PRINCIPLE OF SUPPLEMENTATION

Our body is a machine for living. It is organized for that, it is its nature. Let life go on in it unhindered and let it defend itself, it will do more than if you paralyze it by encumbering it with remedies.

—LEO TOLSTOY

Sometimes Less Is More

Joe came to my clinic because he wasn't feeling his best. Strong, athletic and in his forties, he was very proactive about his health. He was absolutely certain that his problem was something significant because he was doing everything he was supposed to be doing, yet he felt tired all the time as though, as he put it, "something's missing." This issue had progressively worsened over the last five years or so. He was following most of the 9 Steps already and was highly confident that he was getting everything he needed nutritionally. He was the kind of person who had gone to every website and read every book on health and created his own health dossier.

Because I like to approach health from a global perspective, I asked him how he could be so sure his problem wasn't a lack of nutrients in his diet. "Because I've been taking supplements for twenty years and if I was missing anything, I'd know it," he insisted.

Sometimes having part of the answer can be more dangerous than if you had none of the answer, sort of like the old saying "a little bit of knowledge is a dangerous thing." It's better if someone has no knowledge on a subject than to have a little knowledge and assume they know the answer. In fact, this is exactly what most of us suffer from, and what I warned you about before we started delving into the 9 Steps. We must strive to eliminate the notion that we "already know" so that we may stay in a receptive mode to learn new things. But let's get back to Joe.

At that point, Joe hoisted an enormous bag onto the examination table. It was filled to the brim with an arsenal of supplements. Every vitamin, mineral, herb, protein, biological component and homeopathic elixir I'd ever heard of was in that bag. He had to be taking a $1,000 worth of supplements, if not more, every month. I immediately told him he needed to stop taking all these pills and potions and that I would start him on a few specific things instead. He panicked and said he needed all these supplements. "Plus, I don't need anything different. This stuff works just fine."

"Well, Joe," I responded, "if all these things really were doing you any good, do you really think you would be sitting here in my office right now?"

Joe chose to follow my advice, reluctantly, and decided to go off his excessive self-prescribed supplement regimen. I put him on the best multivitamin I know of (I admit I'm biased since we have it specifically made for our patients), omega fatty acids, our cold-filtered whey isolate protein and our liquid, end chain vitamin B complex. He went from taking more than eighty pills a day to just eight and from numerous liquids a day to just two. He also changed his protein to our brand, which I had specifically designed to meet the nutritional needs of patients suffering from cancer. Everyone who I suspect needs a good-quality protein with a high biological value is put on this protein, and I personally take it myself daily, as does the rest of my family. My reasoning is that because it helps patients with cancer, it's going to help everybody.

After three weeks, Joe told me that most of his complaints had significantly improved or completely resolved. He wasn't tired anymore, and the feeling that "something was missing" was no longer present. Bottom line: He assessed *himself* as being 70 percent improved. A simple change for Joe let him know that when it comes to supplements, it's quality that matters, not quantity, and less is often more.

Times Have Changed

Making the switch to whole, organic foods is a monumental step toward getting well. Just having the discipline to make better food choices and resisting old habitual patterns says a lot about your commitment level. Whether you know it or not, your body will take these essential tools for cleansing, rebuilding and rejuvenating and will begin working to move you back to better health. Organic whole foods are the most potent and purest source of vitamins, minerals and proteins that you can possibly consume. Remember, if God made it, it's the best choice. If organic foods are really that powerful, then why do we need supplements? That's a great question. The answer is because our environment has changed even more than our food.

At least once a month a patient will say to me, "I don't need supplementation. My great-grandfather didn't use supplements and he was fine. So why the heck should I use them?" Well, let's look back at what a typical day might have involved for our great-grandparents. Great-grandpa probably woke up at 5:00 a.m., after going to bed at 8:00 or 9:00 p.m. the night before, and enjoyed a large healthy breakfast of organic, free-range steak and eggs from range-fed chickens, with whole, unpasteurized butter and raw whole milk.

Then, because most people didn't own cars, he probably walked to work, breathing clean fresh air the entire way while getting his muscles warmed up and getting his blood circulating. He didn't have to fight any traffic jams, curse anyone for cutting him off (or be cursed at for cutting someone else off), and didn't have to look for a parking space, all the while trying to get to work on time. At work, he probably ate a hand-packed lunch made by great-grandma with food from their garden. After another walk home, he might have eaten homemade stew that great-grandma prepared while he was at work. Later, the two of them probably either sat on the front porch reading—because no one had TV—or worked in the yard and garden together before going to bed by 9:00 p.m. Sound like your average day? I didn't think so.

Modern Malady

In our modern-day society, we have certain stressors that our great-grandparents never even imagined. We fight five lanes of traffic on the way to jobs we hate, where companies try to squeeze more and more work out of us. We have to balance day-care schedules while we're figuring out how to pay all our taxes as we try to avoid getting mugged going to the grocery store to buy our food, which is devoid of most of the nutrients our bodies require. At the same time, this food is laden with things that our bodies DON'T require—substances that only burden our physiology! Threat of terrorism, retirement planning, funding college educations, compliance with regulatory boards, work evaluations, employee/employer issues, paying property taxes, income tax, payroll tax, this tax, that tax, the tax on tax, etc., etc., take up almost all our conscious time.

Meanwhile, the dentist puts mercury fillings in our teeth because we have dental decay from all the excess refined sugars we consume, which we pick up at the gas station every time we pump gas in our car while inhaling the vapor of the gasoline and the exhaust of the cars pulling in and out of the station. The most exercise most of us get is pumping that gas while we inhale the fumes or picking up the remote as we get a beer during halftime or—the ultimate workout—pushing a shopping cart through a supermarket. All these intense daily stressors, with no exercise or outlet, make us feel as though we're living inside a pressure cooker that's going to explode any minute. The stress levels in our society are higher now than they've ever been.

The problem is that human beings were not meant to live this way. We've created an environment for ourselves that's completely unnatural. Our bodies were designed to process isolated occurrences of stress and then return to equilibrium. When a saber-toothed tiger approached a caveman, his adrenaline and cortisol would kick in, putting him in a "fight or flight" mode. If he was lucky enough to escape, the caveman's adrenal glands would eventually calm down and his system would return to balance as if the incident had never even happened. Until the next time it happened.

In modern society, however, we're in a chronically elevated state of stress. Instead of having a peak response and a return to baseline levels, we are in a constant state of stress, our cortisol levels constantly hovering way above baseline. Today, our poor diets, filled with high-fructose corn syrup in sodas and polyunsaturated fat–laden fast food, further stimulate the already increased insulin that results from the continuous cortisol thrashing our bodies are receiving. Both cortisol and insulin are proinflammatory substances that cause great oxidative damage within the body. Realizing this, we can clearly see why consistently elevated stress has led to so much chronic disease in our society, which didn't exist just a few generations ago. The idea of "killer stress" is not just a metaphor. It's really happening all around us.

A Solid Foundation

Without making the appropriate changes to decrease stress in your life, supplements are likely to do you little good. Remember, healing starts from the inside out; whatever is happening in your mind is happening in your body. We'll discuss some of these changes a bit later. In the meantime, it's essential to ensure you get an adequate supply of nutrients. Obviously, the preferred method is to increase the quality of our food items. Unfortunately, the nutritional requirements needed to keep up with modern society's demands prevent us from being able to consume that amount of food, making it necessary to supplement with good-quality B vitamins, organic-based minerals, clean and rancid-free fatty acids and high-potency antioxidants to counteract any internal damage just from the stress of the modern daily carnage we refer to as life.

The foundation of any good supplemental program is a broad-spectrum multivitamin. A time-released vitamin will ensure that you don't flush it all out in your urine within an hour. You can test your own vitamins for their absorption quality. Drop one in a glass of water. If it doesn't dissolve completely within thirty to sixty minutes, you won't be able to absorb it either. Choose one that best fits your age range and gender. Make sure you're getting enough B vitamins in your multivitamin because B vitamins are the one imperative component you need when you're under undue stress.

Buyer Beware Quality Control

Yes, even children need vitamins. Follow the same guidelines when choosing a supplement for your children. They may not be facing traffic jams in the morning, but they're continuing to develop and grow, which requires a huge amount of quality nutrients. Children particularly need good essential fatty acid supplements that provide omega-3 and omega-6 oils for brain development. These include flaxseed, pumpkin seed and walnuts. These supplements come in liquid form, have little taste and can be easily added to other foods. NEVER use these oils for cooking, as they can become toxic when exposed to heat. Their healing power lies in their raw form. I also suggest using fish oil and krill oil, but you have to make sure you're getting these oils from a highly reputable source because mercury contamination is very common.

As with any product you buy, many supplements are not always as they seem. We all want the highest quality in anything we buy, but when it comes to your health, you cannot afford to be cutting corners. Obviously, everyone would rather drive a BMW than a Yugo, because there's a big difference in performance. The performance range for nutritional supplements is actually even wider, mostly because it's so difficult for consumers to tell what they're getting. There are many brands to pick from, some professional and others over-the-counter. Most brands, however, you should simply avoid.

Many supplements don't even contain their key ingredients. As an example, a study done by the Department of Obstetrics and Gynecology at the University of Washington examined the fifteen top-selling brands of probiotics. Recall that these are the "good" bacteria that populate your intestinal tract and provide you with a healthy immune system, among many other benefits. Results showed that thirteen of the samples didn't even contain a trace of the probiotics that they claimed to contain. Only two were found to contain partial ingredients of those listed on the label. Even worse, all except one contained a significant amount of contaminants.[17]

Even if the supplement actually does contain all the ingredients listed on the bottle, that doesn't mean they are necessarily useful or beneficial. For instance, most active constituents in herbal products are highly fragile. Improperly growing, harvesting, processing and even transporting the ingredients can signifi-

---

17 See the Bastyr Center for Natural Health, http://bastyrcenter.org/content/view/664/.

cantly denature supplements, rendering them useless. I can hear your question coming. "Growing, harvesting and processing may harm herbal supplements, but what possible difference could transportation make?" If you want to find out, fill an unrefrigerated truck with milk and drive across the state and see what happens. Transportation of supplements makes a huge difference in their effectiveness and most of the ingredients in herbal supplements are traveling great distances, from places as far away as the rainforests of South America or China, not just a few hours away.

Batch testing is the only real way to determine if a supplement has all the listed ingredients and if those ingredients are in their "active" states. Sadly, most companies do not perform the necessary tests on their products, sometimes out of ignorance but usually due to cost constraints. Tests such as chromatography, electrophoresis and protein assays are some of the ways to determine the efficacy of the raw materials used to create these products. Because no one—including the manufacturers—really knows if a particular brand of a certain product works or not, consumers often end up having wildly different responses to seemingly the same product. Saint-John's-wort is a terrific example. It's is an herbal plant that grows primarily in North America, Europe and Russia.

Saint-John's-wort had its fifteen minutes of fame about twenty years ago when the news media touted it as a natural cure for depression. People flocked to the product with very mixed results. Some had fantastic results, while others were completely unaffected. What was the difference? In the case of this herb, the time of the season when the plant is harvested makes a critical difference, similar to picking an orange off the tree when it's still green. This subtle difference caused some brands to become popular while others weren't as fortunate.

However, because few people realized this, Saint-John's-wort was written off as "folk" medicine or an old wives' tale. The fact is, if you get a good quality of Saint-John's-wort it works more effectively than the counterpart pharmaceuticals, with no side effects and at considerably less cost. But the appropriate question to ask first before giving Saint-John's-wort to someone would be what's causing their *symptom* of depression in the first place?

A Delicate Balance

Supplements have a synergistic effect. This basically means that certain vitamins, minerals and herbs are more effective and work better in the presence of other vitamins, minerals and substances. They work as a more effective team. Sometimes, they may even be dependent on other vitamins or minerals that may act as co-factors or catalysts in order to be properly utilized, absorbed or digested. For example, taking vitamin C with magnesium makes the magnesium more biologically available to your body. Another example is vitamin D and calcium. Without adequate vitamin D, calcium is not properly absorbed. This balance of elements needs to be taken into consideration when creating any supplement. Without the right combinations in the correct ratios, your supplement could literally run right through you and into the toilet or worse, could create relative deficiencies. More importantly, at least from a financial perspective, your money will be going down the toilet as well. Good supplements aren't cheap, so definitely make sure you're getting your money's worth.

Another example that illustrates the importance of balance is when someone is deficient in a particular vitamin or mineral.

Often they'll run to the health food store, sometimes even at the advice of their doctors, and grab a bottle of the specific item in which they're deficient. But when supplementing our diets with a single element or improper ratios of elements, we can create a "relative" imbalance that can have significant detrimental implications on the overall physiological balance of the system. This improper usage could even result in a "relative" deficiency of an entirely different element. The ratio of vitamins and minerals in the body is like a combination lock to a safe. You need just the right amount to open the combination that allows all the systems to start functioning optimally and humming in perfect harmony.

For instance, it's a common misconception that the majority of the population today is deficient in zinc. This is not necessarily true, however. It all depends upon the region where the individual lives and has previously lived, as well as the genetic predisposition for absorption, elimination and proper utilization of the mineral in question. Very often I see patients who are actually copper deficient but have sky-high zinc levels, contrary to this popular misconception. Residents of the southeastern United States, for example, routinely are found to have very high zinc levels but with deficient copper levels.[18]

The appropriate zinc-to-copper ratio in the human body ideally is maintained around 10:1, as measured in urine. Essentially, this means that for every ten zinc molecules, you need one copper molecule to have a perfect balance between these two particular

---

18   It is important to mention that copper and zinc, along with other minerals such as iron and selenium, are all metals that are essential for life. The "metals" found to be necessary for life are commonly referred to as "minerals." However, very high levels of these essential minerals beyond a certain limit will cause them to act in the same detrimental manner as the toxic heavy metals, and induce the same damage through the process of oxidative damage.

minerals. In actuality, mineral balances are usually dependent on the relationships among any three minerals. To continue with our example, let's say your zinc-to-copper ratio was balanced at 10:1 but your individual zinc levels were low when measured on their own. Because your zinc was low, you or your doctor begins to increase your zinc. You begin taking your zinc supplement as directed. As your zinc levels begin to rise and become normal (as measured individually), you induce a "relative" copper deficiency. In other words, as the zinc level rises, the ratio of zinc to copper increases, and now you only have one copper molecule for every twenty zinc molecules.

Simply telling a patient to supplement with an element in which they might be deficient can often create these "relative" deficiencies in other areas. Unfortunately, most physicians and health-care professionals tend to overlook this fact. With few exceptions, vitamins and minerals should be taken with food or immediately after meals to allow for maximum absorption.

In addition, live-source ingredients are hundreds of times better and far more effective than synthetically derived or inorganic versions found in most of the supplements you could take. Without going into too much detail, the live-source products have a biophotonic (body of light) frequency that is exclusively found in once-living things. This biophotonic resonance matches our own human energy signature and makes the end product far more utilizable and able to assimilate into our own physiology. There's an entire course I teach based on this concept, marrying quantum physics with medical science, but that's a subject for another book. More information on this course is provided in the resources section at the end of this book. For now, let's just say that medical science and nutrition will change radically in the coming years—particularly as people discover what their bodies truly need.

Trusted Advice

Who thought picking a simple multivitamin or supplement could be so complicated? The truth is, it's not. You just need the right knowledge, and now you have it. Nevertheless, I would strongly suggest that before you pick something off a shelf you consult a trusted health-care professional. Don't be shy about asking what they take, but do make sure that they understand the underlying principles of nutrition and detoxification. If they don't seem to think detoxification is an issue, find a different doctor. With any product, it's always best to stick to pharmaceutical grade or reagent grade if you can because the standards for these categories are usually much higher. Although you can find this information on product websites or by calling the companies directly, don't trust any individual or company to give you all the information you need. Consult that health-care professional or the knowledgeable individual with experience that you trust.

Invariably, I'm always asked what brand I recommend the most. At my clinic, we use a unique line of supplements that I helped develop, some of which have been registered with the FDA, and many of which have previously been assigned national drug codes. Unfortunately, this line is only available to doctors for their patients. However, a few trustworthy brands of good-quality supplements are out there. It may seem overwhelming at first, but once you do your homework, you'll likely be able to stick with one or two suppliers for most products.

You can get further information on recommended brands of vitamins, minerals and other supplements from our website and in the resources section at the end of this book. Just remember that although even the best supplements aren't silver-bullet cure-alls, they are a necessary part of modern life if you want to stay as healthy as possible to compensate for all the excess stress and toxicity we are exposed to on a daily basis.

> *He that takes medicine and neglects diet and*
> *nutrition wastes the skill of the physician.*
> —CHINESE PROVERB

FAST WRAP
Step 2: The Principle of Supplementation

What's the difference between supplements?

There's a big difference between supplements. Most nutritional supplements don't contain many of the ingredients they claim are in their products. Ingredients may also be denatured, grown improperly, harvested at the wrong time, extracted improperly or transported inadequately. Unfortunately, most companies don't conduct the appropriate tests to verify the effectiveness of their own products.

Why do I have to take them?

Modern society has increased stress levels unheard of just a few generations ago; at the same time, environmental toxicity has increased. This has led to increasing requirements for nutritional support while getting lesser nutrients in our diet due to lack of nutritional density in the foods we eat. Supplements are necessary because they fill this void. Quality supplements also create a strong buffer against this modern onslaught as well as widen the gap between chronic disease and optimum health.

How do I find a supplement I can trust?

Don't just pick one off a health-food-store shelf. Look for pharmaceutical grade products and look at the reputations of various companies. Trust no one because the nutritional industry notoriously exaggerates the value of its products. Test your multivitamin by dropping it in a glass of water. It should dissolve in thirty minutes to be absorbable by your body. Preferably, take gel capsules, powders and liquid supplements to improve their absorption. Rely on your own experience and note the difference for yourself.

If I find a good supplement, how will I know it's working?

It depends on where your personal deficiencies are, but the change you may experience with a new supplement regime could be sudden or gradual or perhaps not even perceivable at all. With the right balance, you may experience some improvements, but the goal of supplementation is prevention. If you're tuned in to your body and you're on a good-quality supplement, you should experience a sense of well-being. The effect, although usually noticeable, is taking place regardless of what you're "feeling." Remember, you can't *feel* prevention.

STEP 3:
THE PRINCIPLE OF WATER

*Water and our necessary food are the only
things that wise men must fight for.*
—PLUTARCH

Out of water, all life comes.
—THE KORAN

Washed Away

Victor came to me basically healthy but with some minor issues. He was concerned about a history of heart disease on his mother's side, had some old sports injuries and experienced intermittent pain in his knees. He went through an appropriate course of detoxification and we worked on getting his GI health back up to par. He improved overall, but his major concern was regarding his knees, which didn't really improve. Victor asked me what he could do to help his knees without a prescription, reminding me that he was not a "pill-taker." He didn't even want to consider trying a supplement, let alone a pharmaceutical. He asked me for my thoughts on the possibility that the solution might involve more activity.

Immediately, the work of Dr. F. Batmanghelidj came to mind. In the 1970s, before the Iranian government was overthrown, he was the personal physician of the Shah of Iran. As a result of being the Shah's personal doctor, he was thrown into prison. While incarcerated for the next few years, Dr. Batmanghelidj met many people who had been in jail even longer than he himself had been, most of them sick and dying because of the very poor conditions. Being a physician, his natural inclination was to try and help. But he had no resources and none were provided by his jailers. All he had was water—and even that was polluted— yet he began treating his fellow inmates with this polluted drinking water. That was all he used, and nothing else. The healing results he achieved were dramatic and are detailed in his book, *Your Body's Many Cries for Water*.[19]

Victor, my patient, was typical when it came to water consumption. He simply drank a glass or two, if that, per day. I had already done some experimentation based on Dr. Batmanghelidj's work. Because of what I had personally experienced, I believed very strongly in the healing power of water. Without telling Victor why, I suggested that he increase his consumption of water

---

19 Fereydoon Batmanghelidj, MD. 2nd ed. 1995. *Your Body's Many Cries for Water*. Falls Church, VA: Global Health Solutions, Inc. p. 186.

to at least two-thirds of his body weight in pounds, applying that number to ounces of water per day. Based on his weight of 240 pounds, for example, he needed to be consuming 160 ounces of water per day. I wasn't sure if Victor would experience what I myself had, but I had a hunch he would. He had no idea at all that I had made this suggestion to see what would happen to his knees. He just knew that I wanted him to begin drinking more water. Fortunately, he was also a very compliant patient.

It took him a good two weeks to work up to that level of water consumption. But once he did, and he had maintained it for a full week, something amazing occurred. His knee pain began to first dissipate and then eventually disappeared entirely. When I asked him how his knees felt, he was surprised because he hadn't thought of his knees for the previous few days. The truth was that the hydration significantly increased the volume of his joints, alleviating the stress his knees had been experiencing.

By the time he had reached thirty days on the new regimen, he was surprised to find that his skin was much clearer and he'd lost some frustrating weight he'd been unable to shake. He'd made no other changes to his exercise or nutritional routines. He also mentioned that drinking that amount of water had become much easier over time because for some reason he felt thirstier. In actuality, his body had begun craving more water because he had essentially rehydrated his thirst receptors, causing the natural thirst response to reactivate.

Out of curiosity, I asked him to stop the water consumption. He first asked why. Then he agreed, but within two days he had to give up because he simply couldn't go without his water. He reported that he constantly felt parched and his body craved the water it had always needed but not previously perceived. Once his thirst receptors were hydrated and functional, the satiation centers in his brain had readjusted. His body just seemed to "soak it up," and the water provided him with healing powers to every part of his body. Water is so much more than just a "tasteless substitute" when soda or fruit drinks aren't available. We're just beginning to see the problems water can wash away in a world population that's essentially chronically dehydrated.

Sacred Signs

There is a studied discipline throughout history known as sacred geometry. It's not like your high school geometry class, so don't worry. I don't want to trigger any traumatic memories for any of you! Sacred geometry is more an observation of specific patterns that occur in nature. For example, honeybees create perfectly hexagonal cells in which to store their honey. Snowflakes are perfectly symmetrical and mathematically precise. Even the leaves of plants will grow outward from their center at geometrically predictable intervals, defined by a set of numbers known as Fibonacci numbers.

This same series of numbers defines the rate of reproduction in rabbits and the ratio of the spirals in a seashell. These kinds of mathematical patterns apply to the creation of the greatest art, architecture and music for thousands of years, even so far as defining the ratio of our arm length to leg length and the mathematical relationship of our various facial features to each other. You don't need to be a mathematician to see that we live in a universe designed for balance and based on implicit order. When we look at water, this principle becomes even more evident.

Our bodies are composed of 75 percent to 80 percent water. Every plant and animal cell on this entire planet is composed of 75 percent to 80 percent water. The planet itself is 75 percent to 80 percent water. Do you think God is trying to tell us something about water? Notice I didn't say "tea" or "lemonade." At least once a month someone tries to use the logic that tea or coffee should be fine since it's composed of water. Nonsense! Sure, coffee has water in it, but coffee can never replace the purity of natural water. If God had wanted us to be 75 percent to 80 percent coffee, He'd have made us that way. (There's more to come on the drawbacks of drinking coffee later.)

Pump Up the Volume

When it comes to water, we need to take the hint from the Creator and increase our water consumption. How much? My rule is simply to calculate one-half to two-thirds of your body-weight number in ounces to determine your minimal intake of water per day. For example, if you weigh 150 pounds, you need to drink between 75 and 100 ounces of water each day. To get an idea of how much water this is, a half-gallon is equal to 64 ounces of water. So, for a 150-pound individual, you would want to consume a little more than a half-gallon to three-quarters of a gallon of water per day. For most people that's going to seem like work, but believe me, once you do this for thirty days, you won't be able to stop. We're nearly all in a chronic state of dehydration.

If we approach the ideal ratio that the Earth needs to maintain a balance of water, and you're in this world, doesn't it intuitively make sense to consume an amount of water that would, at the very least, amount to the same ratio of water on the planet?

Luckily, the human body is very intuitive despite the mind getting in the way. So, you don't have to take my word for it; listen to your own body. The more water you consume, the better your body will feel. Every single function, from digestion and elimination right down to the electrical impulse exchange between cells, will become more efficient.

Drinking this much water will be difficult at first, but you should begin building up to your appropriate level. I carry a water bottle around the office with me. I even take it into the actual office visits with my patients. Sometimes we may be in the office for two hours, so having my water with me is not only convenient so I can consume my 160 ounces daily, it sometimes becomes necessary because I simply get thirsty. My staff members call me Dr. Water because I'm always filling up my water bottle. Okay, that's not true. My assistant is always filling it up.

But the point is to keep your glass with you, and each time you pass the water cooler, fill 'er up! Apply this to your situation, whatever it is. Regularly fill your glass each day and this step won't be hard. You won't even have to think about it. The problem only arises if, at 8:00 p.m. after getting home from a long hard day at work, you try to consume all of your allotted water before bedtime.

Ultimately, you'll saturate and rehydrate your thirst receptors, and when that happens, your body will actually begin craving water. Trust me. Once you hit your appropriate water consumption level, maintain that level for thirty days. Then, just as I had Victor do, try to stop drinking your water. Your body won't let you stop. It's finally being rejuvenated with its most elemental component and it's not about to give it up. That's when it becomes easy because now you're simply just fulfilling a craving.

Which Water?

If oxygen is the breath of life, then water is the blood of life. With something that important, you definitely don't want to be drinking just anything, especially tap water. In fact, **stop drinking tap water immediately!** This is especially important if you live in a major metropolitan area. Most urban water has added toxins, including fluoride and chlorine, among others. Remember from our discussion about the Three Foundations, our primary goal is to detoxify. Well, one of the easiest ways to reduce your toxic load is to interrupt the supply of that toxic load entering into your body. Keep the garbage from coming in at this stage by eliminating tap water. And there are plenty of toxins in tap water. However, don't be lulled into a false sense of security by thinking that all you need to do is drink bottled water. Statistics show that 70 percent of bottled water came from a municipal water supply and was just filtered and put into a plastic bottle. So bottled water, although a bit better, is not that much better and certainly not good enough.

If you can't drink the water from your own faucet, what type of water should be consumed and where can you get it? Who would have thought that something as simple and as pure as water could be so complicated? But the truth is that water is more expensive than gasoline now. At the time of writing, a gallon of gasoline was $3.75 for premium gas. A 32-ounce container of bottled water at the same gas station cost $1.59 (or $6.36 for a gallon). That makes water more than 40 percent more expensive than gasoline. Isn't that shocking? Twenty years ago, if anyone had talked about bottling water for a business, they would have been laughed out of town. But today it's big business.

The only ones who could exploit something as basic as water are the big corporations, and there are plenty of them trying to convince you to drink their "healthy" water. The grocery store shelves are overflowing with various water products. There's water with electrolytes, water fortified with vitamins, ionized water and even flavored water. Some waters come from glaciers, some from springs. Some come from artesian wells in faraway places. A lot of them carry fancy names that contain derivatives of words like *aqua*, *crystal*, *clear* and *pure* to convince you that what's in that plastic bottle is true water.

Think again. Many TV newsmagazine shows have featured profiles about the scientific analyses conducted on many of these products. The shocking part is that regardless of the fancy names, many of them contained nothing but tap water. You could have just saved yourself three bucks and loaded up on your own toxins free of charge in the convenience of your own home.

Just in case you haven't caught on to my sarcastic sense of humor, that was a joke! We're working hard to take toxins *out* of our bodies, so the first place to start is to reduce what we're putting into our bodies. Would the safe answer be to drink distilled water? There are a lot of proponents of distilled water who say that it's the best choice because it's the only true "pure" water available. Distilled water comes from boiling regular water. The steam condenses on receptacles above the boiling water, is cooled and then bottled. It contains only hydrogen and oxygen. The solids and impurities are all left behind as sediment.

The opponents of distilled water, however, claim that due to the property of hypo-osmolarity, distilled water can actually leach important minerals from your body, acting sort of like a magnet and pulling the minerals out of our systems. I don't know if I necessarily agree with this rationale, but I haven't seen any comparative studies that looked at this issue. Regardless, I don't recommend distilled water, but for a much simpler reason. With the exception of rainwater, distilled water is virtually impossible to find or drink in nature. Even when rainwater comes into contact with the earth, it mixes with natural minerals. The other issue is that the majority of rainwater is polluted with the acids found in our environment. Bottom line, if distilled water is the only clean source of available water you have, simply add a pinch of sea salt to the water and you'll have remineralized it.

Water Filter Facts

The best type of water is that which has been detoxified but still contains its important minerals. Unless we're living in the Alps or Himalayas, holding a cup underneath a melting glacier, the best source of water is filtered water from a reputable filtration system—not to be mistaken with water softeners or the gadgets you attach to your water pitchers or kitchen faucets. I'm referring to professional filtration systems designed specifically for the purpose of removing heavy metals, persistent organic pollutants and so on. I've evaluated more than forty different types of water filtration systems and have found one that is above and beyond all the rest. It's called the Wellness Water Filtration System, and I use it exclusively in my own home and my office. My reasons are not only based on the science behind the Wellness Filter but also on the philosophy behind it and the philosophy of the man who developed this unique filter.

The Wellness Water Filtration System was developed by a Japanese scientist named Harusuke Naito. Haru (pronounced Ha' Lu) was a world-record-breaking athlete at the State University of New York–Oneonta and then pursued his PhD in sports physiology at Indiana University before he returned to Japan to continue his work in hydrodynamics as a professor at Tokyo University. When I met Haru, he was fifty-two years old, and it was an amazing experience to interact with a human being of his caliber. There are not many people I've met whose spirit has left me standing in awe.

When he was just twenty-one, Haru discussed with the Dalai Lama his decision to adopt a baby. The Dalai Lama, who later became Haru's personal friend, encouraged him to choose a child who no one wanted to adopt. Haru took his suggestion and adopted a ten-year-old who was begging on the streets. He was only eleven years older than his son! When I met Haru, he had sixty-three children, four of them biological. Over the years, Haru has continued to adopt homeless, orphaned children who were usually begging in the streets, from Laos to Cambodia, India to Vietnam. The most amazing thing is that forty-seven of these children, who had no hope of a future, are doctors today.

After Haru became interested in filtration, he developed a breakthrough system and discussed it with the Dali Lama. His Holiness said, "I know where you received the secret of this invention. You received it from the Muslim holy book, the Koran." Haru said, "Yes, that's correct." Even though he's a practicing Buddhist, Haru initially had a Muslim mentor named Dr. Hakim Mohammed Said, a renowned Pakistani scholar and philanthropist and former governor of the province of Sindh.

Both Haru and Dr. Said shared a passion for hydrodynamics and for helping orphans. Dr. Said was becoming very popular in Pakistan for his humanitarian work, and his popularity among the population was rapidly growing. Because the reigning political party in Pakistan at the time felt threatened by Dr. Said's popularity, he was assassinated. Haru continued Dr. Said's work by transforming the hell these children had been living in to heaven on earth, one child at a time, one day at a time and one drink of pure water at a time, concentrating his efforts in the most impoverished countries in Asia.

Does It Work?

More than 100 hospitals in Japan exclusively use the Wellness Filter systems as their method of purifying water. In 2005–2006, the headmaster of Sea Coast Christian Academy, a special needs elementary school in Jacksonville, Florida, decided to put the Wellness Filter to a more rigorous test. He had Wellness Filters installed on all of the school's water fountains and instructed each teacher to have all of their students (grades 1 through 6) drink four ounces of Wellness filtered water each hour of the school day.

Student behavior indicators, such as the number of students sent to the principal's office, the number of disturbances and the number of children taking medication for ADD and ADHD, as well as the grade point average across all 165 students, were monitored. At the end of the year, the results stunned the faculty and the headmaster. The grade point average had increased from 2.9 to 3.3, and all the incidents of misbehavior declined significantly (reductions ranged from 44 percent to 78 percent). The really incredible result was the 88 percent decline in the number of children being medicated for behavioral issues (from 34 students down to 4).

It's obvious that the Wellness Filter, with its superior water quality, was able to assist in detoxification. During my surgical training, we had a little saying about irrigating wounds to prevent infection that also applies to areas of the body with better blood supply, such as the face: The solution to pollution is dilution. So if the dilutant (water) is cleaner, even more pollution is flushed away. Now you understand why I refer to the Wellness filtered water as "amazing" and why it's the water filtration system I personally use and recommend to my patients.

You can also find many other types of water filtration systems in grocery stores and various retail locations. These other machines purify the water through reverse osmosis, which is a reasonable and affordable second choice. A filtration system can be costly. Like organic food, however, it's definitely worth the investment. From a preventive standpoint, it potentially means the difference between success and failure or, in this case, health and illness. Look in the resources section for more details about the Wellness Water Filtration System. Due to space constraints, discussion of well water can't be included here. However, I myself am on a well at home and there will be additional discussion regarding well water in the members-only area of the book owners' website. Some of the most exciting advances being developed in water purification and even better, "water optimization," will also be revealed for the first time ever on that website.

Water Speaks

When most children are growing up, their parents teach them not to fear water but to respect it for safety reasons. That's an interesting choice of words. Respect water. Water demands our respect, not just because of its power but because of its intelligence. Water is alive. Japanese researcher Masaru Emoto knows this better than anyone. His book, *The Hidden Messages in Water*, is probably one of the most important books published in the last hundred years.[20] When pure water is frozen and viewed

---

20 Masaru Emoto. 2004. *The Hidden Messages in Water*. Korea: Beyond Words Publishing, Inc. p.175.

through a microscope, it forms breathtakingly beautiful, perfectly symmetrical ice crystals, each with a starlike, individually unique shape. Remember the sacred geometry I discussed earlier? Well, what Emoto discovered was when the water was toxic or unclean, such as tap water or polluted water from lakes, it failed to form the uniform crystals when frozen. In fact, most of the time the frozen toxic water formations appeared "torturous."

More important, he discovered that water, whether pure or polluted, could change its crystal structure to reflect the events and people with which it came into contact. Remarkably, he found that even the energetic vibrations from certain words simply imprinted on the containers housing the water were powerful enough to actually change the physical conformation of the crystalline structure of water. Two vials of exactly the same water could have a drastically different result in crystal formation just by changing the words on the labels. A vial labeled "I Love You" showed beautifully complex crystal patterns, while a vial labeled "I Hate You" would not crystallize and looked gray, disturbing and chaotic under the microscope. There was a clear absence of the beautiful uniformity and symmetry found in the frozen water that came from the container labeled "I Hate You."

Emoto conducted an experiment in Japan in the late 1990s at the Fujiwara Dam, which is infamous for its pollution. The water would never form crystals due to its level of contamination. A group of monks were taken to the site and asked to offer respect and prayers of gratitude to the water. After less than an hour of their praying, a sample was taken and frozen. Sample slides of the specimen showed the formerly polluted water now presenting prism-like geometric shapes that were clear and lacked the cloudy characteristic of the previous samples before the monks had chanted their prayers.

Equally surprising is the fact that Emoto got a phone call days later from the administrators of the dam, telling him that a young girl had been murdered and her body found at the dam just days before the experiment. Only days after the blessings were made and the water cleared, a man turned himself in for the crime. Emoto's books are full of these amazing experiments. It truly is a testament that water, whether inside or outside your body, is to be honored and respected.

I first read Emoto's book while on a trip to Spain with my wife and my two youngest children. Abie was just five at the time, and I thought it would be tough to convince such a little boy to read the book with me, but to my amazement, he would actually ask me if we could look at the pictures in the "water book," as he referred to it. He would ask me to read it to him. The fact that Abie, who is truly my teacher in more ways than I could ever adequately articulate, resonated with this book tells me all I need to know. It is the truth. To understand this truth, you must *feel* it.

Some of the most exciting and promising work in advancing water technology is related to the process of "water optimization" as I previously mentioned. This should not be mistaken for a new process of "filtration" or cleaning water. Unfortunately, at the time of writing this book, the information was not ready to be released. Suffice it to say this particular advancement in "water optimization" will take what Dr. Batmanghelidj and Dr. Emoto discovered to newer and great heights and strongly promises to render the medical pharmaceutical model completely obsolete, at least when it comes to chronic disease. For me personally, it's among the three most exciting advances that will change the world and will be easily accessible to any individual. As information becomes available, it will be released in the members-only area of the book owners' website at www.The9Steps.com.

Water is one of the best conductors of energy. It gives energy and transports energy. Your very thoughts are energy, energetic signatures that you are imprinting on yourself. And the water in your body is conducting that energy like electricity throughout every cell, tissue and organ system in your entire system. So think positive thoughts before you drink your water. Respect water! Not just the water you take into your body, but also the water that's already in your body. It's listening.

> *Your body cries for water; you are not sick, you are thirsty; don't treat thirst with medications!*
>
> —F. BATMANGHELIDJ, MD,
> AUTHOR OF *YOUR BODY'S MANY CRIES FOR WATER*

FAST WRAP
Step 3: The Principle of Water

What's so important about clean water?

Water hydrates your body and makes it possible for all your cells to function and communicate better with each other. Filtered water, unlike tap water, carries far fewer toxins, provides you with nourishing minerals, and helps dilute toxins in your body so they are easier to flush out via the kidneys and the GI tract. Remember: "The solution to pollution is dilution."

Why do I have to drink so much?

Even if you think you drink enough water, you're still dehydrated. Ideally, drinking two-thirds of your body weight in ounces of water per day is the *only* way to ensure both that your cells are being nourished properly and adequately while ensuring the toxins are being ushered out. Every process in your body requires water, and we live on a planet that's more than two-thirds water. Listen to what the Creator is trying to tell us! Water is extremely important . . . even more so than you think!

How can I find the best water?

A home water filtration system is best. If your budget is tight, bottled water from the grocery store may be adequate, but you could consider opting for the distilled water with a pinch of all-natural sea salt, which may be the better option, simply because at least you know the toxins have been removed from it. Don't drink distilled water without adding some minerals, however. Natural spring water is good and glacier water is better. But beware of marketing rhetoric. Read labels and make sure the water really does come from the source that's claimed. Avoid regular tap water unless you're getting it from a reliable well. And stay tuned for the release of information on "water optimization" that will soon be available on the book owners' website.

If I drink more, what can I expect?

As you drink more, your thirst receptors will start functioning again and your body will begin to crave water. It will actually become difficult to reduce your water intake once your body begins to be adequately hydrated. Increasing water consumption will assist with a tremendous number of things, from proper elimination and improved focus and concentration (your brain is more than 80 percent water) to improved joint flexibility, clearer complexion and more supple skin, to name just a few.

STEP 4: THE PRINCIPLE OF EXERCISE

Lack of activity destroys the good condition of every human being, while movement and methodical physical exercise save it and preserve it.

—PLATO

The Story of Dan

"What are you talking about?!" The outburst was so jarring, it knocked me right off my train of thought. I was thirty-one years old, standing in front of a group of about sixty people in my local community, having just recently opened my practice after leaving the U.S. Army. The educational lecture I was giving was actually on the same topic as this book, although back then, there

were only five steps, having now evolved into the 9 Steps. I was searching to find where the voice was coming from in the audience. The woman's voice continued to rant in the darkened room while the bright light of the projector facing me kept me from seeing exactly where the sound was coming from.

"How dare you? This is ridiculous. You make exercise sound like the be-all and end-all of health; that if you don't exercise, nothing else matters." I followed the direction of all the heads in the audience turning toward her and spotted a heavyset woman in the fourth row from the front, almost all the way to the extreme left of the room. She had stood up and was flailing her arms about in protest like I'd just spewed profanities at the audience.

"Did you have a question?" I asked the woman, who was completely flushed in the face with anger.

"How can you stand up there and claim exercise is so important to healing? What about the people like me who can't exercise? I've had multiple back surgeries, with two rods and screws inserted into my vertebrae. I *can't* exercise. It's too painful. But you make it out like I had a *choice* in the matter. How irresponsible for you to sit on your high horse and not take into consideration those who can't exercise because we've been injured! What kind of doctor are you?"

She was really upset. But there was only one word I really heard: the "C" word: *"can't."* I could see that this woman's anger was completely misplaced and I was the target of her years of frustration for making whatever excuse after whatever excuse she'd made to herself to justify her failure to take charge of her own life.

Judging from the steam coming out of her ears, I could also tell that nothing I said would register with her, so I just waited until she ran out of steam. It just so happened that the stars were aligned (again), and my friend Dan from the gym had taken me up on my invitation for him to attend the lecture. I looked further out into the small dimly lit conference room and called, "Dan, can you come up here?" There was no response. I finally spotted him, bowing his head, trying to hide. "Dan, come on up here." He sat looking at the floor, shaking his head "no."

"Come on, let's go, Dan!" He already knew where this was going. And he didn't really want to do what he already knew I was going to do.

Twenty-seven-year old long-haired Dan planted his cane firmly on the ground and pulled himself up. He slowly began making his way toward the front of the room, right leg dragging behind him, swinging the left leg in a wide arc in front while supporting himself with the cane, and then repeating the sequence all over again, step by step. By now, someone had turned the lights back on, and it was obvious to the audience that there was something terribly wrong with Dan. One step at a time, Dan made his way down the middle aisle and came up to me, back facing the audience. Before he turned to face the audience, he looked up at me with a half smile and shook his head "no." I smiled back and shook my head "yes." Dan turned around and stood next to me. Needless to say, you could hear a snail move, it was so quiet.

Looking directly at the woman who now looked like a deer caught in headlights, I said, "Dan, can you tell this kind lady who you are?" He responded with a small smile, looking at everyone in the audience, "I'm Dan."

Everybody laughed. "Great. Thanks, Dan. That was very helpful. Now, can you tell everyone how we know each other?" Time for games was over. We both knew it.

"I know you from the gym, Dr. Buttar," Dan said, with partial reluctance but now resigned, knowing that we were going to do this.

"And can you tell everyone how we met, exactly?" I asked.

"I asked you to help me," Dan explained.

"And what exactly did you need my help with, Dan?" I pressed.

"To help tighten the straps on my wrists."

"And why did you need straps on your wrists, and why did they need to be tight?" I continued.

"Because I need the straps to help hold the dumbbells in place because I have a very weak grip," Dan responded in a flat, emotionless way.

"What kind of a wimp are you that you need to have straps in place to pick up some silly dumbbells, Dan?" I pushed him.

"The quadriplegic kind," he responded, again wearing a half smile, looking toward the floor in front of him.

"The *quadriplegic* kind," I said, so loudly that Dan moved an awkward step away from me while smiling broadly. After my prompting, Dan told his story of how he had been involved in a motorcycle accident at the age of twenty-three and completely severed his spinal cord at the C4-C5 level. He became a quadriplegic and was told that he would *never* walk again but he would be able to control an electric wheelchair using a strawlike device controlled by his mouth.

Any Excuse Will Do

It was absolutely silent as the audience sat motionless in their chairs listening to this amazing story. But here was Dan, a quadriplegic, told he would never walk again, who had just walked in front of them all. By this time, the lady in the fourth row, who had been desperately seeking to become a victim, was now sitting down, wearing an embarrassed look on her face. It probably didn't help that different members of the audience were occasionally glancing her way to see her response. I wasn't trying to embarrass her or to put my friend on the spot. My point was simply that if you really don't want to do something, any excuse will do! I don't care what the excuse is. The truth is if you worked even half as hard as trying to come up with the excuse, you'd have already done the task. People work *really* hard to justify why they *can't* do something. If I could, I would have the word "can't" struck from the English language!

"And what did you tell the doctors when they said you would never walk again, Dan?" I asked, looking out at the audience.

"The same thing I tell you every day in the gym," Dan replied, still smiling at me.

I just smiled back and shook my head from side to side. "And what exactly is it that you say to me in the gym every day, that you said to them, Dan?" By now we both had huge smiles on our face and Dan started to laugh.

"That they were full of *shit*!" Everybody broke out in laughter. Everybody, that is, except the lady in the fourth row.

There are two key points to Dan's story. First, if anyone ever had a reason to make an excuse not to work out, it was certainly Dan. Still, there he was, doing whatever it took to improve his life, working out five days a week. After his workouts, he would shift himself from a collapsible wheelchair, which he occasionally used, into his own car that had been custom fitted with hand-controlled brakes and acceleration. After pulling himself into his car, he would then pull the collapsed wheelchair in after him and drive off. Nothing stopped this guy. He absolutely refused to quit. And that leads us to the second point, bigger than the exercise issue. Dan *chose* not to quit on life. He simply made a choice! Failure was just not an option. Never being able to walk again just didn't exist in the playbook of his existence.

Everyone can do *some* kind of exercise. It doesn't mean you have to win a gold medal in the 100-meter dash. Exercise is about challenging yourself to move yourself to your own next level. It takes self-motivation, effort and overcoming resistance. Each of these 9 Steps is the same, in that it will take initiative on your part to make it happen and then, and only then, will you reap the incredible rewards of excellent health. Exercise is about resisting the urge to sit and watch TV. Exercise is to your body what a positive mental attitude is to your mind. What exercise is *not* about, is excuses.

Better Dividends with Age

As you've probably guessed by now, exercise is *not* an option. If you don't use it—the "it" here meaning your whole body—you're going to lose it. No question. Most people exercise because it's trendy or they want a beautiful body. While reshaping your body is a great dividend, you should exercise because it's good medicine. When you exercise, every fluid, organ and system in your body begins to work more efficiently. Exercise increases growth hormone (GH), which is essential for tissue regeneration in every cell of your body. GH is good for you, but the answer is *not* to inject GH into our bodies. All that will do is increase the chances of getting insulin-dependent diabetes and cancer later on in life. There is a proper way and an improper way to achieve anything that is desired. The difference is the expensive consequence of doing it the improper way.

Exercise produces and maintains lean body mass while keeping insulin levels in the moderate range, preventing the peaks and drops associated with hyperinsulinemia. Exercise stimulates bowel regularity and facilitates proper joint and lymphatic function. It's also nature's antidepressant because it stimulates endorphin receptors inside the brain. Let's admit it. No one really loves to exercise. But we all love the way we feel when we're finished exercising. That's reason enough to get a move on! For me, personally, I focus on how good it's going to feel when I'm done and how good it's going to be for me over the long haul.

The more we use our bodies and the more experiences we garner with age, the better we become. But that's contrary to nearly everything you've probably heard. The vast majority of people have accepted the idea that as they age, they'll slowly fall apart more and more because that's "just the way it happens." In fact, most people have come to *expect it* because that's what they've been programmed through the media and by their physicians to believe. But that's absolute, pure nonsense! Anyone who says that is clearly ignorant of the most fundamental aspects of physiology.

Even economically, "retirement" is sought as the ultimate goal so that you don't have to work anymore. Yet, studies clearly show that the earlier a person retires, the greater the likelihood the person will die within just a few years after their retirement. A study of an oil company's employees showed that people who retired at age fifty-five and lived to at least sixty-five died sooner than people who retired at sixty-five. After age sixty-five, the earlier retirees had a 37 percent higher risk of death than their counterparts who retired at sixty-five. But that's not all. The study showed that the people who retired at fifty-five were 89 percent more likely to die within the ten years after retirement than those who retired at sixty-five.[21]

The fact is the human body is the most sophisticated and perfect machine ever created. It's designed with systems of healing and regeneration that modern science isn't even capable of comprehending. Those who continue working beyond retirement and keep their minds and bodies moving live far longer, if for no other reason than because death can't catch up!

The very same day I wrote this section of the book, I read about the release of findings from a new Israeli study assessing exercise in the older adult population. The study clearly revealed that older adults who get regular exercise live longer and are at lower risk for physical disabilities. The research included almost 1,900 people born between 1920 and 1921 who were assessed at ages seventy, seventy-eight and eighty-five. Those considered sedentary (less than four hours of physical activity per week) were compared to those who exercised. A physically active individual was defined as someone who participated in a minimum of four hours of vigorous activities (swimming or jogging at least twice weekly) or who regularly engaged in moderate exercise (walking at least an hour a day).

The researchers found that 53.4 percent of participants were physically active at age seventy, 76.9 percent at age seventy-seven and 64 percent at age eighty-five. The findings revealed that physically active people were 12 percent less likely to die between the ages of seventy and seventy-eight, 15 percent less likely to die

21 Shan Tsai, Judy Wendt, Robin Donnelly, Geert de Jong, Farah Ahmed. October 2005. Age at Retirement and Long Term Survival of an Industrial Population: Prospective Cohort Study. *British Medical Journal.* 331 (10): 995–997.

between the ages of seventy-eight and eighty-five and 17 percent less likely to die between the ages of eighty-five and eighty-eight. Notice, the older the group that exercised, the lower the incidence of death.

Dr. Jochanan Stessman from the Hebrew University Hadassah Medical School in Jerusalem made the following brave statement:

> Despite the increasing likelihood of comorbidity, frailty, dependence and ever-shortening life expectancy, remaining and even starting to be physically active increases the likelihood of living longer and staying functionally independent. The clinical ramifications are far-reaching. As this rapidly growing sector of the population assumes a prominent position in preventive and public health measures, our findings clearly support the continued encouragement of physical activity, even among the oldest old. Indeed, it seems that it is never too late to start.

Dr. Stessman's study went on to show that physically active adults were also less likely to be lonely or to rate their own health as poor; were able to perform daily tasks far more easily than their sedentary counterparts; and were more likely to be able to live independently. The findings were published in the September 14, 2009, issue of the *Archives of Internal Medicine*.[22]

Later on when we discuss the ninth step, I'll describe in detail the finding of a small private study I did in my clinic to assess

---

22 Jochanan Stessman, Robert Hammerman-Rozenberg, Aaron Cohen, Eliana Ein-Mor, Jeremy M. Jacobs. 2009. Physical Activity, Function, and Longevity Among the Very Old. *Archives of Internal Medicine*. 169 (16): 1476–1483.

the effects of exercise on aging, and how we then reproduced the same results with 117 patients in a follow-up study conducted in seven different clinics. Exercise alone increased endogenous (your body's own) GH by more than 118 percent compared to sedentary people. Furthermore, exercise resulted in improved lean body muscle mass, reduced body fat, improved cardiovascular fitness and improved immunity, all of which were effected to some extent by the reduction in total inflammatory process. There is no doubt that exercise *will* delay the onset of the rapid decline we observe in the geriatric population, that is, the time when an individual is no longer able to perform daily tasks.

For those who found this intriguing, you'll really want to learn how we took this 118 percent GH level and further improved these findings (as compared to exercise) using a proven and reproducible method leading to an increase in physical performance, functionality and endogenous GH levels up to a range between *609 percent* and *1,754 percent*. And this was achieved without drugs, using an all-natural protocol, and achieved within five to eight weeks of protocol initiation. Improvements of 118 percent from exercise alone suddenly aren't as exciting. But these findings are critical, nonetheless. More on this when we discuss the ninth step.

Think about exercise again for a moment. What happens to a car when you store it away in a garage for a year or even over the course of a single winter? It begins to deteriorate. That's because it was designed with parts that need to move in order to function well. You're exactly the same way. You have parts that must move in order to function at an optimum level. But if you don't move them, the parts will begin to deteriorate, just like that rusting automobile. In fact, your body *is* rusting; oxidative injury is the rusting process in humans as we've previously discussed.

Let me repeat, the biological system is the only machine that's designed to get better the *more* you run it. I used to say that about "the human body," but it's applicable to all biological systems. Look at how a racehorse can be tuned into an incredible machine that consistently performs at amazing speed. A truly beautiful thing to watch. Comparatively speaking, cars eventually break down and need their parts replaced. If you run most appliances or electronics too much, they'll burn out far sooner than their already short shelf life. But not the biological system. It gets leaner, faster, stronger, better, more efficient, more capable and lasts longer with use. If there's anything close to a Fountain of Youth, exercise is one of the *two* things that will lead you there.

The Simple Truth

Exercise, like nutrition and water, is really a simple idea that's gotten far too complicated in a society crazed by advertising mania. Everybody's got the best way of doing something or the newest device to make exercise better. It's no wonder most people's eyes just glaze over during all those infomercials for ab crunchers, butt blasters and thigh pushers. I can *almost* understand why someone would just switch the channel and stay stuck to the couch.

The truth is that exercise is very simple. Notice I didn't say that exercise is easy to perform; I mean it's an easy concept to understand. The basic rule is that no matter whether you're doing cardiovascular (aerobic) or resistance (anaerobic) exercise (yes, you need to do *both*), you must be exerting a certain level of effort to reap the best benefits. *What* you're doing or the equipment you're using isn't nearly as important as the *effort* you're expending while you're doing it. There's no difference between a bodybuilder lifting a sixty-pound dumbbell in each hand or an eighty-year-old woman doing her reps with soup cans. As long as they're expending energy to the peak of their capability, they'll reap the same benefit, biologically speaking.

If you belong to a gym, get your membership card out, dust it off and make good use of it. If you don't, don't worry about it. You don't have to spend hundreds of dollars on a home gym or even a weight set. You can do pushups, pull-ups or even deep knee bends while holding a small stack of books. Did you know Olympic gymnasts don't lift many weights? They can't, because they'd bulk up too much and lose their flexibility if they overdid weight lifting. They get their amazing physiques simply by supporting their own body weight during their routines. Another great choice for resistance is isometric exercises. You don't need any weights at all. Specific exercises show you how to push and pull against two separate parts of your body at the same time to create a sizable amount of resistance. These kinds of exercises, pioneered by bodybuilders in the early twentieth century and made famous by Charles Atlas, are respected for their rapid ability to increase physical strength.

I used to lift weights and to use various other pieces of equipment in my exercise routines, but my lecturing schedule and travel obligations were so great between 2004 and 2007, I rarely got to the gym. So I had to find something that worked just as well without having to rely on a gym. My personal choice now is no longer lifting weights but bodywork resistance exercise. Part of this is convenience, but part of it is also because Abie and I compete in martial arts, so I need more flexibility and less mass. No matter what you choose for resistance exercise, the point is to do *something*, preferably three to four times a week, and to change it around. Once you do, your entire hormonal cascade will begin to increase and flow better. Testosterone levels increase, as do GH levels. Every system of your body depends on the ebb and flow of the tides of your hormones. Thus, to up-regulate this area but keep it within balance and within normal physiological range is very important. That's why increasing resistance exercise improves every body function.

Let's go back to the analogy of the car for a second. Think of your body's systems as an engine. When you rev an engine and then take your foot off the gas, the engine idles lower, uses less fuel and uses it more efficiently. Similarly, after you rev your internal engine with exercise, your metabolism increases but your idle (resting heart rate, respiratory rate, blood pressure, etc.) is lower. Your blood pressure, pulse and respiratory rates all reset lower, which in turn leads to less physical effort needed to perform normal functions, making your engine last longer.

Get a Move On

The other component of exercise is aerobic activity. You should understand one thing about me and aerobic exercise. I absolutely hate it. I'm not some know-it-all who gets up and runs ten miles each and every morning and then looks down on you, wondering why you can't do the same. I'm the guy who's in awe that he's still alive after doing hill sprints and pats himself on the back the rest of the day because he survived it. Still, hands down, it's the best thing you can do for your entire circulatory system, respiratory reserve and blood pressure. Running faster is better because it also provides less strain to the joints. Dr. Kenneth H. Cooper, in his book *The New Aerobics*,[23] effectively outlines the reason

---

23 Kenneth H. Cooper, MD. 1968. *The New Aerobics*. Dallas: Bantam Doubleday Dell. p. 192.

for running faster (and alternating with walking, if necessary, as opposed to running slowly without stopping) and how this is actually *better* for joint health.

Exercise leads to many benefits. When blood is pumping freely through your vessels, oxygen and nutrients are getting where they need to get faster and more efficiently. The lymphatic system, a vital component of our circulatory system that my conventional colleagues seem to have forgotten, is also being stimulated. It's important to mention that the lymphatics are one of the most crucial but completely ignored components in cancer prevention and treatment. Yet, doctors, conventional or alternative, rarely discuss lymphatics. All this naturally leads to an accelerated rate of healing. And that's fantastic. I still hate running, though.

But . . . I still *do* it. No excuses. Do I do it every day? No. But I do it regularly. Or I do one of my other exercise routines regularly. Like the endorphin rush after resistance exercise, nothing destresses me like aerobic exercise. As I mentioned earlier, my divorce was like a train wreck inside a hurricane. Even ten years later, it's still a potential source of conflict that I have to consciously avoid. The only thing back then that kept me calm and allowed me to survive was periodic intense aerobic exercise.

Interval Intensity

The good news about aerobic exercise is that you don't have to spend two hours of your day huffing through a ten-mile run. By performing interval aerobic training you can burn many more calories, increase your aerobic capacity and amp up your engine in far less time than through traditional jogging. Here's how it works.

Pick a location where you like to walk, perhaps a park or the sidewalk of a street that's not very busy. Begin walking at a natural, slightly brisk pace. There's no rush here. After a couple of minutes, find a spot that's approximately 30 to 100 yards ahead of you, depending on your current level of fitness. The target may be a tree, a water fountain or some other landmark you can keep your eye on. Once you've chosen that spot, sprint for it as quickly as you can. If you can't run, that's fine. Just increase your walking pace to as fast as you can go. Once you reach your target, drop back down to your original walking pace. Let your breath even out. Don't stop!

Continue on for another two minutes, then find another target ahead of you. The key is that the sprinting portion should last about sixty seconds and be followed by two minutes of brisk walking before repeating the cycle. If sixty seconds is too much, drop it down to thirty seconds or even fifteen seconds. Start at a point that is comfortable for you. Whatever that point is, remember to just walk for double that amount and then repeat the cycle.

If space is limited, you can perform this exercise in a single location. Find an open area that it takes you two minutes to cover by walking briskly. Walk briskly to the end and then sprint back to the starting point as fast as you can. Then repeat this cycle, catching your breath while you're briskly walking back to the beginning. Repeat this process five or six times. If that's too difficult, start with three cycles or even one cycle and work up to five or six cycles. You'll be amazed at the changes. When you're ready, you can have your sprint going up a hill and then walk back down in the rest phase. My personal routine is five or six cycles of sprinting uphill for sixty seconds and walking back down the hill in two minutes.

What this routine will do for your ability to breathe is simply extraordinary. At age forty-three, my ability to last a round in sparring went from wanting to grab my opponent's fist and hit myself in the chest—just to end the fight so I could sit down and breathe—to becoming a state champion and making the top ten in the world list in my age group. I was able to achieve this simply by increasing my respiratory reserve by improving endurance using the technique I just outlined. Having now experienced these rapid changes by running hill sprints, I now understand why my college football coaches made us run sprints. The only difference was that at seventeen I didn't feel or appreciate the changes or improvements. Now, in my forties, I'm nothing short of amazed at the rapid improvement in my endurance and breathing.

Remember the analogy I used about your internal engine being like the engine of a car? Constant changes in speed require using more fuel than if you just cruise along at fifty-five miles per hour in your car. Similarly, when you train aerobically using alternating intensity intervals, you'll naturally change your internal gears and burn more fuel. You'll see significant improvements in your aerobic capacity and internal functioning just by training this way three times a week. Do this just six times in a two-week period and you'll see a difference in dropping body fat and increasing respiratory reserve. As you do, believe me, I'll be out there hoofing it up the hill right along with you in spirit, wishing I were somewhere—*anywhere*—else! Actually, the total workout lasts only fifteen minutes, and you can do *anything* for fifteen minutes. That's what I tell myself, and by the time the internal argument gets heated up, the sprints are already over. Of course, you could just follow the typical advice spouted by trainers or medical staff about cardio workouts needing to last twenty minutes to be effective and continue to watch the American society get sicker and fatter. The choice is yours.

By the way, don't just start doing this if you haven't exercised recently. Get yourself checked out by your own health-care provider to make sure there isn't any health reason preventing you from starting on a rigorous exercise regimen. Once cleared and you start your program, you can keep your doctor away. But this disclaimer *has* to be made because, obviously, I don't know the state of your health. So please, use common sense and first make sure you are able to tolerate this program or any other steps suggested in this book. Start with baby steps, first with just walking and then gradually working up to the desired level. I don't expect everyone to be running hills as I do, but I do expect many to implement some level of this program to experience some remarkable improvements.

A colleague of mine by the name of Dr. Al Sears has also developed a phenomenal exercise program, also based on the principal of intervals and intensity training. Dr. Sears' program is actually the only exercise program that has been issued a patent by the U.S. government. You can actually obtain the Dr. Sears' eBook and begin learning the program right away. Space limitation prevents me from going into detail, but suffice it to say, it will be well worth the few dollars the eBook will cost you, assuming you will put into practice what you've learned. There is a special discount to get this eBook for book owners of *The 9 Steps to Keep the Doctor Away*. Details can be found in the members-only area of www.The9Steps.com.

The Inside of Aging

As far as exercise goes, I'll leave you with an image that has stuck with me for better than twenty-five years. As a teenager, I used to play basketball in the park with my friends. Every day I'd see an elderly man come down and shoot hoops right next to us. I was impressed, not just because he was good, but to my young eyes he looked ancient. One day I asked him why he came down to the park every day and played so hard. His response to me was, "Son, if I *didn't* do this, I'd never be able to get out of bed."

That image of this elderly man playing against people a fraction of his age has stuck with me all my life. He could play and keep up with us because the truth was that, internally, he *was* less than half his age. Putting two seventy-year-olds side by side, with one regularly exercising and the other who doesn't, we no longer have to wonder which one is younger, speaking from a physiological perspective. So, with regard to exercise, my simple question to you is, exactly how old or *young* do *you* want to be?

If you don't use it, you're going to lose it

—COMMON SAYING, AUTHOR UNKNOWN

FAST WRAP
Step 4: The Principle of Exercise

What's the best way to exercise?

Before undertaking *any* form of exercise or specific physical program, be sure to consult your regular physician. And remember, the best exercise combines both cardiovascular (aerobic) and resistance (anaerobic) training. What you do and how you do it isn't as important as the *level of effort* you expend while you are exercising. Exercise isn't a casual activity. The idea is to continually challenge your body and mind to reach the next level of health and fitness.

Why is exercise important to my healing?

Exercise dramatically elevates hormonal levels that govern every process and function in your body. Everything runs better. Increased growth hormone (GH) is essential for tissue regeneration in anyone participating in a healing program, but *not* by injecting it into our bodies. Exercise reregulates your heart rate to a lower resting level, allowing the heart to function at an easier pace. Stress-relieving endorphins are released, putting you in a better psychological space in which healing can occur. And lymphatics are stimulated, alleviating stagnation of the one system that is crucial—yet ignored by clinical medicine—in the prevention of chronic disease.

How do I begin if I've not exercised before?

Start where you are. If you have a gym membership, good. If not, lift soup cans in each hand overhead ten times for three sets. Do pushups, pullups or isometric exercises. Make sure you're exerting a level of effort beyond your normal, everyday strength demands. You can do interval aerobic training running back and forth in your backyard. Do resistance and aerobic exercise three times per week each, minimum. You can alternate days. And consider Dr. Sears' eBook. It breaks everything down to a step-by-step program that is easy to follow.

If I start exercising this way, how soon will I see changes?

Very quickly. Within a week you'll feel better, and within two weeks you'll begin looking and functioning better. Your strength will increase as well as your lung capacity. Bowel movements will become more regular. Metabolism will increase. Most of your "aches and pains" will amazingly start to disappear (although some new ones may take their place while your body gets used to your new exercise routines). Oh . . . and you'll start to lose body fat!

STEP 5:
THE PRINCIPLE OF VICES

The unfortunate thing about this world is that good habits are so much easier to give up than bad ones.
—SOMERSET MAUGHAM

Up in Smoke

"You're gonna love this one, Doc." Floyd, my ER nurse, laughed while motioning with his head to the cardiac room as I passed him. I wasn't happy. I wasn't even supposed to be working. I had already worked seventy-two hours so far that week and it was a Saturday night. The waiting room was packed beyond capacity. People were sitting on the floor in the hallways. The emergency department (ED) was a rough department, understaffed, over visited and with too many patient complaints. Months later, I'd be appointed the chief of this same Emergency Department at Moncrief Army Community Hospital.

I'd like to think it was because I was the best man for the job, but the fact is no one wanted the job, including myself. It was the Army, for God's sake. It wasn't like we got paid more or received any additional benefits, just more responsibility and more hours at work. Plus, we had to answer to the big man upstairs, the hospital commander. The hospital just needed a big mouth to be the fall guy who could take the heat from the Quality Assurance Committee, and senior command needed someone to blame when things weren't going well. That fit me to a T. I had a big mouth, and heat seemed to follow me wherever I went. Come to think of it, nothing has changed.

"Dr. Buttar, I need you in cardiac." Another one of my nurses' voices jolted me back from my disgruntled daydreaming. I walked into the cardiac room and immediately recognized the patient. People, including my staff, are amazed when I can't remember my own neighbor's name and yet I can remember the entire medical history and lab values of a patient I may have met only once. Actually, I have no idea how I do this—it just happens. It's not as if I try to remember the information. Just don't ask me their names!

The EKG showed severe inferiolateral ischemia with T-wave inversion (part of the heart wall wasn't getting enough blood, and the patient was in the early stages of a heart attack). I knew him well. I had taken care of him during the last two of his three heart attacks. His wife was crying, being held by his daughter, and his son was standing close by with a worried look on his face. The patient's color was ashen, a classic sign of a heart attack victim. As I leaned over the gurney to listen to his heart, I was repulsed by the stench of stale cigarettes. He recognized me at the same time. "Am I glad you're working tonight, Doc," he said in a weak voice. "Don't worry, Mable. He saved me before. I'll be just fine now," he said to his wife, who was now lightly sobbing into a tissue.

"Are you still smoking, sir?" It was clearly obvious he had not stopped, but I asked him anyway, almost in a confrontational manner. He knew it was pointless to lie. "Please tell me you're not still smoking."

"Well, I really cut down like you done told me, Doc. Maybe half a pack a day or so now." He seemed to want me to know that he had at least heeded some of my previous advice. All of a sudden I just felt exhausted. I was going into my eightieth hour of working that week, but my exhaustion wasn't from work. I had spent hours with this guy the last time, preaching, teaching, inspiring, even going to the point of showing him photos of diseased lungs and telling him patient horror stories to help him change his behavior. His daughter had even thanked me the last time for taking so much time to help educate her father. Even after surviving three previous heart attacks, this guy *still* didn't get it. I'd asked him to choose between cigarettes and his life just months earlier, and he had told me he'd chosen life. Yet, here he was.

I wondered, of the fifty-four thousand people who came through that ED each year, how many actually took my advice and quit smoking. I looked down at the patient as he looked back with guilty eyes. His wife had suddenly begun sobbing again. His son looked away in disappointment, and his daughter appeared to be on the verge of her own breakdown.

I hadn't said anything else; everything in my head screamed for me to keep my mouth shut. But I couldn't. "Sir, why don't you do yourself and your family a favor? Just buy a gun, put the muzzle in your mouth and pull the trigger. You'd save your family a hell of a lot of pain and save the army some money. It's a much faster way to kill yourself, but most important, you'd save me my time so that I could take care of someone who really gives a crap and *wants* to live."

The patient was treated. We initiated thrombolytics, stabilized him and admitted him to the CCU, and he was discharged seven days later after surviving his fourth heart attack. I was just waiting for the ax to fall and get reprimanded for what I'd said. I knew my remarks had been harsh. Eventually I was called into the commander's office and verbally reprimanded, as I deserved to be. But the hospital commander had served with a line unit, as I had in Korea, unusual for medical officers. And my officer evaluation report (OER) ratings were the highest possible, all from senior line officers, also highly unusual for a medical officer. Maybe that's why I got off easy. Still, I justified my outburst in my own mind. Maybe, just maybe, my harsh words had finally gotten through to the patient. And maybe, just maybe, I had now finally saved his life.

What a Drag

With the exception of doing illicit drugs, the worst thing you can do to yourself is to smoke cigarettes. It's absolutely the most disdainful and wretched violation anyone can commit against their own body. It's like spitting at God and tempting fate. It's also rude and disgusting. If people really want to kill themselves slowly, there are other ways to achieve the same result without afflicting others with secondhand smoke and polluting the atmosphere.

One drag on a cigarette generates in excess of 1 trillion free radicals within your body. Just *one* puff! That's more than 1,000,000,000,000 free radical reactions, if you need to see zeros to be impressed. And recall the earlier statement that free radicals cause oxidative injury, the same rusting process that causes a banana or an apple to turn brown. In fact, oxidation is the cause of aging, decay and breakdown. The negative effects of smoking just *one* cigarette take 7.4-plus years to get out of your system. Not a pack or a carton! Just *one* cigarette.[24,25,26]

A Fish Out of Water

I've heard many of my medical colleagues and friends say that Americans don't care how they "feel," just how they "look." It's sad, but true. Many people don't care about how they feel, physically, or their internal state of health. They only care about how flawless their skin looks or how few wrinkles they have. Even so, it's these same people who do the one thing that will absolutely trash their skin. They smoke! Women are typically far more concerned about their appearance and aging than are men. Yet, the difference between smoking and nonsmoking women is startlingly obvious just by looking at their skin.

When I was Nick Perricone's "opening act" on his South African tour in 2002 for his first book, we spoke before many affluent

24 Daniel F. Church and William A. Pryor. 1985. Free-Radical Chemistry of Cigarette Smoke and Its Toxicological Implications. *Environmental Health Perspectives.* 64 (1): 111–126.

25 Thomas M. Flicker and Sarah A. Green. 2001. Comparison of Gas-Phase Free-Radical Populations in Tobacco Smoke and Model Systems by HPLC. *Environmental Health Perspectives.* 109 (8): 765.

26 M. Ghosh and P. Ionita. 2007. *Investigation of Free Radicals in Cigarette Mainstream Smoke.* Available: http://www.bat-science.com/groupms/sites/BAT_7AWFH3.nsf/vwPagesWebLive/5FB7A11D49832F1FC125 73E9003D7869/$FILE/%5B13%5D%20Published%20Paper%20SFRR. pdf?openelement. Last accessed November 11, 2009.

women in that beautiful country. And they all wanted to get the secrets of looking their best. However, during the breaks in the lectures, almost all of these very attractive and affluent women would light up a cigarette. There is just one thing worse you can do for your skin than smoke cigarettes, and that's to douse yourself with gasoline and set yourself on fire.

Human beings were not designed to ventilate smoke. Look at a fish. It ventilates water by separating it into hydrogen and oxygen through its gills. When you take it out of water, it flops around for a while, gasping, until it becomes someone's dinner. It can't ventilate air, only water. If someone slammed your head into a bucket of water, could you ventilate water? Why not? Because you weren't designed to ventilate water. Humans don't have gills. Similarly, when you smoke, it's as though you were slamming your head into a bucket of water and trying to breathe. Eventually, you're going to drown. With smoking, it may take a bit longer, but the result is still the same. You *are* going to drown.

I'm certain that some of you reading this right now will say, "Well, we're all dying." And you would certainly be correct. But that doesn't mean we need to accelerate the process. If you're a smoker, *stop now*! If you're not willing to stop smoking right now, this entire book is a waste of your time.

A patient who had stopped smoking nevertheless once said to me, "Well, even if you do all these steps and don't smoke, you're eventually going to die anyway, so what's the point?" That's true, but assuming that most people don't fall off the side of the Grand Canyon or get run over by a steamroller tells me that we all have a significant amount of control over when and how we return to the Creator. You can die today by slamming your head into a bucket of water. You can die a little every day until you end up gasping out your last decade, tethered to an oxygen tank. Or, you can die a normal, painless death from natural causes after living 120 years or more.

Sure, we all *have* to die. In fact, a friend once told me that he told his patients who were preoccupied with death, "Don't take life too seriously; no one gets out alive." While this is true and I agree that you don't have a choice of escaping the dying process, what's far more important is that you *do* have a choice on *how* you want to live! It's up to you to choose *how* you want to check out. In fact, everything in life comes down to your *choice*.

The people who really don't have a choice about smoking, however, are children who are exposed to secondhand smoke. If you do smoke and have children, I would urge you to immediately stop smoking in their presence. If you're trying to cut down and are making a sincere effort to quit, smoke outside on a patio or on your porch. Never, ever smoke with children in the car, even with the windows down. The data has been available for years about the severe toxicity of secondhand smoke.[27]

A child's lungs are still developing until late adolescence. In fact, almost *all* organ systems continue to mature up until the early twenties, depending on sex and biological individuality. Science has known for decades that a child exposed to cigarette smoke, especially in the womb, won't be as fast, strong, intelligent or resistant to illness as a child raised in a smoke-free environment. They will be more prone to allergies, may have develop-

---

27 A.M. Ford, M.M. Khaled and M.A. Morsy. August 22–26, 1999. *Symposia Papers Presented Before the Division of Environmental Chemistry, American Chemical Society: EPR Detection and Properties of Naturally Occurring Free Radicals in Mediterranean Tobacco Blends.* Available: http://www.envirofacs.org/Pre-prints/Vol%2039%20No%202/Papers/p 114. PDF. Last accessed October 10, 2009.

mental delays and may exhibit behavioral problems associated with environmental toxicity.

Overall, there will be a "failure to thrive" as is evident in a child born from a woman who is an alcoholic or on illicit drugs. Some may presumptively assume that the correlation with cigarette smoke and the health issues I just described is an overstatement, since many variables could contribute to the problems mentioned. However, all the variables are directly a consequence of increasing oxidative load on a developing system. The oxidative load can come from any source but it just so happens that cigarette smoke is one of the most significant.

In fact, the 2006 Surgeon General's Report, "The Health Consequences of Involuntary Exposure to Secondhand Smoke," concluded that there is no safe level of exposure to secondhand smoke and that children are exposed to more secondhand smoke than adults. The report goes on to discuss associations between secondhand smoke and low birth weight, sudden infant death syndrome, cognitive impairments, behavioral problems, acute respiratory disease, asthma and further health repercussions later on in life.[28] An excellent synopsis of this report with detailed references is available on the members-only website.

Making Commitments

In my practice, we refuse to take anyone who smokes. If a patient is not willing to take the most fundamental, commonsense step toward improving their health, how can they expect us to help

---

28 Americans for Nonsmokers' Rights. September 2009. *Health Effects of Secondhand Smoke on Children.* Available: http://no-smoke.org/pdf/shs_children.pdf. Last accessed February 18, 2010.

them? I simply refuse to waste my time or effort. I'll see a smoker only the first time, but they are told beforehand that we don't treat smokers. If they have a sincere desire to stop smoking, I will accept them with the strict understanding that the first thing they have to do is stop smoking. Believe me, I have an immense amount of compassion for anyone trying to shed such a destructive, addictive habit. I've never been one to assume it's easy, but I'm also not interested in all the rhetoric and excuses. There is no greater force than a deep conviction in your soul to change your life for the better. But if a person can't commit to improve, I certainly am not going to waste my time.

More than 95 percent of the smokers who have come to my clinic have stopped smoking. I have no special secret. They're simply told they must stop smoking within the first thirty to forty-five days after their initial visit, and we provide them with whatever they need to accomplish the task, be it acupuncture, Nicorette gum, Zyban, hypnotherapy or, on occasion, a swift kick in the pants. Ultimately, however, it's the patient who is responsible for his or her own health, not the doctor. And the credit for stopping this terrible habit goes to the patient, not us.

This book is about "keeping the doctor away," but in some circumstances, a good doctor may become necessary. With your doctor, you can form a team that can return you to health; it won't happen, though, unless you're willing to do your part. This goes not only for smoking but also for any other medical situation requiring a partnership with your physician.

Acid Trip

Assuming you don't do illicit drugs, the next most destructive vice you can have besides smoking is drinking coffee. It's about at this time during my lectures when hundreds of doctors try to hide their Starbucks coffee cups under the conference room tables at which they are seated. You may have thought the next worst vice was alcohol, right? Wrong. Barring a severe alcohol addiction, I'd much rather have my patients drink a glass of organic red wine once every few days than to drink a cup of coffee every morning. Caffeine has nothing to do with it, actually. If you want caffeine, go to a drugstore and get caffeine tablets. I do *not* recommend this for many reasons, but it would be better than having a cup of coffee.

The reason you should abstain from drinking coffee is because it contains 208 different acids. Decaffeinated is no better. Even though the caffeine is gone, it still contains the full original acid profile. These acids wreak havoc on the insulin and glucose levels in your body. Health is all about body chemistry, and the easiest way to change your body chemistry, either for good or for bad, is by what you put in your mouth. Your body must maintain a serum pH level of approximately 7.35 to 7.45 (slightly alkaline) to be healthy. In fact, each individual organ system of your body has its own regulated pH level, with the entire body averaging out around 7.2. When you ingest acidic items like processed foods and coffee, you begin to skew your entire body chemistry from alkaline to acidic, creating perfect conditions for diseases that need acidic environments in which to thrive.

We buy alkaline batteries because they're *energized* and have the power to run our appliances. But have you ever opened the back of an old radio you haven't used for a long time and looked at the batteries? Often they are crusty, discolored and oozing strange fluid. When an alkaline battery loses its power, it becomes acidic and dies. A similar type of thing happens to the "batteries" in your body when you drink coffee. I don't recommend tea, either. Even though it may have some beneficial herbal ingredients, tea still contains upward of 170 different acids. Even red wine contains acids, but not nearly as many as coffee. Green tea is the best bet, containing just under 100 acids. If you must drink tea, do so in moderation.

Soda Saturation

The following are some interesting facts you may not have known about the phosphoric acid within your favorite cola soft drink:

- When transporting the concentrate from which sodas are made, the trucks must carry the "hazardous materials" placard reserved for highly corrosive substances.

- The pH of phosphoric acid is 2.8 and it can dissolve a nail in about four days.

- Mechanics have used cola to eat the corrosion off car battery terminals.

- Cola has been used effectively to dissolve rust stains from toilets and clean road haze from windshields.

Aside from the additives—artificial colors and phosphoric acid—the biggest killer in soda is the sugar. We've already talked about the dangers of sugar and its effect on the body. Did you know that a single twelve-ounce can of cola has thirty-nine grams of sugar in it? That's over nine teaspoons! Try to put *that* in a glass of water and drink it. Even worse, those twenty-four-ounce convenience-store plastic cups hold seventy-eight grams of sugar, or almost twenty teaspoons! Enough said.

Just by eliminating the habit of drinking sodas, one of my nurses lost seven pounds in less than a week. Another employee who suffered from constantly cracked and bleeding hands had the condition clear up almost completely within two weeks of stopping her soda habit.

I hope you don't make a habit of eating at fast-food restaurants, but if you *drive by*, notice the typical customer. It's not a pretty sight. As much as I hate soda, it is definitely better than diet soda. It's no accident to see countless people struggling with body fat issues, most at obese levels, ordering huge hamburgers, large orders of French fries and sugar-laden desserts along with . . . a diet soda! God bless these people, but do they really think one diet soda is going to cancel out this avalanche of sludge they're dumping into their bodies? Aside from all the synthetic compounds in these artificial sweeteners and the dangers they pose, researchers are just now discovering how these sugar substitutes actually contribute to not only weight and body fat gain by inhibiting metabolism, but also contribute to overall chronic disease!

A study done at Purdue University and published in the *Journal of Behavioral Neuroscience* examined two groups of rats given yogurt to eat. One group received yogurt with sugar. The other group received yogurt with saccharin. In a short time, significant changes were identified in the rats consuming the artificial sweetener. Over the fourteen-day test, the saccharin rats began to eat significantly larger amounts of food as their appetites became overstimulated. As a result, the rats gained a huge amount of weight, mostly as fat.[29]

Most important, the core body temperature of these rats decreased, meaning their metabolism *slowed down*! When you consume something sweet, the body recognizes the sugar and

---

29 Susan E. Swithers and Terry L. Davidson. 2008. A Role for Sweet Taste: Calorie Predictive Relations in Energy Regulation by Rats. *Behavioral Neuroscience*. 122 (1): 161–173.

mobilizes all its resources to begin burning off the extra fuel. If what you eat tastes sweet but there are no calories in it, your metabolism gets confused. The next time you eat something genuinely sweet, your body's burn-off mechanism never gets triggered and fails to engage. Do yourself a favor and switch to water. It really is the best *real* thing. Or try club soda (carbonated water) instead if you must have carbonated beverage.

"Juiced" on Juice

Why would I include juices in the same category as other vices? After all, it's not like people get addicted to orange juice. The truth is that juices contain just as much sugar as sodas do. Don't believe me? Check the nutrition labels. No matter where it comes from, sugar does the same negative things inside your body. Juice has vitamins, right? Maybe, but the detriment far outweighs the benefit. When you eat whole fruit, the skin and fiber in the whole fruit prevents the sugars from entering your system too rapidly and getting you "juiced" from the rush.

Even so, overconsumption of carbohydrates leads to hyper-insulinogenic states, further resulting eventually in many chronic diseases, including diabetes, heart disease and cancer. Juicing at home with your own juicer, using organic vegetables and fruits, is different, however, and actually highly beneficial. Try and get most of your supplementation needs from your vegetables and whole fruits and take an additional good-quality supplement for added measure. Unfortunately, just 17 percent of the U.S. population actually gets the recommended five servings of fruits and vegetables per day.

On a side note, let me mention the many fruit-juice blends now available on the market. Most of them, unfortunately, contain high-fructose corn syrup, artificial sweeteners and added synthetic ingredients. However, believe it or not, a limited few of these companies actually have good-quality products. Generally speaking, the greater the number of fruits within a blend, the better and healthier the blend is due to synergism. Read the labels and check the contents yourself.

My particular favorite, and the one that my family and I have consumed for two years now, is available from independent distributors. I am somewhat biased so you'll have to choose and determine your own truth. However, I believe the discerning individual will agree that a delicious blend of nineteen fruits in a bottle—without any refined ingredients and providing in a four-ounce serving the equivalent antioxidant profile found in eighty-nine apples—is a very good choice. (The company boasts that four ounces of this juice is equivalent to thirteen servings of fruits and vegetables.) See the resources section for more details.

I literally used to drink a gallon of orange juice daily when I was growing up. Now I can't stand it because it's just too sweet. If I do have some freshly squeezed juice, I have to water it down. If you eliminate all sweets from your diet for several months and then try to drink a glass of juice, you most likely will be unable to do so. You'll probably feel nauseated, perhaps even becoming sick and experiencing an upset stomach with cramping. If you choose to discipline yourself and stick with this program of abstaining from sugar and juice concentrates, one of the first things to disappear as a result of being on a healthy and balanced diet will be your sweet tooth.

You should also know that most juices are not fresh but are made from concentrate. The true juice is boiled down to its basic elements for processing. Once the concentrate reaches the appropriate spot in the assembly line, water is added back to restore it to its fluid state. Do you think they're adding pure water from an artesian well on a tropical island to reconstitute your apple juice? Hardly. Consuming pure water is essential to healing, as we've already discussed. That's another reason to stay away from fruit juice and anything made "from concentrate."

If you're looking for a substitute sweetener, remember to stay with "God-given," not "man-made" substances. For instance, honey has lots of benefits, such as the antioxidant and antimicrobial components (but it's still sugar, so be careful). The advantage is that honey has enzymes that are still intact and has a greater fructose rather than glucose component so it will metabolize more slowly. Another good natural sweetener is stevia, an herb that comes from Japan. Today you can find stevia in its powder or extract form everywhere, including the regular grocery stores. The extract is a good choice; if you choose the powder, stay away from the overly "white" versions, which signify they've probably been overprocessed. There are many strains of stevia as well, some of which have an aftertaste. With some trial and error, you can find the right one perfect for yourself.

There are many other topics and options related to natural and synthetic sweeteners, discussing the pros and cons of substances such as xylitol, brown sugar, sugar cane and others. However, due to space limitation, these options are discussed in more detail on the members-only website. Additional updated information will also be provided as it becomes available.

Alcohol? Chocolate?

Believe it or not, alcohol may be the lesser of the vices you can consume. Go ahead—I'll wait until you stop cheering and jumping up and down. Understand this isn't a license to go get hammered every Friday night after work. Alcohol has got plenty going against it. For instance, alcohol turns to formaldehyde as it passes through the liver. For the most part, though, it's a God-given product: the fermentation process wine goes through, for instance, is a natural one during which most of the sugar is removed. Red wine, specifically, has some beneficial properties and antioxidants such as oligomeric proanthrocyanadins and res-veratrol components.

Beer, on the other hand, is very high in carbohydrates. Hard liquors are even worse due to the effects on the liver and of course, the long-term neurological implications. Hard liquor is absolutely *not* good and highly detrimental. The major point to keep in mind with regard to consuming any alcohol is active moderation with judicious selection regarding the type of alcohol consumed. And in the interest of full disclosure, in case anyone cares to know, I do not drink, nor have I ever drunk any type of alcohol. Yes, I was made fun of all during my fraternity years because I didn't drink. However, I was more popular with the girls as a result and I've retained more brain cells than my fraternity brothers. Those are just some of the benefits of not drinking alcohol.

A lot of people consider chocolate a vice. In fact, some people are nearly addicted to it. Of course, anything in excess is bad for you, but chocolate has some excellent antioxidant properties. A study done at the University of Cologne in Germany and published in the *Journal of the American Medical Association* showed that ingredients in chocolate could significantly lower blood pressure.[30] Another study performed at Cornell University and

---

30 Dirk Taubert, MD, PhD, Renate Roesen, PhD, Clara Lehmann, MD, Norma Jung, MD, Edgar Schömig, MD. July 4, 2007. Effects of Low Habitual Cocoa Intake on Blood Pressure and Bioactive Nitric Oxide. *The Journal of the American Medical Association*. 298 (1): 49–60.

published in the American Chemical Society's *Journal of Agriculture and Food Chemistry* showed that chocolate is loaded with antioxidants that prevent cancer, heart disease and other conditions. In fact, the levels of phenolic phytochemicals, or flavonoids, were found to be nearly twice as high in chocolate as those found in red wine or green tea.[31]

Keep in mind, all these studies were done on *dark* chocolate. Milk chocolate has much more sugar added to it, along with dairy products making it over processed and nutritionally void. Dark chocolate naturally contains more cocoa, which is where the antioxidants come from and what gives chocolate its unique, bitter flavor. Once again, eat chocolate in moderation. The higher the cocoa content, the better the chocolate is for you. You can find many bars now that contain up to 85 percent cocoa. A one- or two-square serving daily is best, because the flavonoids contained in chocolate are very powerful and a little goes a long way.

Indulgence Options

Contrary to what some experts may say, sex is *not* a vice. This is one area where you *can* indulge, assuming of course you're with a consensual partner. Sex, in actuality, fits within Maslow's hierarchy of physiological needs along with air, water, food and shelter. The need to have sex and to procreate fulfills a deeply ingrained instinct that allows all species to survive and thrive. It has more physical, spiritual and emotional benefits than I can list in this entire book. I'm sorry but if you need me to encourage

---

31 Joe A. Vinson, John Proch, and Ligia Zubik. 1999. Phenol Antioxidant Quantity and Quality in Foods: Cocoa, Dark Chocolate, and Milk Chocolate. *Journal of Agricultural and Food Chemistry.* 47 (12): 4821–4824.

your significant other on this subject, it falls outside my scope of practice. However, feel free to refer them to this page. Book owners who need help or enhancement in this arena will find some intriguing and exciting information on this subject at the members-only area of the website.

> *Ill habits gather by unseen degrees—*
> *As brooks make rivers, rivers run to seas.*
>
> —JOHN DRYDEN, *ABSALOM AND ACHITOPHEL* (1681)

Fast Wrap
Step 5: The Principle of Vices

What's considered a vice?

A vice is any food, beverage, chemical or product you use or behavior you perform consistently over time that creates toxicity or increases toxic load in your body. Some substances and behaviors that become addictions or very strong bad habits are smoking tobacco, drinking coffee, soda or alcohol and eating excessive sweets. Sex is *not* a vice.

Why do I need to stop enjoying these things?

You may not feel it right now, but the toxins from these substances and behaviors, in excess, accumulate in your body, leading to eventually devastating results. Sugars, in particular, change the body's chemistry from an alkaline to an acidic state and flood the system with huge amounts of unnecessary refined carbohydrates, creating an ideal environment for every major disease. Rampant free radical damage from smoking tobacco is another example of toxin burden exponentially increasing within your system. Stop every source of detrimental accumulation of toxic substances within your body.

How can I change my habits?

Change isn't always easy. If you're looking to get away from diet soda or to curb alcohol usage, you can begin by phasing out just one serving each day until you've eliminated it from your life. Find a new hobby. When it comes to bad habits, you need to make sure your time and mind are occupied with new habits that are beneficial. If you can't quit smoking cold turkey, check into acupuncture or hypnotherapy. It works for many people. The key, however, is for you to first *choose* to quit, *believe* that you can quit and then *take action* to make it happen. Apply these three steps to anything in life you need to accomplish, and as long as you do all three consistently, you'll succeed. You'll also find two tools in the members-only website that will help you conquer any bad habit.

If I stop these behaviors, how will it help me?

You may not recognize it right away, but your body will begin to applaud you. You'll easily see an improvement in your skin as nicotine and alcohol's drying effects are reduced in your system. Skin inflammation and acne will begin to disappear. The bottom line is that you're reducing toxicity. Your cardiovascular capacity will improve, increasing your body's total oxygenation. Most of the dietary vices discussed are loaded with refined carbohydrates and simple sugars. Reducing them will automatically result in improved "prevention." However, remember that prevention doesn't *feel* like anything! These steps *leading* to prevention will allow you to improve your body's balance and, among other things, actually shed body fat and improve body composition. These are just some of the inevitable benefits that will occur when you follow the 9 Steps.

STEP 6: THE PRINCIPLE OF RELAXATION/STRESS MANAGEMENT

How much more grievous are the consequences
of anger than the causes of it.
—Marcus Aurelius

Role Reversal

Gordon brought his wife, Linda, to me because she'd been having hormonal issues, anxiety and weight problems, and she was concerned she may be toxic. Gordon was a nuclear engineer in his early sixties and deeply in love with his wife—so much so that he referred to her as "my bride." She was fifteen years his junior and very motivated to get better, but she had also been spoiled by her husband in the sense that she relied completely on Gordon, and he in turn insulated her from everything. The degree to which he enabled her dependence on him was almost disturbing. Linda did not work outside the home. My nursing staff told me that apparently Gordon even helped Linda with housework, drew her bath for her and often cooked for her, all the while maintaining a full-time job as an engineer.

During a scheduled office visit with his wife, I noticed that Gordon himself didn't look so well. I asked him if he was feeling all right. He shook off the comment, saying that he was fine and that his main priority was his wife's health. He squeezed her hand and smiled at her.

I could clearly see that Gordon's stress level was high, and I asked one of my nurses to take his blood pressure. As I suspected, it was elevated. I made some suggestions to him about making certain life changes and taking some time off from his responsibilities. I also suggested that he slowly begin some form of exercise. No matter what I suggested, everything came down to an issue of time, because he spent *all of it* taking care of or being concerned about his wife.

Since Gordon wasn't my patient, I told him that he needed to follow up with his own doctor. Over the next several months, I would mention the issue to his wife as well. Her response was one of concern, but the idea that dominated Linda's thinking (and Gordon's too, for that matter) was that as soon as she got better, they would focus on Gordon.

Late one evening I received a phone call from my on-call staff member, telling me that Linda had called, crying, from the emergency room of their local hospital. Gordon had suffered a massive stroke. As a result, he was completely paralyzed on his right side, had lost his ability to speak and had become completely incontinent. I had told Gordon just a few months earlier to slow down and start taking care of himself, but he hadn't listened.

In the six months following Gordon's stroke, Linda's hair literally went from black to gray as she now had to assume the role of caregiver and provider. She aged so rapidly that even other patients of mine would ask if she was all right. Often, people charged with caring for elderly parents or sick children experience such a great emotional and physical toll that it's the caregiver who often dies before the one who "needed the care."

It was such a tragedy that Gordon never learned—until after it was too late—that the one most loving and unselfish thing he could have done for Linda was to take care of *himself.* Luckily, Gordon did begin treatments at our clinic, and he improved significantly. But he'll never work as a nuclear engineer again, and his life—and Linda's as well—has forever been impacted.

In the Background

Everybody knows that stress is bad. Yet, it's virtually impossible to get away from it with the daily demands continually placed on us. As we've learned, chronic stress elevates cortisol and insulin, which ultimately leads to devastating oxidative injury within our bodies. In fact, every organ system in your body has to overcome a great physiological burden when you're under emotional stress. It's as though you were used to carrying a burden, but now you have to carry twice as much as normal, up a hill twice as long, in half the time, and you're expected to return in half the time as well. In more than just one sense, stress is absolutely the most damaging component to assault your health that you can experience.

As much damage as a jelly doughnut can do, with all its sugar, processed flour and hydrogenated oils, it's a one-time, isolated attack on your body. Psychological stress, however, can be relentless, and it can go on for days, months or even years, constantly wreaking internal havoc. When we think of stress, we tend to imagine the typical type A ultra-ambitious personality or the person who creates his or her own drama and is always freaking out over nonissues. The person who's rapidly puffing on a cigarette and repeating, "I'm so stressed," is not the person with whom we need to be concerned, however.

The most pervasive, insidious kind of stress is the type we're all under, the low-grade sense of urgency or worrying about our lives that we've become all too accustomed to and almost now expect. It lingers in the background of our minds, keeping us up at night sometimes, to the point that some of us don't even know it's there anymore. It's "normal." Yet the damage is occurring on a daily basis and slowly accumulating, until one day your doctor tells you he's sorry but you've got cancer. Or, like Gordon, you have a stroke. It's this type of person, the one who never complains, with whom we need to be most concerned.

What About Me?

I've met nearly four hundred women with breast cancer over the last two decades—some patients, others just in social settings and still others simply in passing. The one thing common to all of them, besides being women and having breast cancer, was their personality profile. This became even more evident when their spouses or partners were questioned. Nearly all the women were constantly giving of themselves and were always worried about something. They had daily stress about their children, spouses, church, business, Little League, whatever. The stress never ended. If one thing they had worried about was resolved, they found three new things to replace it. I also noted that they never, *ever* took any time off for themselves.

If there's good news here, it's that my ex-wife will never get breast cancer! It's okay; go ahead and laugh. Laughter is the eighth step. She's in on the joke anyway. At least, she was last week.

But, I digress. I believe that the low-level stress from the constant demands these women put on themselves, along with perhaps some unconscious resentment for never getting any personal time—which I believe contributes greatly to their eventual common condition—promotes their common disease. That's why it's essential to take time out of every day that's *just for you.* Taking the kids to the park doesn't count, because that's not time *just for you*—unless taking the kids to the park absolutely and sincerely makes your heart sing. If that's the case, then you may need psychiatric intervention, because taking the kids to the park can be a nightmare!

I'm sure you understand what I'm saying. Taking twenty minutes out of every day for yourself means *taking* twenty minutes out for *yourself.* Whether it's enjoying a bowl of ice cream, a good book, a hot bath or sex with your significant other, or even if it's enjoying a bowl of ice cream *with* a good book *while* having sex in a hot bath, it all counts (although that *may* be a little too stressful). Even if it's just taking the kids to the park because *you* really enjoy it (as long as you're truly enjoying yourself), it counts. Just be cautious not to indulge to the point of inducing self-created stress. The goal is to relieve stress and remove the sense of deprivation (mostly unconscious) we all experience in our daily routines and give ourselves a short little daily reprieve to remind ourselves how good it feels to be alive.

Yeah, but . . .

It never fails. There's always someone who gives me the "Yeah, but . . .": "Yeah, but I'm the only one who can do this job." "Yeah, but I've got to finish this project by Friday." "Yeah, but I have three kids to take care of." Let me give you a valuable bit of advice. Your life is all about *you* . . . and that's *not* a selfish thing. There's nothing noble about dying at your office desk or dropping dead at a church bake sale. If you don't take care of yourself, you won't be around to take care of your kids or your family! Then who takes care of them? Taking care of yourself makes you better physically, mentally and emotionally, which automatically translates into you becoming a better parent, spouse, sibling, provider, employer, leader and so on.

It was between Thanksgiving and Christmas in 1997, and it had been sleeting continuously for a few days. It seemed as though everyone was sick with the seasonal "sniffles and a cold." I was working a night shift in the ED at Richmond Memorial Hospital in Rockingham, North Carolina, when a man in his late twenties came into the ER. His complaints were a cough and "freezing." He had a 103-degree fever and looked very sick, but he insisted that all he needed was a shot of antibiotics. His tests came back showing a white cell count over thirty-five thousand and bilateral infiltrates on chest X-ray. Essentially, he had a "double" pneumonia and was severely septic, meaning that he had a blood infection that had spread from his pneumonia. Even though he was a nonsmoker, his pulse ox (oxygenation measurement) registered at 89 percent, an ominous sign for a person his age.

I told him that his condition was extremely serious and that he needed to be admitted to the hospital. Suddenly, out of nowhere, this guy unloaded his anger and frustration on me. "You %$#@in' doctors think you know everything. How the

%$#@ can you sit there and tell me I need to be in the %$#@in' hospital? I'm workin' for a %$#@in' living, man. I got %$#@in' responsibilities, man!" That was the PG version.

I calmly told him that he needed rest and fluids along with intravenous antibiotics. He was still very agitated about work, but when I offered to write him a note for his employer, he wasn't the least concerned. "My boss man, he don't need no note, man! He hates payin' me overtime anyway." His concern turned out to be for his own two children and his brother's three children that he was raising. His brother was apparently serving a prison sentence, and it was clear that every bit of his focus was on the children.

Number One

I could tell he was going to be a tough one. He was a proud man. I began to discuss the care options his children would have through the state and social services. He looked at me with a confused look. When I brought up temporary foster care, I thought he was going to attack me. He unleashed another tirade, demanding that *he* was the only "%$#@in' one" who would ever take care of those children. He had taken the bait. And it was my turn now.

"No! Social services will *have* to take care of them because they won't have a father anymore. Because *you'll* be dead in a week! Because you were too damn stubborn to listen! Unless you do exactly what I tell you to do, you're going to die! Are you hearing me? You're too busy being a 'man' and being tough, going back to work with double pneumonia, and now you're gonna die because you were being an idiot. Don't give me this bullshit about the 'kids.' Those kids will have to fend for themselves the rest of their lives because their dad wasn't bright enough to keep himself alive!"

The patient just sat there staring at me with his mouth open, shocked because he'd never heard a doctor talk to him that way.

"Well, which one do you want? You wanna die being an idiot or you wanna fight to live so you can raise those kids?" He still just sat there, staring at me. I softened up and told him that he had to let us take care of him for the next few days if he really loved those kids. We admitted him to the hospital.

About a month later, just after the New Year, he came back through the ED, but this time not as a patient. I came out to the front after being paged and there he was, just standing there. After an awkward silence, it was obvious he didn't know how to say what he wanted to get off his chest. I said, "You don't have to say anything." His eyes began to tear up. All he said was, "Thanks!" and then he was gone.

I'm grateful that the situation worked out the way it did, for both of us. His children still have a devoted father who will raise them with the right work ethic and love, and I got the first glimpse of the fact that I didn't focus on my *own* health nearly as much as I should. I know what it means to be a devoted father, but I learned that the best thing I could ever give my children, besides my love and affection, is *my* health. The concept of the 9 Steps had been born.

A Second of Eternity

Besides always remembering that you're "number one," you also need to remember that life is about the "now." In his book *The Power of Now*, Eckhart Tolle[32] does a beautiful job of giving us the crucial message that the truest path to happiness and enlightenment is in living in the moment. I had intellectually understood

32 Eckhart Tolle. September 2004. *The Power of Now: A Guide to Spiritual Enlightenment.* San Francisco: New World Library. p. 224.

this message long ago, but I didn't really *understand*. Remember how we *think* we understand?

I still recall the exact moment when I truly "got it." I was lying on the floor in my living room with my youngest son, Rahan. He was six months old, and he was lying on his stomach, arching his back, holding his head and legs up at the same time. We had nick-named him "Monkelfin" because he acted half like a monkey and half like a dolphin, clicking and chirping when he was in the bath and kicking his legs in tandem like a dolphin.

I reached toward him as I lay on my side, just watching him being entertained by . . . nothing, actually! He had the biggest smile on his face, looking at nothing. He turned with a jerking movement toward me and grabbed my little finger as I was reaching toward him. Our eyes locked for a moment . . . and in that very instant, I experienced what I can only describe as "eternity." I finally understood. It was so overwhelming it literally brought me to tears.

Everything that had happened before didn't matter. It was forgotten. And everything in the future was irrelevant. Now was everything! That moment as Rahan held my fifth finger in his little hand, smiling at a string on the carpet, cooing and babbling, was when I finally, for the first time in my life, really understood what life was about. I wanted that feeling to last forever. It *was* forever, even if it was just experienced for a moment. And yet, I had experienced everything there was to experience in that moment that lasted forever. It was 2005 and I had just turned thirty-nine years old.

Some of the greatest lessons and some of the most thought-provoking proverbs I've heard come from children's movies. I heard one of the best ones from the ancient and wise turtle master in the movie *Kung Fu Panda*. There's a scene in which the turtle is trying to teach the Panda the importance of living in the moment. The turtle says to the Panda: "Yesterday is history. Tomorrow is a mystery. But today . . . today is a gift! That's why we call it the present." That's "the power of now."

Think of those moments when you've enjoyed life the most, which make life worth living. Then go and find them again. Experience them again. Savor them again. Savor all that life has to offer. Enjoy the journey. You've heard all the advice such as you should "stop and smell the roses." Well, *stop and smell the roses*, for God's sake! I mean, literally. Find a garden or go to a florist shop. Find some roses, anywhere! Then just savor and bask in the exquisite scent of those roses for a moment . . . before trying to recall what was so important you almost passed on this little indulgence. Don't make the mistake of thinking this is "silly" and not participate in this simple exercise. I promise, you'll regret that you *almost* didn't do it.

The Gift of Forgiveness

The last portion of this chapter is universally applicable to everyone and is probably the single greatest cause of stress in virtually every human being today. For my patients suffering from cancer, it's actually the one component I now routinely take them all through personally. I do this myself because I find it to be an extremely significant event, and most often, the most crucial and critical turning point in their recovery. It's the principle of *forgiveness* and its power should never be underestimated. In fact, I cannot stress enough the importance and the power of forgiveness.

I would highly recommend that each person reading this book get a copy of *Island of Saints* by Andy Andrews.[33] Read this

---

33 Andy Andrews. 2005. *Island of Saints*. Nashville: Thomas Nelson, Inc. p. 245.

book and it will bring home this crucial principle, which is absolutely necessary before any effective and permanent healing can ever occur. Andrews presents the powerful message of *forgiveness* in an equally powerful and unforgettable manner appropriate to the subject. As Andrews' subtitle for the book states, it's *"A Story of the One Principle That Frees the Human Spirit."* To truly heal from a real, chronic, "you're-going-to-die" terminal type of disease standpoint, you must forgive all those who you believe owe you an apology; that is, if you want to live. By the way, just so we're clear, you're not forgiving them because *they* deserve to be forgiven. You're forgiving them because *you deserve it!* Whether they *do* or *don't* deserve it, is actually completely irrelevant. The point is that *you* deserve it.

Oftentimes, we may feel that someone has done us a great wrong and we harbor resentment and deep-seated anger toward that individual. But what we fail to realize is more often than not, the individual whom we feel owes us an apology isn't even aware that they have done anything wrong. Believe me, I realize the situation may not always be as simple as described, but it *is* always simple to fix.

In my own personal life, my separation and divorce created such a powerful negative image that it was virtually impossible to even contemplate forgiveness. Interestingly enough, my ex-wife felt the same way. But with time and maturity, we both have come a long way and I can honestly say that I want nothing but the best for her and I would hope she feels the same way. Our attempts to work together for the benefit of our children shows me that this is truly the case, and I am deeply grateful for having reached that point. Everybody *can* reach that same point, as long as they are willing to truly forgive. Mind you, I never said that it would be easy or that it wouldn't be a constant challenge. But it *is* achievable.

Final Note

It would be easy to look at what I've recommended in this chapter and think, "Just twenty minutes for myself . . . that's all I need to relieve my stress? That's ridiculous!" And I certainly understand that sentiment. After all, we're sold a gazillion things to reduce our stress: meditation programs, yoga DVDs, herbal teas, exotic baths . . . the list goes on forever.

I'm not against any of those things! But I am against overcomplicating things to the point where a person gets frustrated or confused and does nothing. I've seen that more times than I'd care to admit in my patients, and even in myself. We create a goal or intention, and then we begin by developing lofty, intricate ideas or programs for how we will accomplish everything. We think, we formulate, we contemplate and then . . . nothing.

To avoid this tendency, I recommend keeping things simple. The unfortunate fact is that most adults do not take twenty minutes purely for themselves (and their greater mental and emotional well-being) every day. Just implementing what I've advised in this chapter will be a monumental step forward for most people. What you do during those twenty minutes is entirely up to you. Read, meditate, do yoga, take a walk—it really doesn't matter. And if you can use those twenty minutes correctly, you'll find that you actually become more efficient. You'll free up more time for yourself every day by *gaining* more productive time than the twenty minutes you spend indulging yourself! You'll be in a very elite group of people who *get it*. Until you're at that point, please take my advice and begin with twenty minutes designated entirely for you, each and every day. You'll know when you finally *get it* because that's when you'll begin setting aside more than just twenty minutes a day for yourself.

Man needs difficulties; they are necessary for health.
—CARL GUSTAV JUNG (1875–1961)

FAST WRAP
Step 6: The Principle of Relaxation/Stress Management

What's considered stressful?

Stress is the prolonged burden of anxiousness, anger, resentment, depression, worry or any other negative emotion compounded over time. It creeps into our lives from financial distress, job issues, health challenges, old wounds and relationship problems, among other things. Failure to forgive and/or live in the moment simply adds to this emotional mess.

Why is stress so dangerous?

Because we're so used to living with continuous low grades of stress in our lives, we don't recognize it anymore. We think it's "normal" to live in a slightly agitated, worried or hurried frame of mind. The anger, resentment and fear, however, result in stress, which has serious physiological implications for our bodies. This can lead to extensive damage and the opportunity for disease. Furthermore, these emotions, if left unattended and unresolved, begin to form an abscess, just like a "pus pocket" in a wound. And like a pus pocket that isn't opened up and drained, this emotional abscess will become painful as the pressure increases and eventually spread the "infection" throughout the entire body. This may be graphic for some, but it is this emotional abscess that results in the cancer that no one understands why it occurred, despite eating well, abstaining from vices and trying to live a clean life.

How can I manage my stress when I'm so busy?

By taking twenty minutes out of every day to do something exclusively for your own selfish enjoyment, you will help to reduce your stress level. Make sure that whatever it is, it truly is for you and that you really enjoy it. It's an opportunity for you to reset your psychological stress meter. Read a book. Play basketball. Ride a bike. It doesn't matter. The key is that you take twenty minutes regularly and make a habit of it. Let it become your daily sanctuary. Stop and *actually* smell the roses. Literally! Lean over and inhale their gorgeous and rich scent. Taking twenty minutes to relax and recharge makes you better in all areas and relationships in your life. Savor life. And forgive all whom you need to forgive as a gift to yourself.

If I can take twenty minutes to relax, how will it impact my life?

You'll take yourself out of the "fight or flight" mode and reset your entire emotional, psychological and physiological systems, including the adrenal glands. Every system will be able to recalibrate to its normal functioning state and redirect newfound energy to the needed functions of healing and living, as opposed to being constantly drowned by the mundane. Strangely enough, you'll find when you begin applying this particular step that things begin getting clearer. The insignificance of the unimportant things in life we place emphasis on, and to which we give far too much importance and power over ourselves, become clearly revealed.

STEP 7: THE PRINCIPLE OF PRAYER/MEDITATION

Our prayers should be for blessings in general,
for God knows best what is good for us.
—Socrates

Prayer requires more of the heart than of the tongue.
—Adam Clarke

A Stroke of Luck

Most of the memorable cases I've had have occurred during holidays, with Thanksgiving having more than its share. Holidays such as Thanksgiving and Christmas in the ER are usually very slow during the morning and for most of the day. Then, as the football games are ending and people have just finished gorging themselves on Thanksgiving dinner, people start experiencing chest pain because of overeating. Usually it's just heartburn, but sometimes it's a real cardiac issue caused by overeating. The blood supply to the heart muscle gets shifted to the digestive tract to help digestion, causing "ischemia," or lack of blood flow to vital organs like the heart muscle or brain. This often results in a heart attack or stroke. Having worked over a decade on every holiday on the calendar in various emergency rooms, I knew the routine like the back of my hand.

It was a typical Thanksgiving Day. The North Carolina Panthers' game had just finished (and they had lost). The ER had started getting crazy, following an almost precise, timed, scheduled ritual. As the storm of activity began picking up, the ER doors flew open. Paramedics wheeled in a middle-aged man who had suffered a pontine stroke. Pontine strokes are very severe, and few people survive them. Those who do survive usually end up with extensive disabilities. The family was understandably in extreme distress after a neurosurgeon I had contacted at the higher-level support hospital had told them there was nothing he could do except "wait and see." The patient had one pupil dilated and was totally unresponsive.

The family was asking questions that I couldn't and wouldn't answer, such as, "How much time does he have left?", a pet peeve of mine. How does any doctor know how long any other human being has left? Those doctors foolish enough to predict death are playing "God," and my personal belief is that that may be the most reprehensible and unforgivable component of my profession. The power of words is tremendous, beyond our comprehension, and we should never forget that the most important thing we can offer those who seek our help in living is to offer them *hope*. Believe it or not, I've actually been accused of giving "false" hope by the North Carolina Medical Board, despite having helped hundreds if not thousands of patients from all corners of the world, even when all hope was lost to them.

Hope by definition can't be false. If it is false, then it *cannot* be hope! Think about it. "False hope" is an oxymoron, and anyone who verbalizes such absurdities is an idiot. At the very least, the notion of false hope defies the age-old wisdom—popularized by one of my heroes, Napoleon Hill—of maintaining a positive mental attitude (PMA) in life, especially in an adversity. It certainly raises the question of the motivation behind those who argue against hope by propagating it as false hope. Their reasons become even more highly suspect when proof is shown that the "hope" in question became not only reality, but the person who was supposed to be dead is now, years later, doing well and thriving. Of course, those cases are conveniently attributed to being "anecdotal" and the issue of hope is ignored.

On June 14, 2009, Dr. Ron Davis, president of the American Medical Association, gave his final speech to the AMA House of Delegates in Chicago. He had unfortunately been diagnosed with pancreatic cancer, and at the age of fifty-two had decided to step down from his presidency. What was most moving was what Dr. Davis said about hope. "As a physician, I know the survival statistics for someone with stage 4 pancreatic cancer. But if the five-year survival is 5 percent, that's not zero. . . . So, never take away someone's hope." Unfortunately, his statistics were wrong. But his point was not.

If a doctor could truly predict when someone was going to die, believe me, they would not be practicing medicine; instead, they'd be predicting the stock market and living somewhere on their remote private island. I personally believe that when a doctor opens their mouth and makes statements like these, they have done nothing more than create a self-fulfilling prophecy because the patient now believes what was said by the greater perceived authority: the doctor. Individuals like Dan, who defied his quadriplegic status in the face of doctors, are a rare breed that thrives on proving that the impossible is possible.

As the family asked me about the patient with the pontine stroke, these thoughts ran through my head as they had numerous times before. The CT scan clearly showed where the "bleed" was in the brain. There was no way to get to the "bleed" without causing almost certain death to the patient. And to make matters worse, the patient was an alcoholic and had fallen during his stroke. I told the family that the most important thing they could do now was pray. I went back to discuss the patient's condition with the staff. When I got back to the trauma room, the nurses were openly talking about how this man was "dead." I immediately put an end to that nonsense and ordered any nurse ready to write this patient off to get the hell out of that room.

No one left and the attitude in the room changed. Their actions were apologies enough, and by staying in the room, they signaled that they had chosen to fight for this person none of us knew from Adam. Statistics and rationality were discarded and replaced with PMA, hope and even prayers. Two of the nurses came to me later and asked if I would join them in a prayer for the patient. I didn't bother telling them that I had been praying ever since I had reviewed the CT scan. We joined hands and prayed.

No one really knew if the patient was aware of anything going on, but that wasn't the issue. He still deserved to be treated with dignity and given every possible chance to survive. By writing him off, we would have essentially been killing him. To some that may sound harsh, but it doesn't change the reality. There is no gray zone here. If you're not fighting for whatever you believe in, then the lack of fighting is allowing the opposite side to win. To put it another way, if you're not fighting to save a life, then the lack of fighting on your part is allowing death to win.

The patient was stabilized and I convinced the neurosurgeon to accept him as a transfer to the larger hospital, where more resources (such as the presence of a neurosurgeon and a neurosurgery ICU) were available if things changed. Throughout the patient's stay in our hospital, every so often I'd lean over him and look into his fixed eyes, telling him, "Just hang on, it's gonna be okay, just hang on."

Three months later, I was paged to the front of the ED and told that someone had requested to see me, by name. As a doctor or nurse, you have to be extremely cautious when going out into the ED entrance because you never know who might be there. It could be a disgruntled person or one of the "drug seekers" who fake pain to get narcotics or even a gang member irritated that the doctor saved his opponent's life. You may have noticed that security in emergency facilities is always prominent, and more so at night. As a result, security for staff is always an issue for most ERs, and policy dictated that the ED staff at our hospital not go into the waiting area even if someone had requested them to come out.

I was so busy that it was four hours later before I could walk out into the waiting room. The man was still waiting so I assumed he didn't fit any of the previous mentioned categories. As I approached, he looked up and, seeing me, immediately struggled to his feet. He was holding a cane in one hand, and as the person next to him tried to assist him, he put his hand out to stop them. He pulled himself up and had a huge smile on his face as he moved toward me with measured and difficult steps. I racked my memory, but there was no instant recall. As he slowly approached, I noticed two things that made me even more curious. First, his eyes were filled with tears, and second, his eyes were very familiar to me, although I still couldn't place him. As he got to me he almost fell into my arms, throwing his arms around me. The sheer emotion he was emitting caused me to tear up myself, still not sure who this man was or what was happening.

"You don't remember me," he said, sobbing. I had to admit that I didn't. Then he told me he was the patient with a pontine stroke whom I had taken care of a few months earlier. I was awestruck! He told me he didn't know my name or who I was, but he just remembered a "Mexican" doctor with a "white patch of hair" leaning over him, telling him to "hang on" and that everything would be okay. He said that I was the only thing he could see because I leaned so closely to his face. But he remembered almost everything that had been said. It had taken some detective work on his part to finally determine my name.

He relayed to me, between sniffles and holding my hand, that it was my words encouraging him to hang on and the sound of my voice that became his lifeline. Although I'd like to take credit for helping this man, it had very little to do with me and everything to do with the Creator. It was the intense amount of prayer being offered by all involved that had kept this man alive. I've always known that the power of prayer is what has pulled many people through critical moments in life when I've evoked it, while they were under my care. When anyone comes back from such a dire condition, there's just no explanation other than the amazing power of prayer and intention.

Don't Wait for Science

Debate has long raged about whether or not prayer is truly a scientifically proven modality of healing. University of California–San Francisco School of Medicine and Arizona State University have done studies that show prayer works, while others like the Mayo Clinic and Duke University claim that their research denies the power of prayer. Of course, we know Mayo and Duke's record. Just ask Ellen or Morgan's family. But I digress again!

I never get involved in this debate, however. Besides the positive impact I've personally witnessed prayer to make in my patients, I'm 100 percent certain of the power and effect prayer has on those who *know* they are being prayed for as well as those who actually *do* the praying for others. Prayer connects you and reminds you of something greater than yourself. It focuses and calms you, relieving stress and improving your peace of mind. Prayer gives you perspective and hope that cannot be achieved any other way. And most important, prayer allows you to let go, to yield.

What's more, whether science can measurably verify the power of prayer or not, those who are prayed for—particularly those who know they are being prayed for—feel the difference. Just like you know when someone is looking at you, I believe those who are prayed for are touched in a similar unique way. It's almost like Pascal's famous wager about whether or not God exists. Sure, you can't prove that God exists. But you also can't prove He doesn't! If He does, there are many, many benefits to believing He exists and living accordingly. If He doesn't, what have you lost by living your life with morality, faith and hope? As for me, the Creator most certainly *does* exist! If He didn't, I wouldn't be here and you wouldn't be reading this book. I should have been dead long ago. Some may say it was coincidence or luck that I survived whatever particular situation being discussed, but the sheer number of times that I should have left this world but was kept safe far supersedes any level of coincidence. For those who may not believe, if you can quiet the skeptical part of your brain and truly tap into the power of prayer, you will see the proof for yourself throughout your life. By the way, don't let semantics get in the way. Whether you choose to refer to the Creator as the "Greater Good" or "Source Energy," Allah or Jehovah, the Universal Consciousness or Mother Nature, it is all the same.

Hope, Prayer and Intention

Instilling hope is nothing more than giving or helping someone harness the power of positive thought. Positive thought resonates at a higher vibrational state and attracts the positive thoughts of others, virtually collecting the power of the universal consciousness and focusing it in toward one central point, whatever that target may be that you've chosen.

What is a "thought"? A thought is nothing more than an intention. What is a prayer? A prayer is nothing more than an intention, a thought with a specific purpose to positively impact something or someone in a selfless manner. It is asking without any selfish agenda, asking for the best for all, regardless of the outcome. It is trusting and having faith, yielding and getting out of the way to allow the power of Source energy, the God energy, Universal Consciousness, whatever you choose to call it, to do its thing.

Remember, the idea of prayer is to invoke hope and change the vibrational frequency to one resonating on a positive note. It has nothing to do with coming up with a laundry list of a hundred things you want for yourself. In fact, in prayer you shouldn't ask for anything for yourself at all. With the exception of asking

God for guidance and wisdom and the best outcome for all concerned, I never ask for anything. We already have too much. We need to simply be grateful for what we already have. And we need to ask that the Creator bestow His gifts on others we love and cherish and for whom we are responsible.

Just sit quietly and bring images to your mind of all the things you're grateful for in your life: your wife, your husband, your beautiful and special children; your comfortable home; the vacation you took this year; the fact that you can see, to read this book; your arms, with which you can feed yourself, and your legs, with which you can move without assistance; your health, the food that sustains you, the heat that warms you, the cold that cools you, air that sustains you; the mere fact that you are aware of His existence, that you have been blessed with the freedom to do what you choose. As you see each one of those images in your mind, without verbalizing it, express your gratitude and thank the Creator. If it's hard to do this, simply imagine how you would feel if you didn't have any of these things, and the gratitude will come flooding over you.

One of the easiest things to do is just sit quietly where you won't be disturbed for about twenty minutes. By the way, this is different from the twenty minutes you take for yourself daily. Focus on your breath. Don't try to "do" or make anything happen. Just be aware of your breathing. Make sure that with each breath in, your belly goes out and with each breath out, your abdomen comes in. As you focus on your breath, let all the thoughts drain out of your mind. Experience how good it feels to get "out of your head" and just let your body be.

Mind you, this will be very difficult to do in the beginning. Many strange thoughts will come into your mind, but focus simply on how grateful you are for what you have. No matter how bad you think your situation, whatever it may be, there are always those who have far less than you or are in a far more difficult situation than yourself. Think of them and be grateful for what you have. Our bodies are much healthier when our minds are in a state of gratitude and our brains are not overstimulated. For those who like direction, you'll find some guided meditation and sleep-induction programming CDs in the resources section at the end of this book.

Divine Direction

As we've seen, the most potent agent of oxidative damage and the biggest threat to your health is stress in all its various forms. Powerful nutritionally based antioxidants and lifestyle changes are available to reduce oxidative stress. All of these are excellent tools to eliminate stress and reduce the physiological damage in your own body, a result that in itself is quite empowering. But even more important, the absolute most powerful weapon against all stress, oxidative damage and the resulting chronic disease is something available to you anytime, day or night, and it is absolutely free. It is prayer and/or meditation.

I'm not referring to specific prayers of individual religions or specific creeds. In fact, you don't have to subscribe to religion at all. The idea is to find whatever in life you see as bigger than yourself, whether that be God, the universe, source energy or something else, and then sit in quiet contemplation of that essence and try to achieve oneness with that force. As already mentioned, they are all the same, regardless of the label. If you pray in the traditional sense, that's great! Do that. If meditation works for you, fantastic! Go for it. The benefits of prayer and meditation are the same and are actually twofold.

Let's go back to the car we've been using as an example. When you pray or meditate, you're no longer revving your engine. Instead, you're "down regulating" every system in your body. Depending on your depth of prayer or state of meditation, you can easily eliminate virtually all psychological and physiological stress in your body, at least during that specific time period. It's that rare, precious time your body uses to heal, while your mind is not getting in the way, that we want to achieve as often as possible.

The second and bigger benefit you'll receive is the connection you make with your higher power. I wrote this book to give the best health advice I can give, not to preach a sermon. However, having said this, and at the risk of sounding as if I'm preaching, I will . . . preach! Through the fantastic work of people like cell biologist Dr. Bruce Lipton, author of *The Biology of Belief*,[34] and Dr. David R. Hawkins, author of *Power vs. Force*,[35] and other researchers, we've come to discover the line between science and spirituality is slim at best.

In fact, for me this line does not exist. There is no distinction between science and spirituality. You must be deeply spiritual to appreciate the wonder of science, and all scientific understandings lead to greater spirituality. Mind you, I'm referring to true science based on observation as opposed to the archaic definition of science used and often abused by modern medicine. So much for centuries of conflict over who was "right."

---

34 Bruce Lipton. 2008. *The Biology of Belief: Unleashing the Power of Consciousness, Matter, & Miracles*. United States of America: Hay House.
35 David R. Hawkins. 2002. *Power vs. Force: The Hidden Determinants of Human Behavior*. United States of America: Hay House.

The Quantum Connection

Everything on Earth you see as physical matter, from your car, to your body, to this book you're holding in your hand, isn't really solid. At first, this may sound totally ludicrous. But bear with me for a moment. I assure you I haven't lost my mind. I don't think anyone would argue the point that the smallest complete unit of matter is the atom (assuming we don't include subatomic particles). We also know that the atom is made up of a proton, a neutron and a surrounding electron that orbits the proton and neutron in a highly specific path. It's almost akin to a minute solar system, with the protons and neutrons being like the Sun and the surrounding electrons being like the planets orbiting the Sun.

Virtually every aspect of an atom is comprised of the same components as that of a solar system, just on a far smaller scale. Without going into quantum physics, it's been proven by at least eight Nobel Laureates that the particulate component of an atom actually has wave properties and that the wave components of an atom have particulate properties. In fact, it was Louis de Broglie, as far back as 1925, who postulated that electrons are actually not particles but are rather a nonmaterial wave.

An atom, therefore, is really nothing more than a flux of energy, consisting primarily of space between the electrons, protons and neutrons that make it up. Now remember, it's just energy . . . the same energy vibrating at different frequencies to produce a book, a car, a body. Everything we touch, see, eat, wear and so forth, is made up of atoms. And all of these atoms consist partially of nonmaterial waves and partially of particulate matter. So what's all this got to do with prayer and meditation?

You've probably heard the metaphysical concept that everything is "connected" and that "we are all connected." Well, allow me to scientifically prove this to you once and for all. As already stated, everything, including us, is made up of atoms. Remember, atoms are made up not only of electrons, protons and neutrons but also of the space in between them. Thus, the smallest sub-unit of all matter (atom) is made up of a flux of energy (electrons flying around protons and neutrons) and the space in between them. As Broglie stated, these electrons are not particles but, rather, nonmaterial waves consisting mainly of space. Later on, Albert Einstein showed that the behavior of any particle is *not* independent of the field in which it exists. Paul Dirac, another Nobel Laureate and one of the first pioneers of quantum field theory, further theorized that particles cannot be separated from the space that surrounds them.

This work was continued by other notable Nobel Laureates, including Richard Feynman, who created the concept of quantum electrodynamics, which described the interaction between light and matter with remarkable accuracy; Carlo Rubbia, who postulated that matter constitutes less than a billionth portion of the universe; David Bohm, who first described the highly specific path followed by electrons and also described "implicate order"; Fritz Albert Popp, who described the ideal resonant frequency of live cells; and Timothy Boyer, who described "Zero Field" or "Zero Point," an exceedingly important yet virtually ignored concept when applied to clinical medicine.

Beginning from the premise established by Broglie, Einstein and Dirac, that particles cannot be independent of the field in which they exist and cannot be separated from the space that surrounds them, we can establish that the individual parts of the atoms (the electrons, protons and neutrons) cannot be separated from the space between them. As a result, these subunits are part of the space that makes them up, and the space that makes them up, in turn, is part of the atomic substructure itself.

As already established, atoms are the fundamental building blocks that make up everything, including us. Thus, each of us is a mass of literally billions of trillions upon billions of trillions of atoms. To be specific, a 155-pound (70 kg) person would consist of $7E + 27$, or 7,000,000,000,000,000,000,000,000, 000,000 atoms. We, by definition, cannot be anything else but what makes up our own individual subcomponents. Therefore, we consist of $7E + 27$ fluxes of energy, each made up of electrons flying around protons and neutrons, all a part of the space that makes up the individual atom. The conclusion we are led to, based on Bohm's "implicate order" as well as intuitive observation, is that we, too, follow the nature of atoms, simply because we're made up of atoms.

The same thing holds true for the subatomic particles making up an atom, that is, the particles that make up individual atoms cannot be separated from the space that surrounds them, ad infinitum. This, by the way, is an example of Bohm's "implicate order." A simpler way to understand implicate order would be to watch the children's movie or read the book *Horton Hears a Who*.

Understanding this, and based on Dirac's work, we know the atoms that make us up are part of the space within which they exist. And the space within which these atoms exist is an integral part of the makeup of the atoms themselves. And if we are made up of atoms ourselves, then by Bohm's implicate order, we likewise are part of the space that makes us up, just as the building blocks that make us up (atoms) cannot be separated from the space that surrounds them.

Now, here is the key. We've clearly established, using hardcore quantum physics, that we "cannot" be separated from the space that surrounds us, just like the atoms that make us up cannot be separated from the space that surrounds them. This means we are *part of* the space that surrounds us. The stranger sitting next to us in the theater or walking by us in the park also cannot be separated from the space that surrounds them; thus, they are *part of* the space that surrounds them. Obviously, the space surrounding both you and the stranger is one and the same. So if you are both part of this same space and this same space is part of both of you (which cannot be separated from either of you), then by definition, you *must* be a part of each other.

We are, indeed, all connected, and it is this very connectedness that allows for an explanation of many of the things we can't explain. For instance, answering the question of a loved one . . . but the loved one *only thought* about asking the question! Or knowing that the phone was going to ring and a certain person would be on the other line . . . and the phone rings! And it's that certain person. Or when something happens to someone halfway around the world and at that exact moment, a sibling or a parent or a close friend wakes up from a dead sleep, feeling something significant just happened.

Most of us have experienced these types of things, some more than others. This real phenomenon, which is often attributed to coincidence, has now been scientifically explained by the preceding explanation. Even so, a few will argue with this reasoning simply because their agenda is to prevent this sentiment from growing. The truth is that only a foolish person of insufficient intellect and lacking sequential logic, or someone with an agenda that is highly suspect, would attempt to argue with the logical conclusions we have just reached.

This is the foundation from which we begin to show how the important specific components we intuitively believe in, but that are considered impractical or unreasonable by society, are in fact the most essential. Virtually all these components are easily explained through the better understanding of science. And if "science" just can't currently provide an explanation, it does *not* invalidate the observation. It merely means that we have not yet evolved to the point of understanding, comprehending or deciphering the science. In other words, it's not science's fault that we can't explain it. It's our own fault that our science is not sufficiently mature enough to be able to explain it. Yet the tendency for those of higher station and limited intellect is to immediately hide behind the inadequacy of current science to justify their own obsolete existence.

The point of explaining how all of us are connected is to scientifically show you the basis of prayer and meditation. Your thoughts generate powerful amounts of positive energy, far stronger than any herb or drug, and will significantly affect your state of mind and ultimately your body and overall health. Prayer and meditation are among the most powerful tools you have to continually generate positive energy and life force within your body. These practices help you clear away the "mental noise" and eliminate fear and anxiety in order to connect to a place inside yourself that holds the answers you're looking for and the strength that exists within each of us.

Chronic disease, in part, is related to a lack of this positive energy. On reviewing, observing, and studying the characteristics common among those who are successful at overcoming chronic disease, it's surprising to note that the principles of achieving success are common not only in health and longevity but also in achieving success in all arenas of life, including the spiritual, financial, professional, personal, emotional and psychological arenas. To overcome any chronic disease, the universal principles of success, which I like to refer to as the "science" of success, are all identical. And to achieve these universal principles, we must reduce the noise, attain as much silence as we can and down-regulate our systems as much as possible. We reach this through prayer, not placation; we accomplish this through meditation, not medication.

A Wing and a Prayer

Before I started medical school, my father taught me this prayer: "Uz Ha Biel Ba'as, Rub Bin Na'as." In Arabic it means, "God, please heal this person and allow me to be the conduit." I've silently said this prayer to myself for years, almost every time before I see a patient. On several occasions, I'm certain it was the intervention from this prayer that saved a patient's life, especially when there was nothing more that modern science or I could do.

In 1998, Richmond County in North Carolina reportedly had among the highest incidences of penetrating trauma in the state. I was working at Richmond Memorial Hospital in Rockingham when a twenty-seven-year-old black man was rushed in after being shot in the chest at point-blank range; he was bleeding to death in front of us. We were rapidly transfusing him with blood, but he was bleeding faster than we could get blood into him. I was literally in this man's chest cavity, as were two other surgeons, but none of us could find the source of the major bleeding. We had suction devices going that couldn't even keep up with the bleeding. The color was quickly leaving his face, and I was watching him slip away.

Desperately thinking what I could do, I closed my eyes and said the prayer I've said thousands of times, asking God to heal this patient and allow me to be the conduit. The next thing that happened remains among one of the most amazing professional experiences I've had. I heard the suction devices "gurgle." I opened my eyes to see the last of the blood in the chest cavity taken up by the suction. As it drained away, I looked into this man's open chest to see the major severed vessel responsible for the majority of the bleeding clamped in the hemostat I held in my hand. I looked up at the other two doctors, who were just staring at me. One of them said, "How'd you do that?" My reply was simple. "I didn't do anything."

If the whole idea of prayer or meditation seems overwhelming or new, there is no time like the present to start. One of my favorite prayers is The Serenity Prayer by theologian Reinhold Niebuhr. It's a nondenominational prayer that's a beautiful, simple way to surrender yourself and release the burdens you may be carrying. Just saying this prayer out aloud will fill you with a sense of calm and peace. Go ahead and try it for yourself. Say it aloud, because, believe it or not, it will really make a difference.

THE SERENITY PRAYER

God, grant me the ability to change the things I can change;
the serenity to accept the things that I cannot change;
and the wisdom to know the difference.

Another favorite prayer of mine comes from my uncle, author and former Columbia University professor, Dr. Majid Ali. It simply states, "God, today I ask for nothing. I wish for nothing but only to be in your presence."

The last prayer I will share is the prayer that began evolving when my son Abie was recovering from his vaccine injury.

(I describe that journey and his dramatic recovery in more detail in chapter 12.) We call it the Love and Gratitude prayer, and at first it was simply saying those two words: Love and Gratitude. But while saying it, I want you to think what these words really mean. Slowly, the prayer evolved for us into what it is today.

This is a personal prayer that my daughter, Sarah Aisha (Sarah), and my sons, Abid Azam (Abie) and Rahan Alexander (Hanni), and I say. I'll share it with you so that anyone else who would like to invoke it may share in its power. It is simply twenty-two words, but what's most important is that you need to think what these words mean as you say them. May this prayer serve to guide you and remind you how all of us should live our lives.

> ## THE BUTTAR FAMILY PRAYER
> *Love and Gratitude, Health and Wealth, Success and Prosperity, Peace and Tranquility, Happiness and Contentment, Satisfaction and Fulfillment, Integrity and Honor, Discipline and Courage, Service and Long Life, Intelligence and Wisdom, Spirituality and God.*

Far too often we get wrapped up in our own lives and forget to acknowledge the Creator. A great way to change that imbalance is to spend time alone in nature. No matter how you choose to pray, I can guarantee you one thing. You'll begin to have a deeper appreciation for life on every level once you start. You'll stop fighting and questioning and begin to see the bigger picture. You'll find yourself able to go with the flow of life instead of asking "Why me?" when things don't go the way you want. You'll realize that there are no mistakes and that what has happened, has happened for a very specific reason.

My name in Arabic means "one who stays on the right path of life." You'll probably never meet anyone more off the path than I am, and yet somehow God always straightens me up (sometimes kicks me) and redirects me along the correct path. I planned on being a great surgeon. When I began residency in general surgery, I got into two of the best programs in the country and had my choice of where to attend. I was told by my attending surgeons (senior doctors who teach junior doctors) that I had the most talented hands of any of their residents. I thought surgery was what I was supposed to do. It wasn't.

God (aka Universal Consciousness, aka Source Energy) knows what each one of us is meant to do, where we need to be, and the best possible way for the ultimate plan to unfold. When we don't immediately understand everything that's happening at the moment, we tend to fight, resist and ultimately stop the greater plan from proceeding and flowing. Yield to the greater design. With peace and serenity, you will transcend any circumstance, making every day of your life a joy just because you're alive.

In the words of the great Napoleon Hill, "Every adversity, every failure, every heartache carries with it the seed of an equal or greater benefit." Once you realize this, the pain of resisting because you think you should be "over there" or "doing that" will be replaced by a knowing that all is exactly as it was meant to be. Furthermore, the time to fight and the time to yield will become crystal clear.

> *We need to find God, and he cannot be found in noise*
> *and restlessness. God is the friend of silence. See how*
> *nature—trees, flowers, grass—grows in silence; see*
> *the stars, the moon and the sun, how they move in*
> *silence. We need silence to be able to touch souls.*
> —MOTHER TERESA

Fast Wrap
Step 7: The Principle of Prayer/Meditation

What is prayer/meditation all about?

Prayer or meditation is simply quiet time that you devote each day to reconnect with the Creator. It is the time we allow our spirit, our higher self, to attempt to achieve oneness with God. It has nothing to do with any specific religion. It's a way to check in, allowing our self to connect with the Source Energy that makes up our inner guidance or intuition. You don't have to come from a religious background to practice or benefit from the power of prayer. It is innate within all of us.

Why is prayer/meditation important for my health?

Science has essentially proven that our thoughts generate powerful energy that affects our bodies and overall health. Thoughts are powerful cosmic waves that permeate time and space. A thought with a specific intention behind it becomes a prayer that is oriented in a specific direction. The resulting quietness of prayer and meditation allows you to escape the mental noise inside your head and gives your body a chance to heal without the noise-induced stress causing interference.

How do I pray or meditate if I've never done it before?

Prayer/meditation is mostly about stopping and yielding to the moment. You can recite The Serenity Prayer aloud and the Love and Gratitude prayer several times a day if you choose. You might also find a quiet place to sit for twenty minutes, empty your mind and just focus on your breath. It's a great habit to get into if you're not already doing it, to focus in on your life and think of all you have to be grateful for, and just silently say "Thank You" for each one.

If I pray/meditate, how will things change?

Prayer and meditation will allow you to experience a deeper level of balance, well-being and peace. You'll also understand on this deeper level that all is well even if you can't see it clearly at the time. A greater sense of appreciation for everything in life will fill you when you begin to spend a few minutes each day in prayer or meditation. And perhaps most important, you won't experience the pain of resisting the natural flow of life, nor hesitate from fear to move *into* resistance.

PRAYER FOUND IN THE CATHEDRAL IN CHESTER, ENGLAND

Give me a good digestion, Lord
And also something to digest.
Give me a healthy body, Lord,
With sense to keep it at its best.

Give me a healthy mind, O Lord
To keep the good and pure in sight,
Which seeing sin is not appalled,
But finds a way to set it right.

Give me a mind that is not bored,
That does not whimper, whine, or sigh.
Don't let me worry overmuch
About the fussy thing called "I."

Give me a sense of humour, Lord.
Give me the grace to see a joke
To get some happiness from life
And pass it on to other folk.

—ANONYMOUS

STEP 8: THE PRINCIPLE OF LAUGHTER

The arrival of one good clown exercises a more
beneficial influence on the health of a town than
the arrival of twenty asses laden with drugs.
—Sir Thomas Sydenham (17th Century)

Live a thousand years, not in succession, but in each breath!
The human race has one effective weapon—and that is laughter.
—Mark Twain

Hilarious Healing

Norman Cousins was a famous political journalist, author, professor and world peace advocate. As an adjunct professor of medical humanities for the School of Medicine at UCLA, he was an essential facilitator during the Soviet-American nuclear test ban treaty negotiations in the 1960s, for which he was personally thanked by President John F. Kennedy and later awarded a medal by Pope John Paul XXIII. He received the Eleanor Roosevelt Peace Award in 1963 and the United Nations Peace Medal in 1971.

In 1964, Norman Cousins was diagnosed with ankylosing spondylitis, a condition that causes the connective tissue in the spine to quickly deteriorate. The diagnosing physician, a close friend of Cousins, gave him just a 1 in 500 chance of survival. Instead of simply accepting his prognosis, Cousins did something completely unheard of at the time and became his own health advocate. He discovered that his condition was depleting his body, so he quickly began to supplement with the help of his physician. He also checked himself out of the hospital, saying it was "no place" for a person who was seriously ill. Most important, Cousins found a movie projector and began watching old Marx Brothers films.

Ironically, Cousins discovered that when he watched the movies, he'd laugh so hard that he could get two complete hours of pain-free sleep per night. Soon he found that with each viewing, his blood sedimentation rate and white blood cells (indications of inflammation and infection) were consistently dropping. Ultimately, he was completely healed of the supposedly incurable condition. Cousins wrote an article, published in the *New England Journal of Medicine* in 1976, about laughter being therapeutic[36] and documented the full account of his amazing recovery in his book *Anatomy of an Illness*.[37]

---

36 Norman Cousins. December 23, 1976. Anatomy of an Illness. *The New England Journal of Medicine*. 295 (26): 1458–1463.
37 Norman Cousins. 20th ed. 2005. *Anatomy of an Illness*. New York: Norton, W.W. & Company. p. 192.

The Best Medicine

"Laughter is the best medicine" isn't just a metaphor. It's real science. When you laugh from that deep place within, the real deep belly laughs, an entire cascade of events begins to take place. For instance, CD 3 and CD 4 counts, which determine the body's immune response, have been shown to increase when you laugh. B-cells, which produce antibodies, have also been shown to significantly increase with laughter.[38] Your respiratory rate changes, and the amount of oxygen you're able to process increases dramatically. The blood vessels dilate and allow more blood to pass, while the lymphatics—your "other circulatory system" responsible for removing waste in your system—dramatically improves in functioning. All this is directly related to the movement of the diaphragm, which acts like a pump when you laugh.

As you laugh, you open up, let go, relax and allow your physiology to begin skipping through life instead of continuously dragging. This results in an improved sense of well-being that people can't pinpoint but are adamant they feel. (We'll talk more about this sense of well-being again.) The point is that positive energy begins to flow through your entire body. This positive cascade that you experience also happens to be contagious. When someone else sees you laughing sincerely, they either begin to laugh with you or they have a huge smile on their face because it makes them happy to see someone else laugh.

The mere act of laughing is a way of transferring positive energy life force to someone else. I like to call it positivity—a

---

38 Berk, Felten, Tan, Bittman, & Westengard, "Modulation of Neuroimmune Parameters During the Eustress of Humor-Associated Mirthful Laughter, *Alternative Therapies in Health and Medicine* 7, no. 2 (2001): 62–76.

shift to the bright side of any situation. It has a ripple effect that steadily moves outward from you, just as a pebble falling into a still pond creates the ever-increasing ripples. This ripple effect caused by laughter touches others and fills them with the same positivity. But the amazing part of this entire reaction is that this positivity is like a boomerang. It goes out from you but it comes back and fills you up even more, all in a matter of seconds and with more power than when you sent it out. It's an "exponential" return on your investment.

For example, we all know at least one person we absolutely just love being around. You could be having the worst day imaginable, but when this person walks into the room, he or she lights everything up. That person has a gift of being able to generate positivity and knows how to empower others with it, but the gift isn't unique or rare. The gift isn't the *ability* to do this but rather the *knowledge* of how to harness this universally available and abundant source of energy. You have it, and when you learn how to use it, you can create a healing life force that surrounds you and everyone you come into contact with.

Positivity is a process that is self-perpetuating and grows exponentially. The more you give out, the more you'll get back in return—and it just keeps building. Take the first step in starting this process for yourself, because it's one of the most valuable and precious things you'll ever discover, and the best part is that it's absolutely free. How can you learn to do this? Simple. With the very next stranger you pass on the street, look them straight in the eye and sincerely smile, extending to that person positive thoughts and well wishes silently from inside your mind as you go by. Experiment and see for yourself. I guarantee, as that person passes you, without knowing why, they'll have a smile on *their* face.

Good Vibrations

Every emotion we experience carries a unique and specific vibration, some positive and others negative. For example, when a very negative person enters the room, everyone can tell. The negative individual doesn't even have to say anything, but when they do, it's usually something negative, further adding fuel to the fire. We all know at least one person like this. Some refer to these people as "energy vampires." If they can't be happy, no one else can either, and they'll try to suck all the joy out of your day and more, if you let them. However, each of us has a *choice* in how we allow ourselves to feel every day. We've already discussed how thoughts affect your body, so *choose* positive thoughts that keep you happy and in a positive frame of mind, which in turn will create positive resonance or good vibrations and will help repel the "energy vampires."

Healing in all aspects will soon follow a positive frame of mind, extending beyond your health into other areas of your life even if you didn't realize you needed it. One amazing aspect of laughter is that when you share it with another, the energy expended comes back to you exponentially—just as with positivity. It's multiplied and comes back at a far greater rate than even a bank charges interest. Remember that *energy breeds more energy.* It's just like exercising. You have to expend the physical energy to work out, but then you get that zip in your step, that vitality and sense of well-being in return, even when you're not actively exercising. You'll actually experience more energy, but it doesn't just appear. You have to start up the energy "tennis match," but once it's started, it's easy to keep it going.

One of the easiest methods of creating positive thoughts, which also allows energy to breed more energy, is by surrounding yourself with as much humor as possible. Humor really is infectious and becomes contagious—but only for the good. In fact, regular laughter is far more contagious than any disease or infection. It has a domino effect, with such benefits as increased intimacy, uniting and binding people, creating healthy amusement in addition to all the health benefits mentioned in the preceding paragraphs.

Besides increasing energy and enhancing the immune system, laughter diminishes pain, improves focus, reignites hope, restores connections, enhances relationships, relieves tension, relaxes muscles, optimizes hormonal balance and reduces the effects of stress.

It's interesting to note that infants begin smiling within the first month of life and begin laughing within just a few months of being born. Researchers have studied the release of endorphins, as well as vasodilation of blood vessels resulting in increased blood flow[39] and reduced incidence of heart attack and stroke[40] as a result of laughter. Other studies have shown improvements in mood, reduction in anxiety and depression and shifting perspectives into a positive light when people laughed. For this reason alone, begin setting a goal to make laughter a part of your daily life and to use humor in all your interactions with others.

---

39 Miller, Mangano, Park, Goel, Plotnick, Vogel. *Laughter is the "Best Medicine" for Your Heart.* http://www.umm.edu/features/laughter.htm. Presented at Scientific Session of American College of Cardiology, March 7, 2005, Orlando, FL.
40 Miller, Clark, Seidler. *Laughter Is Good for Your Heart.* http://www. umm.edu/news /releases /laughter.htm. Presented at 73rd American Hearth Association's Scientific Session, November 15, 2000, New Orleans. LA.

Beginning this transformation in your life may seem difficult now, but once you begin, the momentum will carry it forward. Some ways to facilitate this change are as follows:

- Begin by laughing at yourself.
- Make a joke of situations you would normally complain about.
- Watch children and use them as examples of how to laugh and take life lightly.
- Bring humor into conversations.
- Move toward the sound of laughter.
- Spend more time around funny people.
- Read funny jokes and share them with others.
- Watch a funny movie or TV show.
- Read funny stories and comic strips.
- Count your blessings while smiling.

Another important component of humor is how it comes full circle to help overcome challenges that we face daily. We can learn a lot from children and how they naturally approach problems. Even when afraid or confused, they try and make a game of their challenge, allowing themselves an opportunity to experiment with new solutions while also getting some sense of control over the situation. This approach to solving problems naturally utilized by children is heavily based on imagination, laughter, play and fun. Not only does this make life more enjoyable, it also allows for solutions to appear, connections to be made and creativity to flourish. People who daily incorporate play and humor find it also to be highly beneficial in establishing and strengthening relationships.

Unexpected Entertainment

Medical students are first introduced to clinical medicine (see-ing patients under supervision) beginning in the third year of medical school. During the latter part of my third year, while on a family practice rotation, I entered the room occupied by a seventy-eight-year-old male patient. With his full head of thick blond hair, handsome and tanned face, rugged and firm jaw line, flannel shirt with sleeves partially rolled up, he could have passed for Robert Redford's younger brother. I apologized and walked out of the room because I thought I had the wrong patient. The man in the room couldn't, by the looks of him, have been past his fifties. The nursing staff reassured me the man in the room was indeed seventy-eight years old, and two of the younger and very attractive nurses argued over who would be reviewing instruc-tions with the patient after I was done.

The patient had come in for a shoulder problem, and we went over the issues and various options for treatment. After the visit was completed, I got up to leave, and as I opened the door, he said, "Uh, doc, uh . . . by the way, there's uh . . . something else . . ." My ears perked up. Just days before, one of the lectures I had attended during grand rounds had been on how to deal with elderly patients facing their mortality. We had learned that as patients get closer to making the inevitable transition, they need reassurance about the uncertainties surrounding death. However, because the doctor is often far younger than they are and the elder patient is supposed to be the "life expert," it creates awkwardness in the interaction between the two.

Frequently, some simple complaint (like a shoulder issue) would be an excuse for their primary reason for visiting the doctor. We were taught that the patient would usually wait until the visit was over and then, hesitatingly, bring up the real issue as the doctor was preparing to exit the exam room. Being cognizant of this timeline, being sensitive to the needs of the patient and learning techniques on how to deal with these issues were all covered in detail during this lecture.

The patient asked me to shut the door. "This is it," I thought. The instructors had said that these patients *always* ask you to shut the door first! I was so ready to be the "nurturing doctor." This was the mortality issue. I turned around, ready to bestow my recently found wisdom on this patient. The timing couldn't have been better.

"I'm not sure how to bring this up," he stumbled. "It's a little difficult to talk about this with you but it's about . . . "—I decided to make it easy for him, but just as I began to open my mouth to start showering him with my newfound knowledge, he finished his sentence—"oral sex." *Bam!* I was stunned.

I was sitting on the stool, suddenly staring at the ground. I couldn't have been more shocked if I'd been hit by a baseball bat. Once I came to my senses, I hesitatingly started to explain the fine nuances of oral sex and all it entails to this seventy-eight-year-old man who was old enough to be my great-grandfather.

He first looked relieved as I began; then, looking confused, he cocked his head to the side, the way a dog does, before he finally was staring at me as if I were from another planet. "Oh God," I thought, "I've shocked him beyond belief!" And then he burst out laughing.

"Son, I was having oral sex long before your mamma was a glimmer in *her* mamma's eye," he roared, slapping his knee. "I just wanted to know if there were any diseases I need to worry about picking up while having oral sex."

As he left, he gestured toward me and playfully told the nurses, "I can't wait for my next lesson about oral sex!" You know what they say about never assuming anything. Well, I'd learned my lesson. It was with mixed emotions that I handled my new found realization. The generations ahead of me had actually discovered sex as well! Who would have known? It took a few days to overcome my embarrassment before I was able to laugh at myself.

Just for Laughs

This experience was just another example of Murphy's laws. I've always enjoyed the irony of Murphy's laws. A friend sent me the following "Murphy's Lesser Known Laws,"[41] which I thought I would include as a conclusion to this chapter on laughter. Remember, laugh as much as you can and as often as you can. It's totally free despite being one of the most valuable and enjoyable activities you can ever engage in with tremendous benefits from a disease prevention and health wellness perspective.

Murphy's Lesser Known Laws

1. Light travels faster than sound. This is why some people appear bright . . . until you hear them speak.

2. Change is inevitable, except from a vending machine.

3. Those who live by the sword get shot by those who don't.

4. Nothing is foolproof to a sufficiently talented fool.

---

41 Author unknown. November 2006. *Murphy's Lesser Known Laws.* Available: http://www.jumbojoke.com/murphys_lesser_known_laws.html. Last accessed October 17, 2009.

5. The 50–50–90 rule: Anytime you have a 50–50 chance of getting something right, there's a 90 percent probability you'll get it wrong.

6. If you lined up all the cars in the world end to end, someone would be stupid enough to try to pass them . . . on a hill . . . in the fog, and nine times out of ten, they'll have (insert whatever state you wish to insult) plates on their car . . .

7. The things that come to those who wait will be the scraggly junk left by those who got there first.

8. The shin bone is a device for finding furniture in a dark room.

9. A fine is a tax for doing wrong. A tax is a fine for doing well.

10. When you go into court, you are putting yourself into the hands of people who weren't smart enough to get out of jury duty.

Seven days without laughter makes one weak.
—MORT WALKER

With the fearful strain that is on me night and day, if I did not laugh I should die.
—ABRAHAM LINCOLN

Fast Wrap
Step 8: The Principle of Laughter

What's so funny about laughter?

Laughter is contagious. It's an energy exchange that moves outward from you, touches others and comes back to you with twice as much energy as you expended. The energy output from laughter is a powerful healing force, and you *have the choice* to use it every day of your life.

Why is laughter really like medicine?

Science has shown that the immune system's response strengthens when we laugh deeply, from within ourselves. It also creates an entire cascade of chemical events and initiates physiological cascades inside your body that overwhelm you with a sense of well-being while actually stimulating certain processes that enhance your health. For example, laughter stimulates the lymphatic system, increases lung capacity and dilates blood vessels, allowing you to process larger amounts of nutrition and oxygen to feed and regenerate your cells and efficiently eliminate waste and toxins from your body.

How can I laugh if I'm not feeling my best?

Everyone can laugh, at any time. It's simply a choice to allow yourself to laugh. My daughter has refused to smile whenever she's angry with me about something. I'll tell her she can be angry, but she has to smile, and then I'll begin to tease her to the point that she can't help but laugh. Of course, she'll usually tell me, "You're strange, Dad," and point out that she's not laughing with me but rather *at* me. However, she's usually laughing by the time she's telling me this and that was my goal in the first place. Try to sit through a few scenes of your favorite comedy. Watch old movies of your children or grandchildren. Children and animals are great for laughs. Reminisce about funny stories with friends. Soon you'll be feeling too good to feel bad.

If I laugh more, what do I get besides a stomachache?

When you laugh, you attain freedom, relaxation, peace and energy. Your body will feel lighter as you experience the blessed gift of not taking life so seriously. Every cell in your body will begin to expand with positivity while you're laughing, allowing you to heal faster and with less effort. Better yet, you'll become one of those high-energy, positive people everyone loves being around, and in turn, you'll attract only the same types of individuals.

STEP 9: THE PRINCIPLE OF PHYSIOLOGICAL REGENERATION

All parts of the body which have a function if used in moderation and exercised in labors in which each is accustomed, become thereby healthy, well developed and age more slowly, but if unused they become liable to disease and defective in growth and age quickly.

—HIPPOCRATES, GREEK PHYSICIAN

The Last Drop

Several years ago, an elderly lady came to see me at the urging of her neighbor. The neighbor was a patient of mine and believed that I could help this lady. A childless widow, the elderly woman had recently had two stents placed in her heart, and she had a history of congestive heart failure. Her heart wasn't pumping efficiently anymore, which accounted for her shortness of breath and weakness. This was followed by depression, fatigue and a host of other issues. She was too weak to participate in any kind of activity or work and in her words, "had no reason to live."

I started by addressing some of her health issues but, as I do with all patients, I encouraged her to begin the 9 Steps as well. I suggested she start taking a product called Trans-D Tropin® (TransD), the details of which I'll explain shortly. At the age of eighty-two, however, she was existing solely on Social Security, which amounted to just $845 a month, and she informed me quite bluntly she couldn't afford it on her limited budget. Basically, it came down to choosing whether she was going to "eat or take some drug." I reassured her that Trans-D was *not* a drug and that it contained nothing but natural ingredients. Still, she said, "I just can't afford it." I happened to have my own bottle in my lab coat, so I took it out, gave her one application and then gave her the rest of the bottle. I knew she would benefit from it. I asked her to simply continue using it until the bottle ran out, unsure if I'd ever see her again.

Less than one month later, she walked back into my office without an appointment. The first thing she said was, "I can't afford *not* to be on this stuff!" She then proceeded to tell me the amazing changes that had occurred in her life since I had last seen her. Since that time, she'd started breathing better, had more energy, was sleeping better and felt refreshed upon awakening. She felt so much better in fact that she'd taken a job as a transcriptionist, which she said would help her pay for treatments and for her Trans-D. I started her on an appropriate detoxification program and she steadily continued to improve.

Later, she met a gentleman, became romantically involved and eventually moved to Seattle with him sometime in 1999. The last time I saw her, she hugged me and whispered in my ear, "Thank you for giving me that bottle. It saved my life." In fact, one of my staff later told me the woman confessed to having kept that empty bottle, even after the last drop was gone, just to remind herself of how hopeless she used to feel and how her life had changed.

Hormonal Havoc

In chapter 2, we covered the foundation of hormonal optimization, namely, that hormones control the balance and performance of virtually every system in the body. Think of hormones as the musical notes in an orchestra (your body's organ systems) that need to be read in the proper key, at the right tempo and with the ideal volume in order to produce beautiful music (health). As we age, however, many of these hormones decline; it's just accepted as part of the aging process. One important hormone associated with aging is human growth hormone (hGH or GH), which along with testosterone and many others, drops significantly as we age.

As these levels begin to decline, many of our body's systems begin to lose their ability to function properly. The orchestra is now playing from sheet music that's either missing a lot of notes or the musicians are off key. This results in music that's too fast or too slow, too loud or too soft at the wrong times or completely out of tune. What's happening is that the endocrine system, the system responsible for balancing all the hormones in the body, is "off." It's how people feel when their hormonal levels are not being produced at optimum levels—out of tune. It's the malaise most people have just come to accept, because they're told that it's "just the way it is" with aging.

When hormone levels are not at a healthy balance, every system in your body suffers. Your endocrine and immune systems are particularly burdened, creating the opportunity for many abnormalities and subsequent diseases to become established. Recognizing these risks, some doctors have attempted to optimize hormonal levels in ways that, unfortunately, do not work in conjunction with the body's natural design. Their patients end up trading one risk for two others.

As an example, let's look at hGH. Many doctors try to increase hGH levels through the injection of a synthetic version of the hormone. The first problem with synthetic injectable hGH is that it is quite expensive, with the average price exceeding a thousand dollars per month or more. But that's the least of its drawbacks. Far more important is that injectable hGH has some serious side effects and causes some abnormal changes to occur in the physiology. These include joint effusions (swelling), carpal tunnel syndrome, cardiomyopathies (heart disorders) and the abnormal growth of the hands, feet and forehead known as acromegaly. Later, we will also discuss the issue of cancer and the interrelationship between hGH and other hormones and how they may affect the incidence of cancer.

The trend in hormonal supplementation now is leaning strongly toward bioidentical hormones. These hormones are made at a compounding pharmacy and share the same molecular structure as those made by your body. The idea is to eliminate many of the side effects related to synthetic hormones. Although the patients who use these bioidentical hormones are free from many of the noticeable problems caused by synthetic hormones, a far more insidious risk lurks silently in the background for those who use these so-called safer options.

Let me briefly remind you that your body's hormonal system is a complete circle of signals and responses. You will recall from chapter 2 that the hormonal system is regulated by a larger safety mechanism system in your body called the negative inhibitory feedback loop (NIFBL). When your body experiences a specific need, a signal is sent, received on the other end and responded to, all in a matter of seconds. This is how the signal to create hunger, build more muscle mass or jump out of the way of a speeding car operates.

Hormones start their cycle from the signaling source (in the case of hGH, from the hypothalamus) to release hGH from the pituitary gland located in the brain. The pituitary gland sends out many different chemical signals that move through what we call the "hormonal cascade." By the time the signals reach the bottom of this complex chain, the proper glands produce and release varying amounts of the hormones needed by the body, from testosterone to cortisol to insulin to some hormones modern science hasn't even discovered yet.

The problem, however, occurs when we interrupt the NIFBL or short-circuit the hormonal cycle by taking out this regulatory safety mechanism. Earlier, when referring to exercise, we discussed the principle of "if you don't use it, you'll lose it." Exercise creates a constant cycle of tearing down and repairing body tissue, so it's always in a state of growth or regeneration because it's "using" the muscle. *Synthetic or not,* when we introduce a hormone into the system, it causes a disruption in the *end result* of a long chain of other hormonal factors. What happens to the gland that originally produced the hormone we are now replacing with the synthetic hormone or its bioidentical cousin? The gland obviously atrophies because it is no longer being "used." Instead of being in a state of low functioning, we drive it into the state of nonfunctioning or, because we don't "use it," we "lose it."

Testosterone is another example of a hormone that doctors prescribe. Normally, the lower the level of testosterone in a male, the more the hypothalamus sends the message for the gonado-tropin-releasing hormone (GnRH)—the hormone responsible for releasing the sex hormones—to produce more testoster-one. When doctors notice that the testosterone levels are low, they assume the glands (testicles, in this case) are not produc-ing enough, and they prescribe testosterone. The testosterone is taken. The natural monitoring system, again the hypothalamus, sees all this new testosterone coming in. So, instead of sending GnRH to tell the testicles to make more testosterone, the hypo-thalamus says, "Uh-oh, we already have too much testosterone coming in, so there's no need to produce any more."

Thus, no signal is sent to the testicles from the hypothala-mus. The testicles just hang around (pun intended) waiting for the signal to begin producing testosterone. But no signal comes because the doctor is prescribing the synthetic or the bioidenti-cal testosterone. The testicles no longer are being used so, like anything that's not used, they begin to deteriorate and eventually completely stop functioning. The result is testicular shrinkage (testicular atrophy). What the doctor has done, in effect, is to take a poorly functioning system and totally shut it down.

Even minimum testicular function is better than none. Sup-porting the body in the work it's already doing is obviously a better option than shutting down the entire system. This is the biggest risk most users of synthetic or bioidentical hormones are not even aware of, because the concept of hormonal balancing is not the popular message. Instead, the primary focus remains on replacement of the end hormone, with no regard to the serious consequences of this nearsighted strategy. Interrupting the natural flow of any bodily process is never a wise idea. It assumes we know more than the One who created it.

The question that should be asked first and foremost is, what's causing the decline in the testosterone release in the first place? If you *can enhance* the normal physiological processes without causing a shutdown of the organ normally producing the hormone, it is the most desired result. This becomes impossible, however, by giving the end hormone (synthetic or bioidentical). The most desirable of all results would be to achieve the above-mentioned end result by *increasing* the ability of the organ in question itself to make more of the desired hormone without adversely affecting the regulatory system or causing the NIFBL to become initiated.

By understanding the fundamental premise of the "use it or lose it" phenomenon and respecting this fundamental regulatory principle, you have now created something that feeds into the perfect design created by the ultimate engineer, the Creator. A therapy such as this, which respects your body's intelligence and natural processes, is one that will make the orchestra in your body perform flawlessly, creating the most perfect music any ears have ever heard! The fantastic news is that there actually is just one such therapy and it has been available for well over a decade now. The sad news is that there is only *one* such therapy.

I'm about to share with you a new innovation that supports the body in producing more of its own (endogenous) hormones, including hGH, testosterone and other hormones. The profound thing is that this treatment actually stimulates the organs and glands that naturally produce these hormones already to begin producing *more*, thus preventing the atrophy of any of these glands (which occurs more often than not with the synthetic or bioidentical hormonal route). Despite what doctors may say about giving low doses to prevent atrophy from ever occurring, it is nonetheless a very real and often observed phenomenon. Without ever replacing the end hormones, the body itself can be awakened to optimum functioning and, through its own work, can maintain a level of vitality you might not have thought possible into your sixties, seventies, eighties and well beyond. But before we discuss this incredible treatment, which I have personally used for over twelve years, a brief background history is warranted.

Promised Fountain of Youth

With all the incredible advances in technology throughout history, the proverbial "fountain of youth" has continued to evade humanity. In the twentieth century, however, modern medical science stumbled across something that held the promise of a longer and healthier life. In 1934, Mary Crowell and Clive McCay of Cornell University conducted a nutritional study with rats. They discovered that rats fed a severely reduced-calorie (up to 30 percent) diet, while vital nutrient levels were maintained, lived up to twice as long as their counterparts that ate as much as they wanted.[42]

More recently, former UCLA professor and pathologist Gordon L. Walford, MD, and his student, Richard Weindruch, conducted a similar experiment with mice only to find the group that had their caloric intake drastically reduced doubled their life span when compared to mice that ate a normal diet. It was

---

42 Clive McCay and M. F. Crowell, "Prolonging the Life Span," *Scientific Monthly* 39, no. 5 (1934): 405–414.

also reported that the calorie-restricted mice maintained higher energy levels and showed a marked delay in all age-related diseases. More details on the studies of Walford and Weindruch can be found in their book *The Retardation of Aging and Disease by Dietary Restriction* (1988*).*[43]

An article by Donald K. Ingram, Mark A. Lane and George S. Roth, published in *Life Extension* magazine, examined caloric restriction in our nearest genetic relatives, the primates. The article found the monkeys that consumed 30 percent fewer calories lived 30 percent longer. They managed to live to thirty-two years of age, which corresponds to ninety-six human years![44] That's the equivalent of adding twenty-one years onto the current human life expectancy of seventy-five!

It is now widely accepted that the only scientifically established method of truly increasing life span of humans beyond the "accepted" range of seventy-five years is caloric restriction. For the end user, however, the problem may be that life just appears to *seem* longer because you feel like you're slowly being starved.

In all seriousness, however, the most incredible aspect of these discoveries is that all the groups of animals whose caloric intake was restricted experienced an increase in hGH levels while, at the same time, evidenced a consistent decrease in IGF-1, cortisol and insulin levels. Remember that IGF-1 (insulin-like growth factor—type 1), insulin and cortisol are all markers of inflammation. The reason why these animals not only lived longer but

---

43 R. Weinbruch and R. L. Walford. 1988. *The Retardation of Aging and Disease by Dietary Restriction*. Springfield, IL: Charles C. Thomas. p.436.
44 D.K. Ingram, M.A. Lane, and G.S. Roth. 1998. Compelling Evidence in Humans' Closest Relatives: Calorie Restriction in Monkeys. *Life Extension Magazine*. Available: http://www.lef.org/magazine/mag98/july98_monkey.html. Last accessed February 17, 2010.

also with virtually no chronic disease is because inflammation was substantially reduced as evidenced by the reduction of the hormones that are markers of inflammation. These hormones are double-edged swords, like oxygen. You can't live without oxygen, but it's the cause of oxidative stress as well, which as we'll learn in the next chapter, is the cause of all chronic disease.

The findings of these studies did not go unnoticed, and soon public demand created an entire new arena of medicine that became known as "anti-aging" medicine. Ridiculed by practitioners of traditional medicine and ostracized by those who practiced integrative medicine, anti-aging medicine nevertheless received a popular reception by the masses. Unfortunately, the proponents of anti-aging medicine focused on only one component of these studies. It was hGH that garnered all the attention, and that rapidly became the treatment of choice of the rich and famous. Anti-aging clinics have since sprouted up everywhere, and the various "age and longevity management" societies have thrived.

I've been invited to and have lectured at all of these societies. I even served on the Continuing Medical Education Committees for the most reputable of these organizations. However, all of them virtually ignored the rest of the story—the most crucial and more indicative portion that no one wanted to talk about. I was advised on more than one occasion, even by the companies that sponsored my lectures, not to discuss the issue of the rising IGF-1 levels. Yet, these changes are clearly observed when patients are prescribed hGH. Because discussing the increasing levels of IGF-1 threatens to topple the house of cards created by the incredible promise of hGH injection therapy, its supporters would try to silence the most important part of the story.

As time went by, and through some strange medical folklore process, increased IGF-1 levels incredibly became the marker of choice to assess *effective* hGH therapy! And even more preposterous, a lack of IGF-1 increase was interpreted to mean the clinician needed to further *increase* the hGH dose. Like a bad dream, the entire truth went from being blurred to being completely buried, and the public's common understanding about hGH and IGF-1 was turned upside down. The fewer than half a dozen doctors and researchers who were outspoken about the truth behind increasing IGF-1 were gradually distanced from these societies and eventually kept from lecturing or talking about the truth. Their audience was simply prevented from hearing them. But, as with all truths, despite the agenda at hand, the truth about hGH and IGF-1 has sustained itself.

Athletes versus Sedentary Individuals

It all started because I wanted to extend the benefits of hGH to my patients and I wanted to personally benefit from the incredible promise of hGH myself. But there was no way I was going to inject hGH into my patients or myself because injecting hGH clearly increased IGF-1. Remember that IGF-1 stands for insulin-like growth factor—Type 1. It's one of many types of growth factors, but this one is called insulin-*like* growth factor because the peptide sequence is very similar to that of insulin. In fact, the binding sites are actually identical to insulin and are interchangeable.[45]

Looking at the morphological characteristics, the properties of IGF-1 and insulin share many commonalities and are almost

---

45 See the International Society of IGF Research, http://www.igf-society.org.

identical. We've previously identified both insulin and IGF-1 as pro-inflammatory molecules, so just that alone prevented me from giving someone a substance that would *increase* the inflammatory response. We obviously want to *decrease* inflammation. But there were many other crucial assumptions that were being made, something characteristic of modern medicine and very unsettling, especially since the implications are so devastating. To explain this, let's take a moment and look at the type of individual who has high insulin levels as an example of what high insulin levels imply.

Insulin actually acts like a fuel injector to take sugar (glucose) from outside the cell and drive it into the cell. We know that exercise sensitizes the cells to the effects of insulin and therefore the body needs less insulin to accomplish the same effect. As a result, when people exercise they don't need as much fuel injector to push the fuel into the cell because the increased demand for fuel *by* the cell essentially *sucks* up the fuel (glucose). In other words, you have a more efficient utilization of glucose in patients who exercise, thus requiring *less* insulin. A higher metabolism rate, increased lean body mass, optimum cell membrane fluidity and greater level of activity all lead to a decrease in insulin levels. Anyone who understands even the most basic, elementary components of human physiology will *not* argue or contest that exercise increases insulin sensitivity and therefore reduces insulin levels. This is as simple as $1 + 1 = 2$ in the understanding of physiology.

It's also widely accepted that exercise leads to a younger physiological state. A number of studies have shown that exercise naturally increases hGH. In fact, in one of our own studies, we actually showed that the placebo group had more than a 118 percent increase in hGH levels just by exercise and dietary changes alone.[46] We also know that exercise increases testosterone and improves overall hormonal response in the entire endocrine system. Numerous studies have shown that exercise decreases blood pressure, heart rate, respiratory rate and peripheral vascular resistance, making the system more efficient. Exercise is also widely credited with increasing endorphin levels, increasing lean body mass and strengthening immunity, as well as improving range of motion, endurance, recovery, stamina and sex drive. None of these are contested facts among scientists.

Now, if insulin and IGF-1 are very similar to each other—sharing the same receptor sites and morphologically and characteristically almost identical—then would it not be reasonable to conclude that IGF-1 levels should be *lower* in athletes just as insulin levels are *lower* in athletes? This is what you would expect, but incredibly, according to the textbooks and all the "anti-aging experts," IGF-1 is a marker that doctors should strive to *increase.* To me, this is analogous to increasing insulin in patients, which is clearly *not* something any doctor desires to do in a healthy person. Insulin is given only to diabetics, and the resulting side effects are widely recognized, some examples being kidney failure (diabetic nephropathy) and worsening vision (diabetic retinopathy).

Clinical observations provide further validation, showing IGF-1 levels measured in patients to be opposite of what the "experts" were saying. In my own clinic, the younger and more

---

46 Rashid Buttar, DO, James Biddle, MD, Rajiv Chandra, MD, Terry Grossman, MD, Clarence Norris, MD, James Smith, DO, Annette Stoesser, MD, Dean Viktora, PhD. 2002. *Preliminary Results of Multi-Centered, Double Blind, Placebo Controlled, Cross-Over Study Evaluating Endogenous hGH (Human Growth Hormone) Levels With Serial Hgh Radio-Immunoassay Levels After Trans-Dermal hGH Releasing Hormone Analog Administration.* Available: https://www.transd.com/science-of-trans-d-tropin.php. Last accessed August 11, 2009.

athletic the person was, the *lower* their IGF-1 levels were measured. Conversely, the older, sedentary, obese patients had *higher* IGF-1 levels. Now, if we're trying to reverse or at least halt aging, then shouldn't our goal be to achieve the *same* physiology found in a young athlete, namely, lower IGF-1 levels as opposed to simulating the physiology of an older, sedentary, overweight individual? By increasing IGF-1, we would be clearly emulating an older, sedentary person.

Increasing IGF-1 simply made no sense because I was consistently finding IGF-1 to be higher in older, sedentary, obese people and lower in younger, more athletic and in-shape individuals. The few professional athletes in my practice had the lowest IGF-1 levels, under 95 ng/ml. My own IGF-1 was also low at 123 ng/ml, and at the time I was thirty-three and involved in a very intensive exercise regimen. Yet the sedentary people in my practice—all older, nonactive, mostly overweight—all had *high* IGF-1 readings, sometimes triple or more than that of the younger, fitter, healthier and more active patients. As any other reasonable doctor, I wanted all my patients to emulate the physiology of a younger, athletic, healthy and fit individual, not a sedentary obese person who never exercises and has an IGF-1 level of 280 ng/ml. Despite what the "experts" were saying, I was observing the complete opposite in real life.

To resolve the issue of what was a normal IGF-1 level in younger versus older patients, I decided to conduct my own study. We decided on an outcome-based study with thirty-eight patients from my own practice. Criteria to participate included no treatment and no history of manipulation with hormones for a minimum of two years prior to entering into the study. Of the thirty-eight total individuals, twenty-one were sedentary males and females with no previous history of regular exercise for two years. The age range was 30 to 84, with a mean age of 55.3 years and a median age of 57. IGF-1 range was between 61 to 304 ng/ml, with a mean of 153.0 ng/ml and a median of 182.5 ng/ml.

We compared this to a group of seventeen males and females considered athletic, defined as having had regular physical activity for a minimum of two years prior to the study, including aerobic and resistance training conducted at least every forty-eight hours. The age range in this patient population was 25 to 42, with a mean age of 34.1 and a median of 33.5. The mean age in the athletic group was therefore 21.2 years *lower* than the sedentary group. IGF-1 range was between 88 to 196 ng/ml, with a mean of 149.4 ng/ml and a median of 142.0 ng/ml.

The goal of therapy, according to the anti-aging gurus, is to increase IGF-1, which is supposed to be synonymous with youth. Thus, we would expect high IGF-1 to be the normal finding in athletic, younger people and low levels in the older, sedentary population. According to popular belief, then, our younger group should have had a much higher IGF-1 level, especially considering they were twenty-one years *younger*, on average, than our older group. Yet the findings were totally opposite. The highest IGF-1 measured in the young athletic group was 196 ng/ml, compared to 304 ng/ml in the older, sedentary group. This conclusively proved that normal IGF-1 is *lower* in younger, athletic individuals and higher in older, sedentary individuals.

So, why would anyone ask for a treatment that leads to results found normally in older, less active people (*higher* IGF-1)? Wouldn't everyone want a treatment leading to results found normally in younger, more active individuals (*lower* IGF-1)?

My study showed that the promise of "anti-aging," "longevity" and "age-management" medicine, supposedly to help people feel, look and function better, was actually based on a *lie*! And the treatment being promoted to attain these results was, in actuality, geared to do the exact opposite! This small study validated my initial observations and again proved that experts should be approached with caution. The full findings of the study are available online and also covered in detail in one of the "Know Your Options, The Medical Series" DVDs, both listed in the resources section.

IGF-1 and Cancer

I was actually at an advantage compared to most doctors because I also happen to treat patients suffering from cancer. One of the markers I had monitored in all my patients was IGF-1. What most doctors prescribing injectable hGH *do not* realize is that cancer produces its own IGF-1 to increase the fuel uptake of the glucose upon which cancer thrives. In fact, cancer is an obligate glucose metabolizer, meaning it's "obligated" to sugar or dependent on sugar to survive. Without sugar, cancer cannot survive. Remember that insulin's job is to drive sugar into the cells. IGF-1's also serve this same function. In order to grow, cancer cells release their own IGF-1 to facilitate more uptake of sugar for themselves.

At this point you may be asking why doctors promoting injectable hGH continue touting the virtues of increasing IGF-1 levels. Well, when you find out, let me know! In actuality, they have *no* reason except that when you inject synthetic hGH into the system, it's converted to IGF-1 in the liver. But increasing

IGF-1 in a person with cancer is like pouring gasoline on a fire. The IGF-1 simply fuels the cancer by feeding it, pushing more glucose into the cancer.

Keep in mind, we're talking about a hormone that causes *all cells* to grow and build, including cancer cells that we may not yet be aware exist inside our bodies. If cancer cells themselves produce IGF-1, can you logically give *any* justification to increase this level artificially in the body for *any* reason? There was *no way* I was going to be a part of any treatment introducing something into the body of my patients that was going to increase IGF-1 or further propagate any potential cancer that might have been lurking within their systems.

Obviously, the issue is with IGF-1, not hGH. In fact, we know hGH is "good" and begins reaching its peak during the late adolescent years. When plotted on a graph, the incidence of cancer remains the lowest during this period of maximum hGH release. Conversely, during early childhood and after age fifty, hGH levels are the lowest, and we see the highest incidence of cancer in those years. It's important to point out that there is a slow descent of hGH levels after reaching peak around age twenty-one. But this supports the old adage "Where growth stops, decay sets in." The challenge was to raise hGH levels in the body without increasing IGF-1 levels.

After three years in the laboratory and literally over thirty-four hundred trials, we finally accomplished what was thought to be impossible. We were able to increase hGH levels while *decreasing* IGF-1 levels, all using a patient-friendly format that requires no injections whatsoever.

This factor regarding the *reduction* of IGF-1 was something that I only incidentally noticed, but the full implications completely escaped me back then. It wasn't until almost nine years later, after having solved this challenge, that the magnitude of what we had done truly dawned on me. Recall the laboratory parameters measured in the caloric-restricted animals that lived longer. The animals experienced an increase in hGH while at the same time showing a consistent decrease in IGF-1, insulin and cortisol levels!

To clarify, the only scientifically valid and established method of increasing life span (using caloric restriction) *decreased* IGF-1 levels! And yet, here were the "anti-aging" experts injecting hGH into patients and *increasing* IGF-1, a known marker of inflammation, known to be released and produced by cancer cells to feed and propagate cancer, associated with older age, sedentary lifestyle and obesity. All this, in complete opposition of the original work done in caloric restriction, which proved you could increase life span by reducing caloric intake resulting in increasing endogenous (your body's own) hGH while actually *decreasing* IGF-1. The implications are enormous.

Let's also not forget the importance of how injectible hGH is administered. When the negative inhibitory feedback loop (NIFBL) is violated, we now understand the consequences. By giving injectible hGH, we are in fact causing a shutdown of our own endogenous production of hGH, inducing atrophy in the pituitary gland, which is responsible for production and storage of the hHG our own system was meant to produce. Remember, no matter how many signals the body sends out saying "too much hGH" (in the case of hGH, the signal is somatostain), it does *not* prevent or stop the individual injecting the hGH from *continuing* to inject themselves. This violation of the NIFBL is, in essence, nothing less than a chemical castration, the same as what would be induced by a bodybuilder when taking too much testosterone.

From the Top Down

Let's be clear. Just by following the first eight steps alone, you will go a long way in optimizing your hormones. Still, depending on the damage or health issues you've experienced over your lifetime, just following the first eight steps may not get your health to the completely optimum level. If that's the case, your endocrine system and hormones may need a little "boost." The first foundation is systemic detoxification. The second foundation is immune modulation. And the third foundation is what we're going to now discuss, physiological optimization.

This is where TransD comes in. It's the safest and most effective method, not to mention the most affordable and easiest way to naturally up-regulate all hormones—*without* engaging the NIFBL or using hGH. Back in the mid-1990s, the period that saw the advent and growing popularity of hGH, I chose to work toward finding something that could increase endogenous hGH without increasing IGF-1. Not only did we accomplish this almost impossible goal, we were able to measure a consistent *drop* in IGF-1, both immediately as well as over the long term.

TransD is a unique, peptide analog-based, transdermal (applied through the skin) product that my partner and I developed in 1998. Without going into too much technical jargon, we were able to essentially mimic the "in vivo" process of protein conjugation. In other words, we were able to essentially duplicate the process by which the body digests proteins from, say, a turkey sandwich, into the raw amino acids and then reassembles these amino acids into new peptides to make enzymes, hormones, tissue, etc. "That's impossible," you might say. So did everyone else.

Over the years, as we played with this, the realization that the results we wanted might never materialize crossed our minds, but we just continued. We kept trying: batch after batch, month after month. And then, after more than thirty-four hundred different trials leading to over eleven hundred separate batches and a few years, as if by divine inspiration, one of the batches worked. To say we were excited would be an understatement. Over the next forty or so days, I woke up every morning in a cold sweat believing that everything had been just a dream. We are truly humbled by the discovery.

Trans-D Tropin® was developed for use only in my own private practice. By coincidence, however, I also had a number of patients receiving treatment at my clinic who happened to be physicians themselves. A few of them were started on TransD and experienced the incredible broad-based benefits firsthand. Word slowly spread through these patient–doctors, who wanted to provide the same unique benefits to their own patients; the rest, as they say, is history.

In 1998 we applied for registration with the FDA, and TransD was duly registered in 1999. It's important to mention that "registered" is different from being "approved." The FDA does not "approve" products that are all-natural. We initially made TransD available by prescription just because we wanted to distribute the product through doctors and pharmacies, and for the first decade this was the only way one could obtain TransD. It has now officially been on the market for well over eleven years and has enjoyed steady success in the most difficult market in which to sustain an all-natural product, namely, the medical market.

TransD has been recommended by more than 1,880 doctors in twenty-seven different countries and, as of 2008, had more than 22.8 million doses dispensed. Before going any further, I want to make clear to all the readers, if it hasn't already been made abundantly clear, I have a vested interest in TransD. However, even though I personally developed and have a vested interest in TransD, it doesn't change the fact that TransD was created because there was nothing out there that conferred the benefits I was searching for without the side effects. It was something that I very much needed and actively sought to help my patients.

TransD is an hGH-releasing analog, which means it acts like the signal telling the pituitary to release hGH. This function is vastly different from being the hormone itself. Because TransD starts at the top of the hormonal cascade, it doesn't interrupt the delicate balance in the middle or at the end of the cascade, as a hormone itself would do. Another tremendous benefit from TransD is that the signal it mimics is not limited to hGH. Studies have shown that TransD has an effect on many other hormones as well, including increasing such sex hormones as testosterone and decreasing such stress hormones as cortisol.

TransD should certainly not be confused with a class of therapeutics referred to as secretagogues (which I mentioned briefly in chapter 2). TransD mimics the actual messenger that tells your pituitary gland to begin the process of producing more of its own natural hGH. Most secretagogues, on the other hand, are sugar-based precursors that have little if any benefit. Worse, like hGH, they promise to increase IGF-1. The truth is they are harmless and won't elicit anything. In the rare event that you find a secretatogue that may be effective, it will be effective only in creating a problem precisely because these substances promise to increase IGF-1, the same *undesired* effect as that of injectable hGH.

In appearance, TransD looks like a simple off-white runny lotion and is applied directly on the top of the forearms. Very simply, you apply the lotion to the top surface of one forearm and then rub it against the other forearm. There are no needles to inject and no special rituals to follow. You can take a shower or go for a swim within five minutes of applying TransD, but we suggest waiting at least ten minutes to make sure everything applied has been fully absorbed. Best of all, TransD is completely safe, costs far less than injectable hGH, is far more effective and never violates the NIFBL. Preliminary study results and subjective patient responses obtained in three studies done between 1999 and 2003 were nothing less than extraordinarily exciting. But then, again, remember—I'm biased.

Just the Facts

All three studies that we did on TransD showed similar results, and other doctors have since reproduced the same findings in their own patient populations all over the world. Details of all three studies are available online. The largest of these was a multicentered, double-blind, placebo-controlled, crossover study initiated in twenty-five locations throughout the United States. Two groups, totaling 117 patients, were monitored over an eight-week period, and then the control group (on placebo) was crossed over into the experimental group (on TransD) for another eight weeks.

At the time of initiating TransD, there was a 462 percent *increase* in endogenous (what your own body produces) hGH levels just ninety minutes after the first application in the group on TransD. By the end of the second week, the TransD group showed that endogenous hGH had increased to 815 percent from what was measured at baseline to ninety minutes after application. By the fifth week, the TransD group showed there was a phenomenal 1,754 percent *increase* in endogenous hGH from what was measured at baseline to ninety minutes after application. Remember, this is without giving any end hormones and all achieved while respecting the normal, healthy NIFBL.

All hGH levels were assessed by both radioimmunoassay and chemiluminescent immunoassay testing in all 117 patients. Other laboratory findings measured during the same period of time included insulin, cortisol and IGF-1 levels, all of which *consistently decreased,* with all the participating patients reporting subjective improvements in various areas. At the eighth week on TransD, however, we observed an interesting phenomenon, which we didn't anticipate. We actually observed an unexpected drop in the endogenous hGH levels, down to 609 percent (from a high of 1,754 percent) over baseline. We were at a loss to explain this initially.

After looking at the results a bit closer, it became clear there were two very distinct possibilities to explain why the hGH levels had dropped by the eighth week. During the fifth week, there was a tremendous increase in endogenous hGH by 1,754 percent. This means the amount of hGH released by the pituitary was, on average, seventeen and a half times *more* than normally released! So if we're getting such a huge increase in hGH, do you think it's possible that we were *exceeding* the physiological limits? Absolutely!

However, our safety mechanism was completely functional and intact, so the NIFBL kicked in. This is the first of the two possibilities explaining the drop in endogenous hGH levels. The hypothalamus registered "too much hGH" and the NIFBL went into action, initiated by somatostatin, which relays the message to the pituitary to take a break and stop releasing hGH. No matter how much TransD we continue to take or how many signals reach the pituitary as a result, the NIFBL is in control and no hGH will be released. Until the hypothalamus registers the levels of hGH have come back down and stops sending somatostatin (which tells the pituitary to hold back), no more hGH can be released. The beauty here is that it's impossible to be out of balance!

The second possibility for the drop of hGH during the eighth week was that the pituitary gland couldn't keep up with the demand to produce so much more hGH than what it was normally used to producing. Remember, the pituitary gland stores hGH and releases it in a pulsatile manner. But due to the effectiveness of TransD causing a greater than seventeen-fold increase in hGH to be released, the pituitary reserves may have become depleted and additional time was required for the hGH to be replenished.

Regardless of whether it was the NIFBL or simply a depletion issue, hGH levels went from a high of 1,754 percent down to 609 percent by week eight. Study patients were instructed to take two weeks off at the conclusion of the eight-week study, and TransD was then resumed after those two weeks. Findings revealed that the same improvement had recurred, with hGH *increasing* and IGF-1 *decreasing* as had previously been observed before the two-week break. About 20 percent to 25 percent of the patients from both groups were followed intermittently over the following two years, and all subjects reported significant and consistent improvements while continuing to use TransD. There was no evidence of a buildup or of resistance to TransD reported by any of the study groups that we followed.

Taking a one- to two-week break from TransD every eight weeks appeared to reset the hypothalamic-pituitary axis, and the peaks in hGH levels resumed immediately. In fact, I've been on TransD since 1998, and I can still tell the difference between the way I feel when I'm taking it and when I've been off it for a week or two. For me, the effect is highly discernible. Questions may arise regarding what, exactly, the optimum hGH levels are, but the answer actually varies from individual to individual because it's based upon biological individuality and genetic uniqueness.

Defining "optimum hGH levels" also should not be confused with diagnostic versus therapeutic efficacy, that is, the 5 ng/dl levels typically discussed by endocrinologists who are doing dopamine challenge tests for diagnostic purposes to establish hGH deficiency. The point is TransD provides what each individual needs almost in a personalized manner. The results and benefits people report using TransD extend throughout the complete physiological gamut, indicating that optimization of the entire system is taking place. The most common benefits reported are discussed next.

Turning Back Time

People who use TransD have reported experiencing changes they thought they would never experience again. The results indicate the physiology shifting to that of a younger state. Beyond the science, the dramatic results of TransD can be found in what patients are *feeling*. Changes observed usually within the first few days to weeks include improved sleep, increased energy, mental clarity, muscle strength, improved endurance, increased stamina, faster recovery, faster healing, increased libido and improved sexual performance. After using TransD for a few months, additional changes have been reported, including hair re-growth, skin thickness, significantly diminished wrinkles, body contour changes, improved emotional stability, less frequent nighttime urination and the disappearance of chronic pain from injuries that were decades old.

Having said this, I must caution you not to expect the clouds to part and angels to immediately begin singing when you first use TransD. After just the first application of TransD, some patients have experienced benefits in less than thirty seconds, although this is not usually the case. Some people see a faster change than others, but the majority of people begin to experience the shift within the first few days to the first two weeks. However, you need to be in tune with your body. The experience of using TransD will *not* be a euphoric event, nor will it be like a caffeine trip.

To use the example of athletes, they don't *feel* stronger, but they *are* stronger, and they see the difference in the gym. Or runners are not any faster, but they do reduce their recovery time between races from a few days to literally just hours. For those who have argued this to be placebo induced, the same observations have been made in racehorses after administration of the equine version of TransD.

After running a race, a racehorse typically takes twenty-four hours to recover and cannot run again the same day. In racehorses on the equine version of TransD, although no changes in speed were noted, the horses were much calmer and, more important, they were able to run the same race, at the exact same performance level, within twenty minutes of having previously run! Since animals are not capable of being influenced by placebo, I bring this up simply to illustrate that the effects of TransD are not placebo induced.

However, as one of my patients put it so eloquently, "I don't care if it's just in my head, I'll take it any way I can get it as long as I'm *feeling* the benefit." For animal activists, don't worry. The horse is only performing what it's capable of performing. A greedy racehorse owner won't be able to overtax the winning horse any more than they would be able to were the animal not taking the product. In other words, at a certain point, the animal will not be able to run. The TransD will only allow for improvement in function within the confines of the limits of physiology.

Sleep is one of the very first things to change for most people right after they begin using TransD. People report that they don't require as much sleep and that the sleep they *do* experience becomes much deeper and more restorative. People also report that they dream more frequently and with more intensity and clarity when using TransD. In conditioned athletes, besides the improvement in endurance and recovery, strength levels have exponentially increased sometimes up to 40 percent, in *less* than forty-eight hours! But the most important benefit from using TransD hasn't even been mentioned yet.

Second Act

Everyone feels life is too short. For some of us, we simply don't have enough time in one lifetime to accomplish everything we need to do. Time runs out, and people find themselves at sixty-five or older wondering where the years went and what they could have done, where they could have gone, who they could have been. What would you say if I told you that you could have a second act in life that's even better than the first, living with vitality and purpose to over a hundred years of age?

A very famous two-time NASCAR National Champion and the only person to have retired as a National Champion tells his experience, in his own words, about his "second act." And he did this without receiving a single cent in compensation for his endorsement because he feels so strongly about the benefits of TransD and what this unique product has to offer the world. He should know, having been on TransD for almost seven years. I feel virtually certain TransD will become a major key that will not just dramatically improve the quality of our years but also the number of those years as well.[47]

Unlike anything else on the market, synthetic or natural, bioidentical or not, TransD is the only substance available that can optimize your hormones, improve your functioning and reduce your inflammation—all while providing the same benefits as that of caloric restriction. Mind you, I'm not saying TransD will increase your life span . . . yet! However, we know for a fact that TransD increases natural, endogenous hGH levels while at the same time reducing insulin, cortisol and especially IGF-1. These are exactly the same laboratory findings observed in the calorie-restricted animals that led to substantially increased life span.

It appears that TransD has truly been the best-kept health secret in the field of physical rejuvenation. Of course, you can try and reduce your caloric intake by 30 percent if you would like to achieve the benefits associated with this drastic type of caloric restriction, but I think I'll continue to eat a healthy balanced diet and use TransD as I have for almost twelve years now.

It just simply makes logical sense that the findings observed with caloric restriction in animals, if possible to duplicate, would lead to the same observation in humans. I believe history will remember TransD as a significant leap in "smart therapeutics." That's why I truly believe TransD will prove itself as the only practical and viable keystone of quality life extension in the twenty-first century. It's been around for more than a decade, but I'm willing to bet TransD will become the gold standard for effective age management and preservation of functioning in the

---

47 For more information, visit http://www.transd.com/trans-d-tropin-celebrity-testimonials.php.

next decade. Check with me again in sixty years and I'll let you know, if you haven't already found out firsthand for yourself!

With very rare exceptions, TransD is the only hormonal intervention I use with any of my patients. As previously mentioned, I myself have been using TransD religiously since 1998. I can tell you from personal experience there is nothing else that can elicit the type of changes I've personally experienced with TransD. I've made it my business to learn about every single thing that can enhance the body without causing any negative response. The bottom line is that TransD has impacted my own personal life so significantly that if I were stranded on a desert island and could take only three health and nutritional products with me, TransD would absolutely be the first one I would take. But again, please remember that I'm biased.

You can't rely on my opinion. You should evaluate for yourself everything I say about TransD. In fact, this is applicable to everything I've recommended to you in this book. You have been forewarned to do your own due diligence before taking my word for it. People who've used TransD are equally as passionate about this therapeutic intervention as I am, if not more. Although some of the changes may be subtle, many are obvious and clearly discernible because of the functional differences observed by the individual using TransD as well as those around the individual. The benefits discussed so far are just a handful of the benefits you can expect.

To be able to experience these benefits without violating the NIFBL is something that will serve you well over the long term and will measurably increase your quality of life. Statistically, we've followed users of TransD, and in the six-month period we monitored, we observed that 82.9 percent of the people who began using TransD chose to continue using it. TransD has made *that* big of a difference and has created a dramatic shift in thousands of people's lives. On the website where TransD can be obtained, purchasers are given a 100 percent money back guarantee if they are not satisfied with the product. Typically, a return rate for a product is said to be good if it's around 15 percent; 10 percent is considered extraordinary. During 2009, the rate of return for TransD was less than 0.3 percent for the *entire* year!

The normal protocol of using TransD consists of administrating TransD for five days, taking the weekends off and also taking one to two weeks off from the product every two months. The eighth-week drop in GH observed during the earlier aforementioned study is the primary reason for taking the recommended break when using TransD. However, approximately 15 percent of people taking TransD relate that during the two weeks off, they begin to feel bad and seem to lose the sense of well-being they had gained. For these people we recommend they continue using TransD uninterruptedly. But for the people who don't experience anything negative when taking a break from TransD, we recommend taking that short break every two months to allow the NIFBL to reset and/or to give the pituitary adequate time to replenish its stores of hGH.

The only side effects reported have been with acne, in approximately 6 percent of patients and reinitiating of menstruation in 2 percent of postmenopausal women. Although such side effects were unwanted and the patients experiencing these changes were not pleased, it was proof positive that TransD was reversing the physiology to that of a younger and more youthful state. The only other side effect to point out is that approximately 2 percent of the people using TransD experience a temporary mild rash at the site of application that resolves with simply rotating the site of application.

We're used to hearing about the "next big thing" in treatment modalities that unfortunately never seem to pan out. However, I believe that these findings from the study conducted in 2002 although not reported through the popular media, will eventually one day change the way we view and practice medicine entirely.

Did people taking TransD achieve optimum hGH levels? What are these levels? The answer is that the levels varied from patient to patient. That's why the study measured a percentage change, because baseline levels varied among individuals. The fact is that hGH can increase as much as possible and will benefit patients as long as IGF-1 is *not* increased and the NIFBL is kept intact and not violated. Vastly higher hGH levels are now acceptable because the NIFBL will always be the regulator of the hGH production. All these and more questions are answered in detail in a DVD available in the resources section at the end of this book.

I hope that you now see the beauty of God's incredible design. Every system in the body is designed with this level of ingeniousness and sophistication.

Sure, I have a vested interest in talking favorably about TransD. But monetary gain was the last thing on our minds when we created the product. Our motivation was simply to deliver a viable, effective, affordable solution to the hormonal problems I so often saw in my patients. If you lay the foundation with the previous eight steps, and still believe there's more your body can do, then I sincerely invite you to give TransD a try. More information and details can be found in the resources section.

We acquire illnesses from years of environmental exposure and years of bad habits. It took time to get where you are, and it will take time to improve and get back to where you want to be. Fortunately, it doesn't take nearly as long to get better. No matter how long you've been sick or not feeling your best, your body remembers what it's like to be healthy. When you begin to change your life by living these 9 Steps, your body will soon begin to respond. And by turbocharging your progress with the ninth step, you'll be amazed at how quickly you can begin feeling the difference.

Remember, however, this is NOT a panacea, and as with anything else in life, you'll only get out of it what you put into it. Can you get a benefit just from the ninth step, without doing the other steps? Yes, most people do. But you'd be missing the most important essence of the real rewards that await you by following the first eight steps. Do not make this mistake. Begin with instituting the first eight of these 9 Steps. As you start experiencing the changes, only then reward yourself with the ninth step. Follow these instructions and you'll understand why, soon enough.

There comes a time when for every addition of knowledge you forget something that you knew before. It is of the highest importance, therefore, not to have useless facts elbowing out the useful ones.
—SIR ARTHUR CONAN DOYLE, 1858–1930

Trans-D Tropin® [TransD] is the [therapy] we endorse at Los Gatos Longevity Institute. We have probably some of the longest experience with this product and consistently see positive results in a high percentage of our patients. We have seen TransD be the only agent effective in restoring vigor and stamina in some selected patients where all other hormonal interventions were not successful. No one agent, drug or nutraceutical is right for everyone. But we have such a high percentage of positive results and feedback with TransD that we endorse the product without reservation. We never compromise on quality. Of all the various therapies I have utilized, TransD is the only product that has consistently exceeded the manufacturer's claims.

—PHILIP LEE MILLER, MD
FOUNDER AND DIRECTOR, LOS GATOS LONGEVITY INSTITUTE

FAST WRAP
Step 9: The Principle of Physiological Rejuvenation

What makes Trans-D Tropin® (TransD) different?

TransD works *with* your body instead of against your body by enhancing your endogenous (your body's own) hormones *without* violating the essential but ignored negative inhibitory feedback loop (NIFBL). TransD is an all-natural, transdermally applied therapy that rebalances and maximally optimizes the entire hypo-thalamic-pituitary-adrenal axis by mimicking the actions of the "releasing hormones." But the critical difference is that TransD achieves far greater results while *never* violating the NIFBL, an unavoidable side effect with hormonal replacement regardless of whether the hormones are synthetic or bioidentical.

TransD achieves all of its incomparable changes with the greatest safety profile established over twelve years and with far greater efficacy than any other single product on the market—without the inconvenience of an injection, and in a far more cost-effective manner. TransD acts analogous to how the body works (explaining why it's referred to as a peptide analog) and optimizes healthy physiology, diametrically opposed to how we currently approach and treat people with various hormones.

Why do I need to take TransD?

Obviously, you don't *need* to do anything. That's a personal choice. However, for those who wish to optimize their health, you may want to try TransD. *So* far, the only scientifically proven method of increasing life span is caloric restriction. Laboratory changes showed an increase in hGH, with a *decrease* in IGF-1, cortisol and insulin. TransD is the only substance that has been shown in multiple studies to induce exactly the same laboratory changes without having been designed to do so. In fact, this observation was made eight years *after* TransD had been on the market.

In addition, every bit of healing in your body requires the building of new cells and the repairing of damaged ones, all of which is controlled by various hormones. This is a daily process that constantly takes place in your body. hGH is one of the more essential hormones for the rebuilding of all body tissues. Naturally, the closer to optimum your hGH levels are, the faster you will rebuild and heal. However, unlike with injecting the end hormone, TransD works *with* your body's natural hormonal flow, providing *the signal* to optimally produce all of your own body's endogenous hormones, many of which science hasn't even discovered yet.

Because TransD helps your body do its own work and produce all its own hormones, dangerous side effects from hormonal therapies such as glandular atrophy, acromegaly, cardiomyopathies, joint effusions and increased risk and incidence of cancer (due to elevated IGF-1 levels), are completely eliminated. TransD is also far more affordable than injectable hGH and is simply applied to the skin and rubbed in, forearm to forearm.

How do I get TransD?

Visit the members-only area of the book owners' website to get a special offer to try TransD risk free. More information is also available in the resources section at the end of this book and at www.TransD.com.

If I use TransD, what will I feel?

This isn't about feeling like Superman overnight, although some people do notice changes immediately. After the first few days to the first two weeks on TransD, most patients require less sleep and experience a better quality of sleep. Additionally, most people report increased dream activity. As time goes on, you'll experience various other changes, some dramatic and others subtle, including, among others, diminished wrinkles, thicker skin, increased muscle strength and endurance, faster recovery, stronger libido, hair regrowth, increased emotional stability, higher energy levels, body contour changes and decreased chronic pain. In many instances, decades' worth of old aches, pains and injuries begin to disappear!

It's important to remember that you will *not* see *all* these changes. But you may see many of them. Each person responds differently, and the better your body is functioning and the cleaner your system, the more dramatic the result from TransD. The initial eight steps in this book will get you where you need to go. TransD is the ninth step, which will accelerate the process so that you can get to your desired level of health much faster but also extend far beyond what you could reach on your own.

You don't *need* to take TransD, but if you're interested in the possibility of increasing life span, improving functionality and getting healthier, then you need to experience TransD firsthand and reach your own conclusion.

THE 7 TOXICITIES

*There is nothing more difficult to take in hand, more
perilous to conduct, or more uncertain in its success than
to take the lead in the introduction of a new order of
things because the innovator has for enemies all those who
have done well under the old conditions and lukewarm
defenders in those who may do well under the new.*

—MACHIAVELLI, *THE PRINCE*

The Truth You've Learned

Occasionally, patients have told me that they've heard some
of these 9 Steps before, but somehow it was different when I
explained it. I wasn't sure why I'd heard this so often until a new
patient in 2002 made me aware of something I hadn't previously recognized.

I'd known this individual from the gym for two years before he became a patient upon the recommendation of a trainer. He commented that some of the information I was sharing wasn't new but was somehow different when I presented it. When I responded I'd heard this many times before but wasn't sure why, he shared his own insight. *"I've seen how you work out at the gym. At the Christmas party, you didn't even drink a soft drink. I've noticed how you always try and stay positive, smile and take time out to talk to the janitor when everyone ignores him. The reason it's different when you say it is because you live these steps daily."*

It made sense, and from a vibrational standpoint, truth resonates far greater than simple words do. Although I'm not perfect by any means, I do try and live each of these 9 Steps every day. It's easy to miss a step here or there occasionally, so don't worry about that. It's the direction in which you're moving that counts.

A great saying attributed to Confucius is that we should take every single opportunity we're given to preach our message . . . but *never* open our mouths. Setting the example and leading by example should be an inherent part of being a physician. Doctors should be their own best advertisement, but sadly, I wouldn't take an aspirin from most in my profession. Have you noticed the demeanor of most doctors? They're broken down, stressed out, straight-faced; they never smile, laugh even less, are often overweight and have terrible habits. Would you take health advice from someone who lacks the basics of health in their own life? Yet most people do. It's like having a basketball coach who never played or experienced the game, yet is expected to help you and teach you to make three-point shots and win games on the court.

Remember that you do *have a choice* in how you feel. It takes more energy *not* to laugh than it takes to laugh. It takes more effort and more muscles to frown than it takes to smile. *Make a choice* that you'll actively smile at least eleven times a day and laugh as many times as you can. Why eleven? Because it's more than ten. It really *is* that simple, as simple as making the choice! I *choose* to feel good every day, laugh, exercise, have a positive outlook and do everything I can to put energy into the world, because I know it's coming right back to me but in a magnified manner.

These 9 Steps aren't something I learned somewhere or read in some book. They started out as five steps and eventually evolved into the 9 Steps you've learned, each revealing itself and proving its significance over the years as the time became right and I became prepared for the next one. The benefit to you is that all you need to do is simply follow these 9 Steps and allow them to prove their benefits to you directly. Most important, remember that doing just a little every day toward each of these 9 Steps will go a long way, not only toward preventing illness but also toward giving you a life of better quality and far longer duration.

Just pick one thing toward each of the 9 Steps and do it daily. After implementing this one change for thirty days, you'll have formed a new habit. Now add the next component from each of the 9 Steps and do that for thirty days to form additional new habits. If picking one thing from each of the 9 Steps is too much, pick three of the 9 Steps to start with and choose one thing toward each of them. If that's too much, then just choose one of the 9 Steps and pick one thing for that one step and do that for thirty days. The point isn't how *much* you do, it's that you simply do *something*. Take action. Immediate action! The action you take is not important. The simple *act* of taking action is the key.

You've also learned about the Three Foundations upon which the 9 Steps are built. This information is most crucial to achieve the results in health and wellness we all desire. But we need to elaborate on the first foundation, detoxification. In fact, the one underlying component we've mentioned throughout this book that I want you to keep in the back of your mind long after you've finished reading it is this concept of detoxification. We discussed how once the burden of toxicity is lifted by breaking the vicious cycle of oxidative stress, your body can begin to do what it was designed to do—heal itself. But what exactly are the various forms of toxicity from which we must detoxify our bodies?

My experience having worked with several thousand patients from all over the world has taught me that the vast majority of toxins come from seven major sources. I speak from firsthand knowledge when I say that if these seven toxicities are *effectively* addressed and removed—with "*effectively*" being the "key" operative word here—the vast majority of oxidative stress is eliminated. When this occurs, chronic disease, by definition, simply *cannot exist*. It becomes impossible for chronic disease to set up house in a body where the oxidative burden is minimal or nonexistent because the cause (toxicities) are no longer present to induce the increased burden of oxidative stress leading to chronic disease. Let's review and briefly explore these seven toxicities.

The 1st Toxicity: Heavy Metals

Heavy metals include mercury, lead, antimony, nickel, cadmium, tin, arsenic, uranium, as well as a host of others. In addition to causing significant oxidative damage, heavy metals are doubly dangerous because, being metallic in nature, they have the ability to displace many of the essential minerals your body needs to function properly. These minerals include, among others, magnesium, copper, manganese, zinc and selenium. Your body needs these essential minerals to run the various metabolic pathways of your internal engine. Adding insult to the injury of replacing essential nutrients, heavy metals and (mercury in particular) wreak additional havoc on the endocrine system, which regulates hormonal levels. And as if it couldn't get any worse, some people may even have an additional issue due to allerginicity (having an allergy) to the metal in question.

A study published in the *Journal of the American College of Cardiology* by Andrea Frustaci, MD, examined the link between heavy metals and heart disease. Titled "Marked Elevation of Myocardial Elements in Idiopathic Dilated Cardiomyopathy Compared with Secondary Cardiac Function," the article focused on patients with an uncommon heart condition that usually affects younger people. Heart biopsies showed levels of mercury were *twenty-two thousand times higher* than those in biopsies of other tissues in the body. Antimony was *thirteen thousand times higher.* And those were just the top two metals of the many that were present![48]

Another example is a study by Eliseo Guallar, MD, titled "Mercury, Fish Oils and Risk of Myocardial Infarction," published in the *New England Journal of Medicine.* Dr. Guallar's results showed a direct correlation between the level of mercury in toenail clippings and the incidence of heart attacks, with an

---

48 Andrea Frustaci, MD, Nicola Magnavita, MD, Cristina Chimenti, MD, Marina Caldarulo, MD, Enrico Sabbioni, PhD, Romano Pietra, PhD, Carlo Cellini, MD, Gian Federico Possati, MD, Attilio Maseri, MD. May 1999. Marked Elevation of Elements in Idiopathic Dilated Cardiomyopathy Compared with Secondary Cardiac Function. *Journal of the American College of Cardiology.* 33 (6): 1578–1583.

inverse correlation to levels of decosahexaenoic acid (DHA), which is a component of fish oils.[49]

As Chairman of the American Board of Clinical Metal Toxicology, it's my responsibility, along with the rest of the executive board, to help establish educational guidelines for doctors on the dangers of heavy metals, how to identify the presence of heavy metals and how to remove them safely and effectively from their patients. It's also my responsibility to keep up-to-date on the latest research regarding heavy metals and chronic disease. Much of this research is published on Toxline, a search engine that is associated with the National Library of Medicine's website.

Toxline is under the auspices of the Agency for Toxic Substances and Disease Registry (ATSDR), which is a subdivision of the Centers for Disease Control (CDC). As an example, a simple Toxline search on mercury revealed 358 studies linking mercury with heart disease, 643 linking mercury with cancer and 1,445 linking mercury to neurodegenerative disease (such as autism, Alzheimer's, etc.). Keep in mind, mercury is *just* one of the many heavy metals known to have serious health issues. The example used in these search criteria was looking just at mercury.

The search criteria was not looking for *all* metals contributing to these disease processes. Those who argue *against* chronic heavy metal toxicity as a valid concern in clinical medicine have compromised their own integrity, and their motives become highly suspect. The simple facts scream the truth that anyone can

---

49 Eliseo Guallar, MD, DrPh, M. Inmaculada Sanz-Gallardo, MD, MPH, Pieter van't Veer, PhD, Peter Bode, PhD, Antti Aro, MD, PhD, Jorge Gomez-Aracena, MD, PhD, Jeremy D. Kark, MD, PhD, Rudolph A. Riemersa, PhD, Jose M. Martin-Moreno, MD, DrPh, Frans J. Kok, PhD. November 2002. Mercury, Fish Oils and the Risk of Myocardial Infarction. *The New England Journal of Medicine.* 347 (22): 1747–1754.

easily confirm themselves if they would simply open their eyes and put aside their bias.

I chose mercury for this example because it tops my list among the many metal toxicities. Why? Because mercury causes some of the worst damage in the human system and is considered to be the second most toxic element known to man, according to the Environmental Protection Agency (EPA). Only uranium is considered to be more toxic. For instance, whenever we hear of a mercury spill in a high school, the students are evacuated, hazmat teams are rushed in and the immediate area is bordered off as a "hazardous spill area." No one is allowed to return until the Occupational Safety and Health Administration (OSHA) has cleared the building. This, by the way, is when inorganic mercury has been spilled, in actuality the least toxic version of the metal.

Yet, mercury is *still* present as a preservative in most vaccines, including the flu shot. Many people are under the false impression that it was removed from vaccines between 2000 and 2002, but this is not accurate. Thimerosal, or ethyl mercury, is still used in the manufacturing process of almost all vaccines, although since it is no longer "added" as an ingredient and only used during the manufacturing process, it is no longer disclosed on the vaccine labels. As a result, Congressman Dan Burton, during a congressional hearing held in 2003 regarding this specific issue, asked for criminal sanctions to be brought against the head of the FDA and the FTC. Yet, nothing was done. The media failed to report the story and mercury continues to be used in the manufacturing process of almost all vaccines.

Despite being extremely dangerous, mercury is found literally everywhere. Industry mixes mercury with other substances to create more toxic compounds, from the inorganic to an organic form such as ethyl mercury or methyl mercury. When altered like this, mercury becomes more easily assimilated into the body and thus becomes an even worse poison than the naturally occurring elemental mercury. We put mercury in dental amalgam tooth fillings, which are approximately 50 percent mercury by weight.

Combustion of fossil fuels is one of the greatest sources of mercury vapor emissions. Coal plants pump this mercury vapor into the air, which we inhale unknowingly, while corporations dump mercury-filled waste into our rivers, streams and oceans from which we drink water and consume fish. An article published on August 19, 2009, in *USA Today* showed that research conducted by the U.S. Geological Survey found every fish caught in a U.S. stream tested positive for mercury and 27 percent of the fish caught had mercury levels high enough to exceed what the EPA considered safe to consume.[50]

The neurological effects of mercury are very well understood, and as a result, suspicions have swirled for years around the connection between autism and mercury in early childhood vaccinations. Interestingly, the CDC's 2003 National Health and Nutrition Examination Survey (NHANES) study showed that a significant number of women of childbearing age in the USA are mercury toxic. Later, a study conducted under the auspices of the U.S. Environmental Protection Agency and published in *Environmental Health Perspectives* reviewed the NHANES data

---

50 Elizabeth Weise. 2009. *Federal Study Shows Mercury Found in All Fish Caught In U.S.-Tested Streams.* Available: http://www.usatoday.com/news/ nation/environment/2009-08-19-fish-mercury_N.htm. Last accessed February 21, 2009.

from 1999 to 2004 and found that approximately one out of six women of childbearing age in the USA is mercury toxic.[51]

Meanwhile, a study published in the journal *Pediatrics* disclosed that 17 percent (approximately one in six) of U.S. children were reported to have some type of neurological compromise, whether it was ADHD, autism, seizure disorder, cerebral palsy or some other neurological disability.[52]

Closer to Home

My son Abie lost his ability to speak around the age of fourteen months. His limited vocabulary of about fifteen or so words rapidly disappeared within a few weeks of his third set of inoculations. His first word, "Abu" (meaning "father" in Arabic), was the first to disappear. His mother and I had decided we would not inoculate our son due to the presence of thimerasol (ethyl mercury) in vaccinations, which as mentioned, is used as a preservative. As I was considered one of the up-and-coming leading authorities in metal toxicology, there was no way my son would be exposed to mercury.

Unbeknownst to me, however, my now ex-wife had gotten Abie the regularly scheduled vaccines because she had listened to the fear-evoking propaganda fed to her by the pediatricians and the doctors at the hospital when she delivered. She had gone back and gotten the inoculations the day after Abie first came home at the ripe age of one day old, and then had taken him for

---

51 Kathryn R. Mahaffey, Robert P. Clickner, and Rebecca A. Jeffries. January 2009. Adult Women's Blood Mercury Concentrations Vary Regionally. *Environmental Health Perspectives.* 117 (1): 47–53.
52 C.A. Boyle, P. Decoufle, M. Yeargin-Allsopp. Prevalence and Health Impact of Developmental Disabilities in U.S. Children. *Pediatrics.* 93, no. 3 (1994): 399–403.

all his subsequent vaccines. By the age of two, he was considered to be "developmentally delayed."

Abie was born on January 25, 1999. In March 1998, ten months prior to his birth and a month before his conception, I had made the decision I would not see autistic and developmentally delayed patients any longer. Looking back, it's clear that God had a specific plan for me, but I was moving away from the right path. Now I understand that this experience was nothing more than God upping the ante, sending me a clear message: "You're going to do what you were meant to do, what you were created to do!"

It was obvious to me that Abie's loss of speech was more than a transient delay in his development. As time passed, the pediatricians kept saying the same thing. "Oh well, there's probably nothing there. Just wait. Maybe he's a late developer." But I knew there was something wrong because he had *lost* his ability to speak. It wasn't that he never acquired it. He had *lost* it! A twelve-to-fifteen-word vocabulary isn't much, but it's still something! And now those words were all gone.

I didn't know what to do. Although I had treated hundreds of patients with mercury and lead toxicity, I hadn't treated a child this young. I knew from having treated autistic children in the past that his behavior was the same, with the toe walking, hand flapping and stimming—repetitive stereotypic behavior commonly found in developmental delays indicative of decreased sensory input—and that terrified me. I knew my son was *not* supposed to be like this.

I subsequently spent thousands of hours—many if not most of them late at night, sometimes all night—studying, researching, learning, crying and praying that my son would be returned to me. I pleaded, begged and threatened God. I bartered with the Creator, negotiating my arms or my legs in exchange for the return of my son. Throughout this ordeal, Abie always looked at me with his gentle, milk-chocolate-colored eyes that would say, "Don't worry, Dad, I know you'll figure it out."

Eventually I did. Realizing that mercury was the most likely culprit, I tested Abie four times before his challenge test finally came back positive for mercury. As a result, Dr. Viktora and I developed an innovative detoxification method for him, which up until then had never been contemplated. Five months after I began his detoxification, Abie went from no language to a vocabulary of five-hundred-plus words. He was nearly three and a half years old. And, as I shared with you in chapter 2, on May 6, 2004, at the age of five, Abie became the youngest formal witness to appear before the U.S. Congress, testifying in front of the U.S. Congressional Subcommittee on Human Rights and Wellness regarding innovative methods to treat neurological injuries and the dangers of mercury in vaccines.

Today, people ask me if he's "normal." It makes me smile to think about it, because he's anything *but* normal. He's extraordinary, exceptionally handsome, surprisingly gentle, ahead of his peers in school in all subjects and two to three grade levels ahead in math and English, an incredible athlete in every sport he tries, a gifted martial artist who is a triple-crown state champion and ranked among the top ten in the world in both forms and sparring two years in a row and now working on his second-degree black belt in Taekwondo. He touches everyone who meets him, and to know him is to truly love him. Even the parents of the children he competes against come to me to remark on his style, grace and sportsmanship. It is, without any exaggeration whatsoever, truly one of my greatest life blessings to be his father. At the risk of sounding overly sentimental, I have at times literally felt such terrible sadness for the rest of world because they will never know the incredible and indescribable feeling of being Abie's father.

One point about heavy metals I believe is crucial to understand is the synergistically destructive nature of this first category of toxins. In science, a lethal dose (LD) of any substance is measured as the amount needed to kill 1 person out of 100. This measurement is known as LD1. A substance with an LD17 would be sufficient to kill 17 people out of a 100. If you took an LD1 of mercury (sufficient mercury to kill 1 out of a 100) and you took an LD1 of lead (sufficient lead to kill 1 out of a 100) and put these amounts in the *same* 100 people, you would kill *all* 100 people! That's how synergistically dangerous heavy metals are, and virtually everyone is walking around with more than one of these toxins in their bodies.

There is just one study of which I'm aware that has been conducted to assess the synergistic destructive nature of heavy metals. Done in the 1970s, it looked at only mercury, lead and cadmium. So we really don't know how destructive some of these other metals are when combined with other metals within the same individual. However, all these substances are removable through the proper detoxification protocols. In time, the body can completely be cleaned, rebound and rebuild itself, leaving no room for chronic disease to begin, as long as you maintain your body's lowered burden of toxins.

More than thirty-five hundred doctors in the United States address the issue of chronic heavy-metal toxicity. However, most of these doctors don't have any training in addressing this crucial issue of heavy metals and fewer than two hundred of them are board certified through the American Board of Clinical Metal Toxicology (ABCMT) in heavy metal toxicology. I strongly suggest you find one of these board-certified or board-eligible doctors at www.ABCMT.org, the board's official website. Remember that the medical hierarchy does not recognize chronic metal toxicity as an issue that should be addressed and also refuses to recognize ABCMT, an organization founded almost thirty years ago. More information on heavy metal toxicity and detoxification can be found in the resources section.

The 2nd Toxicity: Persistent Organic Pollutants (POPs)

The second category of toxins is known as the persistent organic pollutants, or POPs, because they tend to "persist" in the body and are extremely difficult to get out. Some of these POPs can continue on for generations, being passed from mother to daughter and affecting both sexes while still in utero. Many of these include insecticides from the 1950s and 1960s. While they may no longer be allowed or used, their effects are still causing birth defects in children two generations later.

In 2000, the World Health Organization Congress met in South Africa to discuss the implications of the twelve most deadly organic compounds and pollutants, affectionately named "the Dirty Dozen." There was a concerted effort for industrialized countries to reach an agreement to begin removal of these dangerous elements from the environment because the Dirty Dozen had now clearly been implicated in the causation of numerous disease processes. These deadly organic compounds and pollutants include DDT, PCBs, dioxins, chlordane, furans and a number of other insecticides.

Even if all industrialized countries immediately stopped using these substances, these POPs have already gotten a monumental head start. For example, the "newest" toxic chemical in the Dirty Dozen was introduced in 1957, over fifty years ago, and the oldest has been in use since 1913, almost a hundred years ago. These POPs exist in pesticides, insecticides, varnishes, cleaning solutions and virtually every product in an aerosol can, a bottle underneath your kitchen sink or in your garage right now. Be careful when using *any* chemical product, no matter how safe the manufacturer claims it to be.

In 2005, the Environmental Working Group put out a report by Jane Houlihan and Timothy Kropp, PhD, titled *Body Burden: The Pollution in Newborns.* The placental cord blood of newborn babies was tested for 413 different industrial chemicals and found to be positive for 287 of these substances, which included PCBs, mercury, DDT, dioxins, fluorinated hydrocarbons, organophosphates and many other categories of POPs. This blood was obtained on these infants' very first day on the planet![53] What are the full implications of these and similar toxicities being passed from mother to infant? And what is the global impact of these substances on the biological burden that must be borne? For the full study, visit the members-only website.

---

53 T. Kropp, J. Houlihan, S. Gray, and R. Wiles. Environmental Working Group. 2005. *Body Burden: The Pollution in Newborns.* Available: http://www.ewg.org/reports/bodyburden2/newsrelease.php. Last accessed February 21, 2010.

The 3rd Toxicity: Opportunistics

The third toxicity represents the opportunistic infections, which include bacteria, viruses, parasites, yeast and a host of other critters. I call them the opportunistics because these organisms need an opportunity before they can set up house in the body. The right environment must be created in order for them to survive and thrive. This third class of toxicity is actually heavily dependent on the first and second toxicities, because heavy metals and POPs suppress the immune system and render the body vulnerable to opportunistic pathogens.

Opportunistics are the only class of the seven toxicities that modern medicine has done a reasonably fair job of addressing, with antibiotics, antivirals, antifungals and so on. However, medical professionals have miserably failed to establish *why* there are so many more infectious pathogens today than in years past. No one has considered the first and second toxicities as the cause of the rampant increase in opportunistic infections, further contributed by drug resistance from the over use of antibiotics and other medications.

Moreover, the problem of *why* one person gets a particular infection and another one doesn't has never been addressed. The answer is because of the variance in people's immune systems due to differences in the type and amount of toxic burden that everyone is carrying, which causes the decline in the immune system. The problem, even though these drugs work, is that if you don't address the underlying cause of the immune suppression, the problem (infection) will recur.

The first and second toxicities, which are responsible for the drop in immunity, are ignored by traditional medicine. You can beat back these infections with drugs for a while, but once the drugs are stopped, the problem always comes back. Unless the immunosuppressive cause is removed, these issues continue to recur like a bad dream. This is why conditions like yeast infections in women and jock itch and athlete's foot in men are persistent and are an indication to look much deeper.

The 4ᵗʰ Toxicity: Energetic Toxicity

The first three toxicities discussed are objectively measurable. The remaining four are a bit more esoteric. Energetic toxicity includes all the high-powered energy waves that pass over, under and through our bodies every day. In modern society, our bodies are bombarded by energetic toxicity from things we can't see, including everything from electromagnetic radiation from power lines and microwaves to ambient radiation from cell phones, military radar systems, televisions and computer screens. And this fourth toxicity is increasing at a stunningly rapid exponential rate.

The level of ambient cell phone radiation we are exposed to is just one example of energetic toxicities. What possible implications could cell phones have regarding toxicity? Dr. George Carlo, an attorney and researcher from the Science and Public Policy Institute, conducted a study on cell phone radiation and cancer back in the 1980s, long before the explosion in cellular usage. The study was actually sponsored jointly by the federal government and a cell phone manufacturer. The goal was to prove that cell phone radiation did not cause cancer, but unfortunately, his data proved just the opposite.

Dr. Carlo explained to me in person that from 1984 to 2004, the first billion cell phones entered the global market. It took only the next eighteen months, not twenty years, for the second billion to appear. Less than one year later, the third billion cell phones flooded our airwaves. As a result, ambient cell phone radiation has increased 500,000 percent in the last decade in the average urban area.[54] In his book *Cell Phones: Invisible Hazards in the Wireless Age,* Dr. Carlo reported that the rate of death from brain cancer was higher among handheld phone users.[55] Because the cell phone company sponsored the research, they claimed ownership of the data and prevented its release. But Dr. Carlo wrote several books on the subject that revealed the health and environmental impact of this particular toxicity.

Some readers may be familiar with the increasingly frequent news stories about the drastic reduction in the population of honeybees over the last several years. In fact, the bee populations are rapidly disappearing on four of the five continents. The reasons have been attributed to parasites, pestilence, insecticides and global warming. But in actuality, it has to do with a naturally occurring mineral called magnetite and how the ambient cell phone radiation affects this mineral. Bees have magnetite in their intestinal tracts. Humans have it in their brains. Birds have it in their beaks. Magnetite helps orient us by aligning with the Earth's magnetic grid and allows for direction finding. It accounts

---

54 Personal conversations between author and Dr. George Louis Carlo on November 11, 2007, Chicago, IL.

55 George Louis Carlo and Martin Schram. 2001. *Cell Phones: Invisible Hazards in the Wireless Age.* New York: Carroll & Graf Publishers. pp. 174, 205.

for the ability of animals and birds to find their way back home from thousands of miles away and helps to explain how certain species find their way back to their nesting grounds and follow specific migratory patterns.

The magnetite in the intestinal tracts of the bees, when aligned with Earth's magnetic grids, allows the bees to find their way back to their hives. However, the incredible increase in ambient cell phone radiation prevents the magnetite from aligning correctly with Earth's magnetic grid, so the bees get disoriented and never make it back to the hive. The result is that the bee populations are rapidly diminishing.

Another example is homing pigeons, which have magnetite in their beaks, as do most birds. Racing homing pigeons is an ancient and very upscale sport that challenges birds in races of up to six hundred miles. As recently as a few years ago, the number of pigeons that kept on course and finished the race was 85 percent, but today, an average of only 15 percent make it back alive.

Imagine the catastrophic impact of the disappearance of honeybees. Bees pollinate an immense amount of our food supply. Without bees, most food won't grow. The U.S. Department of Agriculture estimates that about one-third of the total human diet is derived from insect-pollinated plants and the honeybee is responsible for 80 percent of this pollination. A study from Cornell University in 2000 concluded that the direct value of honeybee pollination to U.S. agriculture is more than $14.6 billion, and that was a decade ago.

Before I move on to the next toxicity, there's one last thing I want to mention in this discussion of the fourth toxicity, and that is the use of microwave ovens. Just know it's not a natural way of heating food. The cancer patients we've tested for energetic toxicity exposures have the highest levels of microwave radiation exposure of all the various types of energetic pollution for which we've tested. I personally have not used a microwave since 2002 and don't even have one plugged into the wall at either my home or office. I hope that will convince you to throw *your microwave oven out*. Toaster ovens and convection ovens are fine, however.

There is a tremendous amount of information regarding the fourth toxicity, but space constraints prevent me from going into more details. More information is available for book owners in the members-only area of www.The9Steps.com, which goes into greater detail and provides further references and resources on this subject.

The 5th Toxicity: Emotional/ Psychological Toxicity

Everyone should have therapy at some point in their lives. Some of us may need more than others . . . and I'm being only partially facetious here. It should be a required "emotional boot camp," as long as the therapist is kept from prescribing a drug. I don't care if you grew up like the Brady Bunch and all your family's problems were wrapped up in the course of thirty minutes minus the commercials, emotional baggage is still present for all of us. Actually, if you really do come from one of those "Stepford Families" where everybody's happy all the time and no one ever argues because they're "fine," you should seek therapy immediately!

We as a society have no idea of the power our minds possess to protect us by suppressing emotions and sometimes even hiding them so our conscious mind doesn't have to deal with these painful issues. I was a young doctor in my mid-twenties and had just gotten married for the first time, and my mother did not approve of my wife. Family heritage and cultural passion run deep through most of us, but my family happens to have more than their fair share. My mother was so traumatized by my action that she literally had a nervous breakdown.

She turned my photo face down on her bureau and said that I was "dead" to her, while rocking back and forth on her knees on the floor, crying for *her* own mother. It was a slightly difficult emotional time for me because I was twenty-six years old, stationed in the most volatile area in the world at that time— the DMZ in South Korea—and responsible for the health and welfare of five-thousand-plus soldiers, my bride and I had a new baby on the way . . . and now my mother was disowning me. But I got through it, like everything else, and thought that was the end of it.

More than fifteen years later I was having dinner with my good friend Dr. Bob Marshall, a researcher and chemist. I had invited him to give a lecture at one of my physician teaching conferences (AMESPA courses) and we had just finished the second day of the course when the conversation turned to past traumas. I won't bore you with the details, but suffice it to say that Bob began working on me, unbeknownst to me, and ascertained that I needed some "emotional release" work. I can't fully explain what happened and don't think I would try, even if I did fully understand what happened. But I followed Dr. Marshall's advice to the letter.

He warned me to be prepared for a "cathartic" event. Within twelve hours, this forty-one-year-old, 6'1", 240-pound former college football linebacker, prior military, competitive lifter, black belt martial artist, who had been a bouncer for six years during college and medical school was sobbing uncontrollably for more than one hour straight. Now, after having gone through this release, I can look back and say, yes, there were issues . . . deep and emotionally scarring issues. I can only say the experience Dr. Marshall led me through was not only cathartic and cleansing, it left me lighter, happier and cleared a path within me which previously I wasn't even aware existed, let alone was blocked. My relationship with my mother also drastically improved. At least it had until she reads these last few paragraphs.

Whether you know it or not, your cells have their own intelligence. They also have memory that's completely independent of your conscious intellect. Athletes and dancers know what "muscle memory" is. When you train over and over and it comes time to compete, your body remembers all the actions that are needed, automatically, without your even having to think. Similarly, therapists who deal with trauma and posttraumatic stress disorder often use physical interventions instead of "talk therapy" because that is where those memories are stored, within the body, like muscle memory.

The link between physical health and mental health is not even up for debate anymore. For example, every patient suffering with cancer I have seen, did not begin to recover until they had addressed their emotional issues. Only those who were able to successfully come to terms with and release their anger, to forgive and choose to love unconditionally have a chance of winning the battle.

Dr. Ryke Geerd Hamer, a German oncologist whose son tragically died in a hunting accident in 1978, has done some remarkable work in this arena. He and his wife were intensely grief-stricken with the loss of their son. Eventually, Dr. Hamer himself developed testicular cancer and his wife developed breast cancer, from which she passed away. He ultimately discovered there was a psychological/emotional link to all cancers and eventually healed himself. Tens of thousands of people have read his books and credited their remissions to his work.

Negative emotion is one of the most toxic and dangerous forms of oxidative stress because it's insidious and often suppressed. These emotions fester like an abscess, corrupting the good and rotting away the love. They hide from us even when we think we've dealt with them, and they lurk in our subconscious creating more discourse and pain. Be brave and go to those scary places. I'm a testament that you'll come back very much alive . . . and a healthier person.

For those who may have more of an interest in this particular subject, you'll find in the members-only area of www.The9Steps. com a website listed that deals with this issue in its entirety, including the implications this has on our ability to be successful in all facets of life not only regarding health but also spiritual, financial, physical and emotional. This topic is so crucial in fact that I began concentrating my efforts in this area a few years ago and since have begun teaching a course and conducting an exclusive retreat focused on achieving resolution of unknown conflicts and unblocking areas of resistance to allow a person to achieve success in whatever area they desire. More information is available in the resources section at the end of this book or visit www.BuildASuccessfulLife.com.

The 6ᵗʰ Toxicity: Food Toxicity

The sixth toxicity isn't about the chemicals or additives in our food. Those would be included in the first two toxicities. The sixth toxicity involves the genetic modification of food, the manipulation and irradiation of what we do to the substances we consume, and the immunologic issues surrounding modern food production. The concerns are that these forms of food manipulation are very new and unexplored and we simply don't have any idea of their implications to human physiology. The ramifications could be disastrous.

Who wants to take the risk of consuming these items and then waiting to see what the effects are twenty years down the line? Genetic modification of food manipulates the actual essence of these food substances by altering the DNA. When ingested and incorporated into our bodies, this altered DNA is now becoming part of our own essence. The altered DNA has the potential of damaging or, even worse, becoming incorporated into our own genetic code.

The DNA in corn, soybeans and other produce has already been genetically modified, but the question is, what will it do to the DNA inside of you when you consume it?

In addition, your body may not recognize this genetically modified substance as food, since it has been altered from its original genetic state. Anything foreign to the body is an antigen, to which the body will make antibodies, thus potentially giving rise to a host of new autoimmune diseases. There are just far too many unanswered questions.

The easiest rule of thumb is to completely avoid genetically modified organism (GMO) produce and irradiated produce.

Remember, if it was changed in any way from its original, God-given form, it doesn't belong in your body. It goes back to the same advice: God given = Good. Man-made = Madness.

The 7th Toxicity: Spiritual Toxicity

Spiritual toxicity is my favorite toxicity to discuss and most people's least favorite because it touches on a very sensitive and personal arena of life. Although it's never my intent, someone usually ends up getting offended. So, if you're that person, I apologize in advance—but prepare to be outraged. Most people don't know this, but my second major in college was theology. The trigger that started my search for God was a personally difficult and tragic one.

A little girl I used to babysit was killed in a horrific accident as her father looked on, completely helpless to stop it. She was decapitated after being hit by a bread truck early in the morning as she walked across the street to wait for the school bus. She was just six years old at the time she died, and I was a freshman in college. I experienced what can only be described as a seventeen-year-old having a breakdown, and I completely dropped out of my own life. I disappeared. I didn't tell family or friends where I was going. I missed classes and ended up living on the streets for six days, searching for why a God who loves his creation would allow something like this to happen.

What purpose did her death serve? She'd never had a chance to experience driving a car, her first date or the misery of love! She had been robbed of life, and I was desperately trying to make sense out of this ghastly tragedy. Trying to find balance and truth in my life, I decided to pursue a second major in theology. The years passed as I spent countless hours studying, looking for the "truth," the "true" religion with the "true" God. I read the Torah more than a dozen times, the Bible about thirty times, the Koran an unknown number of times, certainly far more times than most people who practice the religions these books are connected with usually do. But still I had no answers.

I began reading books of other faiths and studied Hinduism and Buddhism. I took every 500-level course offered at Washington University (my alma mater) in Religious Studies. I was six months from graduating college and was just weeks from my twenty-first birthday and had finally reached the point of emotional exhaustion. The more I studied, the more confused I became and the further I felt I was moving from the answer that I sought . . . to find the "truth."

For each major, we were assigned a counselor. My counselor for my theology major also happened to be my professor for the one-on-one independent study 500-level classes I was taking in religion, since I had already completed every formal religion class offered at my university. While sitting in his office one day, I just unloaded on him. "I just don't get this," I said far too loudly. "I've spent the last three and a half years of my life studying the most prominent religions of the world to find the truth, and I feel I know *less now* than when I started."

My counselor, whose faith I didn't know at the time, looked at me with absolute clarity and, in his characteristically soft, child-like tone of voice (which used to infuriate me because his voice always sounded like he knew the answers to all the secrets of life), responded to my obvious frustration. "You, my friend, have just achieved a level of understanding regarding God that very few people will ever attain." I remember those words so clearly, only because they were so amazingly absurd to me at the time.

I literally turned around to see if someone was standing behind me, thinking he was talking to someone else. There was no one there. Even more frustrated and feeling that he was purposely being sarcastic with me, I snapped back, "Did you just hear a single word I said?" He just smiled at me. His reply was so simple yet so profound and within the next few minutes, he was able to take all the confusion I had experienced over three and a half years and in one fell swoop, made it all make sense.

"Rashid, your problem is that you're in New York City with millions of other people," he explained. "It's dirty, crowded and crime-ridden. Everybody wants to get out. No one's friendly and God doesn't live in New York. And everyone, just like you, wants to go where God is."

"What the hell is he talking about?" I thought in my head. "Is he having a stroke?"

He continued. "You see, Rashid, everyone knows that God lives in California, where all the beautiful people live. It's always sunny there and the beaches are beautiful. The climate is perfect because God lives there."

"He's definitely having a stroke!" I thought to myself. The only thing I could picture was an image of smog hovering over Los Angeles.

He continued. "Now you have to go from New York City and get to California."

"Where God is, with the beautiful people, right?" I asked.

"That's right," he said, oblivious to my obvious sarcasm. Great! And then what he said next was as if he'd wiped the mud and grime off a windshield and I could suddenly see the road in front of me.

"You can fly Continental Airlines and stop over in Chicago, or you can fly TWA and layover in St. Louis, or you can fly American Airlines and stop over in Dallas. But the destination is all the same. No matter what airline you fly, Rashid, they're all going to get you to California, where God is."

He then proceeded to tell me that all the faiths have a rich tradition and culture. Although they are all different, they all share similarities. Just like the different airlines, each religion has a different layover, but they all are striving to reach the same final destination. "You should embrace the amazingly rich tradition and culture of the beautiful religion you were born into, Rashid. Islam means to 'submit.' You should submit yourself to discovering all the wonders of God within your religion."

No one on campus knew his religion. It was a great source of mystery which he refused to discuss. I realized after graduating that in his role as teacher and mentor, he didn't want to inadvertently influence an impressionable mind with his own beliefs. A few years later, while home visiting from medical school, I ran into him shopping with his wife in a natural foods store. He was so pleased to see me and told me how proud he was of me. We talked, catching up, until his wife politely interrupted and reminded him that if they didn't hurry, they would be late for the Synagogue. He turned to me and we both stared at each other. My professor's great hidden secret had been inadvertently compromised by his wife who knew nothing of the mystery. We both began laughing.

I've often thought about what he taught me. Since then, I've realized that all faiths are based on two major components: (1) Love one another, and (2) Pay homage to the Creator (what I like to refer to as "Source Energy" or "the Universal Consciousness").

If that same message were taught to everyone on a mandatory basis, how many thousands of lives would be saved every year? How many wars would have been averted? How many millions would be affected? How would the world be? When you consider there is only *one* God, no matter whether you call him Lord, Jehovah, Allah, Yahweh, Eloah, Bhagwan, Ishvara, Vishnu, Krishna, Universal Consciousness, Source Energy, or any other name, what are we all fighting about?

This actually forms the basic premise of the seventh toxicity, which is actually very simple. A person has spiritual toxicity any time they feel someone else does *not* have the right to believe something that contradicts their own personal doctrine. It's this rigidity of their personal philosophy that causes the seventh toxicity. The more flexible and accepting one is, the less likely they suffer from this toxicity.

The actions of someone with the seventh toxicity, at best, are annoying. At their worst, they can be criminal and murderous. In either case, a spiritually toxic person claims superiority over another human being, declaring they have no right to exist simply because they have a different belief. In fact, more people have been killed in the name of God throughout history than all other causes of death combined. So how is it that throughout history, all religions believe God is a loving and merciful God, yet kill each other in God's name???

The great Eastern philosopher and father of Taoism, Lao Tzu, said that as babies, we are smooth and supple, like grass waving in the wind. As we get older, we become hard, brittle like reeds and break easily. To make an interesting analogy here would be that flexibility denotes strength. The stronger you are, the more flexible you are, which would follow that the stronger your belief in God, the more flexible and accepting you must be. Make sure you remain strong enough to bend, no matter what your belief.

An Outside Job

I'd like to leave you with one final note on toxicity. Whether it's a heavy metal, cell phone radiation, negative relationship or religious fanaticism, toxicity is an outside job. Your body is the gold standard in efficient mechanical functioning. It will continue to serve you well all throughout your life unless you allow one or more of these toxicities inside. We've all been taught over and over that we are victims to our genetics. How many times have you heard someone say that their father, mother, brother or sister had a particular condition, and they were just biding their time until they came down with it as well? Science has clearly proven that this simply is not so. *We are not helpless victims of our genes.* Unfortunately, a lot of people almost lay out the welcome mat for disease, in complete resignation. Remember: where attention goes, energy flows!

You are not a single living entity but a collection of 50 to 70 trillion living entities called cells. The famous cell biologist Bruce H. Lipton, MD, PhD, describes in his book *The Biology of Belief* how cells from the same specimen can be divided up into two groups. One sample is placed in a positive environment, while the other in a negative, loud, dark or otherwise toxic environment. The cells in the positive, light, supportive environment thrive. The cells (with the same DNA) in the negative environment become diseased. Healthy cells that build a healthy body are determined by our individual perceptions and the external environment within which we immerse them.

I remember seeing Dr. Lipton's work for the first time and laughing out loud. Here was a man who was validating all my clinical work with a theory that was beautiful and resonated with the truth. Somehow I'd been intuitively making these changes with my patients all along—what I refer to as *shifts*—although they were only partially intuitive. They were mostly based upon the sound principles of human physiology. It's no wonder that most of my patients make some amazing recoveries. From the food we eat to the thoughts we think, we choose, moment to moment, what we put into our bodies. When we choose to remove toxins from our bodies and refuse to allow them back into our own environment, it's impossible for chronic disease to exist. And therein lies the real power.

Each of these seven toxicities warrants far more attention than I can give in the limited space I have available. But a brief discussion of each of them was essential to establish the foundation of all chronic disease. I would encourage you to visit the website www.FactsOnToxcity.com and watch the nine videos you'll find there to better explain the seven toxicities and their relationship to chronic disease. Each of these nine videos is ten to twelve minutes long and is completely free. I just ask one thing in return. If you find these videos to be valuable, I want you to make the commitment to "pay it forward" and share this valuable resource with others whom you love and care about.

Health is a state of complete physical, mental and social well-being, and not merely the absence of disease or infirmity.
—WORLD HEALTH ORGANIZATION

13

BEYOND THE 9 STEPS

*Buttar is the bumblebee of medicine. A bumblebee defies
all known laws of aerodynamics. It is impossible for a
bumblebee to fly! But the bumblebee doesn't know about
the laws of aerodynamics and is too foolish to realize
it's not supposed to be able to fly. So it just flies.*
—DEAN C. VIKTORA, PhD
LABORATORY DIRECTOR, V-SAB MEDICAL LABS, INC.

A Word on Detoxification

Congratulations! I applaud you for getting this far and making
such an enormous commitment to yourself and your loved ones
to take back control of your own health. Embrace these 9 Steps
and your life will never again be the same. You've been given a

road map to optimum health, regardless of your current health status. It's my sincere desire for you to live the life you deserve, one that's filled with vitality and happiness. Every single person *can* have this, but it won't be served on a silver platter for you!

Do these 9 Steps always work? In a word, "Yes" . . . they always work! They are not based on theory or even merely my experience. Rather, they are based on natural law—the immutable laws by which the Creator designed the human body and all its self-healing systems. Depending on your current state of health before embarking on the 9 Steps, it may take you longer than others. You may even need the intervention of a competent and experienced physician who can help you get to this point until you no longer need them. In fact, that's always been my primary goal when I treat someone: to get them to a point where their own innate healing mechanisms become functional again and they no longer need me.

If you fall into this category of having a major medical condition—or having a condition that has your doctor baffled to the point they're trying one medication after another, desperately trying to get you some relief—then this last chapter will be the most important one for you. I would strongly urge you to review the Three Foundations again, especially the first one, detoxification. I urge you to make the commitment to pursue the proper methods of detoxification indicated for your condition. I also strongly suggest that you begin your journey back to health by, first and foremost, understanding the necessity for proper detoxification. If you don't achieve *effective* detoxification, you will *never* regain what you hoped to be able to regain.

If any of the patients' stories you've read here resonate with you, or if you recognize some of their situations, it's in your best interest to find a doctor who understands the seven toxicities. If your story is nothing like the ones you read except that you could relate to the frustration or hopelessness in cases where all treatments attempted simply failed, or if your story is just that none of the specialists can figure out what's wrong with you, then you especially need to see a doctor who understands the seven toxicities.

No matter what you may be dealing with, be it heavy metals, persistent organic pollutants, or one of the other forms of body burden I've mentioned, there are specific detoxification methods to address each individual concern. By ridding your body of these roadblocks, you can make the journey back to health—to a place that's not just a mere existence but one where you thrive and grow and actually *live* your life again. If you're going to such great lengths to reclaim your God-given state of natural health, you need all the advantages on your side.

The only thing that can derail your progress is if your body is not properly detoxified. I cannot overemphasize the monumental importance of detoxification in any healing process. Unless the toxic burden is lifted from your body, your body will not be able to mend itself effectively. That's why many people who make a sincere commitment to reclaim their health finally quit, discouraged and bewildered after failing to see the results they expected. The reason they fail is because they either never knew there was a hidden component sabotaging them every step of the way or they didn't know how to effectively eliminate that sabotaging component. Their body wasn't able to divert resources to getting better and healing because it was too busy trying to simply survive, continuously spending all its resources putting out the internal fires of inflammation and oxidation.

There are two routes that you can pursue to determine an effective course of action for your particular situation. First, review the videos on toxicity as previously mentioned. Next, proceed to the members-only area at www.The9Steps.com, which you have free access to as a book owner. There, you will find the two options you can pursue. The first is using the Advanced Health Evaluation and Assessment for Detoxification, Medical Assessment Program, or AHEAD MAP. The second is finding the right doctor within a reasonable distance who has special training to help you regain your God-given right to live a happy and healthy life. You can choose one of these great physicians to help you begin your journey back to recovery.

I'll just mention here that I personally handpicked this select list of doctors. They were *not* able to buy their position on this list, and they were selected not only on the basis of their medical ability but also on their attitude toward healing. Obviously, I can't guarantee they'll be able to help you, but what I can guarantee is that they are exceptional doctors and they will do everything they can to help you get better.

A Word on the Philosophy of Healing

Make sure that you are comfortable with the physician you choose to help you in your journey to recovery and maintain open lines of communication with them. Never compromise on who your doctor is because a good doctor is as rare of a commodity as a good mechanic. When you find one and you "connect" with him or her, you know you're on your way to regaining your health.

Never take anyone's word for anything, especially when it comes to your health. That goes for me as well. Just because I wrote it here, don't take my word blindly. Do your own research and search for the truth. It will become very evident to you as long as you keep your mind and your heart open and receptive. There are far too many doctors, health regulators, politicians, health systems, insurance companies and pharmaceutical corporations who are willing to compromise your well-being for their personal profit. Hopefully, you didn't need to hear this from me and you were already aware of this intuitively. However, what you may not recognize—yet this is essential in order for you to fully recover—is that you *must* take responsibility. *You* are ultimately responsible for your own health.

To blame a book, doctor or TV show for advice that may not be accurate for you is just an excuse to shift responsibility to someone else. By doing so, you are essentially giving your power away to someone else. When it comes to your own health, don't blindly believe everything you read or see on TV. In fact, don't believe *most* of it. Always challenge the source of the information and trust your instincts when it comes to the validity of the message being presented. Never be afraid to question a doctor. Even me! If a doctor is offended that you questioned them, here's a little advice: Find a different doctor! As physicians, we may be wearing the white lab coat and carrying the big title, but *you* are the expert when it comes to your own body. Only you know how your body reacts and feels "inside."

The most sophisticated piece of machinery God created was the body you're living in right now. Human beings have yet to create anything that comes even close to the intelligence and resiliency of the very body they inhabit. When it comes to sheer efficiency, even the most complex computer systems fade in comparison. Part of the marvel of this machine we call our body is how it was designed to react in certain scenarios. We've come to call the study of these reactions and processes "physiology." Take time to sit quietly and listen to what your body is telling you. Listen to your physiology and let it tell you. Deep down, your body knows what it needs and is speaking to you all the time. Never second-guess it, and always follow your intuition, especially when it comes to asking the questions you need to have answered. Never hesitate to ask and always listen for the answer.

Getting Out of the Way

When the most sophisticated biological organism gives us a message that something harmful needs to be moved out immediately, does it makes sense to block the process? In our arrogance of going against the natural design of the human body, we claim to be more intelligent than the One who created it, and in response, we suffer from the consequences of our meddling. More accurately, the *patient* suffers the consequences. In a situation where the symptom would last only three to four days before the body "self corrects," we arrest the process of correction, forcing the body to keep the toxins inside where they do more damage over a longer period of time.

Let's look at an example using a very common problem that physicians try to deal with to illustrate this point. Let's use a case of diarrhea, for instance. Typically speaking, diarrhea is a natural response to some sort of gastrointestinal irritation. It could be an infection from a bacteria or a virus, or it could be because something you consumed was not fit to be consumed or going bad. Generally, diarrhea is self-limiting, meaning that it will go away by itself and usually lasts just two to four days. In certain conditions, diarrhea can last for far greater periods if there is a serious underlying issue, but this isn't typical.

In the vast majority of cases, the culprit is a virus or bacteria (food poisoning) and the diarrhea is the body's natural detoxifying response to expel it as quickly as possible. In fact, that's how God designed our systems, with a feedback mechanism built in. If you touch something hot, you immediately pull your hand back. Similarly, when you ingest something that is detrimental to the body, it will respond with vomiting or diarrhea or both to get rid of the offending substance you ingested. Still, doctors just love to prescribe medicines to *stop* the diarrhea. Why? By doing so, a condition that would have lasted a few days now takes seven to ten days to resolve.

One of the editors reviewing this manuscript commented that the explanation I just presented didn't address why doctors prescribe the medication that causes the condition to last longer. In the interest of clarity, allow me to explain. Doctor's don't prescribe to make it (diarrhea, in this example) last longer. Doctors are trained *to* prescribe, and that makes the condition being treated last longer.

The Warnings

It's this type of approach in medicine that has gained favor in the last fifty years and has come to be known as "symptom management." Masking symptoms with medication is a dangerous trend that has gone on for far too long. If you keep turning up the radio so you don't hear the knocking in your car engine, the motor will eventually burn up completely. Outside of emergency care for broken bones and trauma, modern medicine has made an art form out of getting *in the way* of the infinitely intelligent processes of the human body—to disastrous effect.

Having said that, however, and in defense of doctors, I have to say that that's all we've been taught to do—how to "block" things. That's why we (doctors) use "beta blockers" and "calcium channel blockers" and so on. In fact, the mechanism of practically every drug is to block something from happening. That's mostly what medicine has become today, getting in the way of the body and preventing it from doing its own work. Common sense dictates that we should allow the "bad stuff" to get out. Who'd want to carry around a backpack full of liquidy, smelly, festering stool for the next seven days?

Yet, that's exactly what tens of thousands of people are doing every day when they are unnecessarily prescribed medication for diarrhea. This holds true for every message your body gives you, whether it's a heartburn, headache, rash, swelling, allergies or anything else. An outward manifestation is *always* a signal to look deeper and find the cause. To cover up the symptom with a drug is like removing the fuse from the warning indicator on the dashboard of your car.

Sure, you don't see the symptom anymore because the fuse was taken out. We're now lulled into our false sense of security because the flashing light on the dashboard is no longer flashing and *annoying* us. But it was that very symptom you covered up (removed) that was trying to warn you that your engine is about to blow. And if you ignore the symptom or cover it up, your engine *will* blow. The body knows what it needs to do. The problem is most of us keep hitting the override switch of our body's signaling systems, and when that's not sufficient, we go to a doctor and have *them* override the system with stronger over riders meant to block even more reactions.

The bottom line is that "killing" the messenger (symptom) with a drug is never the smartest or best course of action. In fact, it's the *worst* possible option you can choose. Listen to your body! Embrace the signals it's providing. Don't suppress the message by covering it up. And run from any doctor who simply wants to flip you a prescription and push you out the door. You deserve better. And if you want to get healthier and stay healthier, you must *demand* better.

Good Medicine Is Your Choice

There are many doctors practicing in multiple specialties with long titles. It doesn't matter if the doctor is trained in cardiology, neurology, rheumatology, gynecology, oncology or anything else. There are really only two specialties in medicine—methods that work *with* the body and methods that work *against* it. Patients continue to leave conventional medicine in droves for treatments that work *with* their bodies, treatments that bring *real* healing. This philosophy has been called a lot of things over the years, from alternative medicine to integrative medicine, from holistic medicine to natural medicine. I simply choose to call it *Good Medicine* or more appropriately, *Advanced Medicine*.

It's true that on the rare occasion (very rare), I may opt to use a drug, but it's always prescribed for a specific limited period of time. Regardless of what I use or how I treat a person, it will *always* be with the understanding of physiology and the intervention that works with the innate intelligence of the patient's body.

Many people think that when they become healthy, they'll be happy. However, it's the other way around. Happy, joyous people are quite often the healthiest. Your attitude has far more to do with your health than you may even realize. The good news for you is that your state of mind is completely within your own control and you have full power to change it however you see fit.

I once read that happiness is governed by the "3 Cs of Life": compromises, choices and consequences. Most people continuously compromise their entire lives, only to find that the choices they *could* have made would have prevented them from having to face the consequences of those compromises. Be brave when it comes to your health. Make the bold choice. It may not be the easiest thing to do at the time, but remember, the universe always gives a reward equal to or greater than in proportion to the risk taken.

Take the risk to be happy—*really* happy! Yes, it *is* a choice to find the good in your day and focus on it all day. We've all seen a person who has had a life plagued with one misfortune after another and yet greets everyone with a smile. How do they do it? It's no secret. They just choose to be happy. A happier person has a happier biochemistry and a happier biochemistry means happier cells, which create a healthier body. This may be oversimplifying things, but you get the point.

There's a saying that goes, "What *you* think of me is none of *my* business." Wiser words were never spoken. People can think what they want about you. They can even say what they want about you. It happens to me ***all the time!*** But just because someone says it, it doesn't make it *true*. Only you know *your truth*. Nothing has the power to change that. It reminds me of a line from another children's movie: "No matter how the wind howls and screams, the mountain will never bend to it." Once you're anchored in your truth, no one can ever make you feel any specific way without your permission. When you allow someone to hurt or upset you, it's not their fault. You just violated your own truth. Take your power back and remember who you really are. How you feel is all about you and up to you.

Empowerment Often Begins in Your Body

One of the added reasons why I emphasize detoxification so often is because by rediscovering and learning to honor the healing power of our bodies, we become aware of something very profound and miraculous within ourselves. Most of us have been raised and (unfortunately) indoctrinated in a way that we've never been conscious of our body's remarkable power to heal itself. To be honest, what makes the biggest difference for my patients is this awareness—that *their body* is doing the healing. I'm actually nothing more than a glorified trash removal expert, a "sanitation engineer" of the physiology, removing toxicities from the body.

The real healing is that my work simply helps them to detoxify; their body's own healing intelligence kicks in and then the miracles take place. It really isn't me at all—and this revelation frees them from depending on me or any other authority for the rest of their lives. If there's one insight you take from this book, I hope it's that your body is a miracle, and it can heal itself from virtually anything. Sure, you may need to assist it by removing toxins or feeding it the right nutrients, but with the right pieces in place, your body will do the healing. Nothing else is necessary—not me, not any drug, not any supplement. Of course, it's one thing to know this and it's another thing to *experience* it in your own actual life.

That, my friend, is what will change everything for you. I promise! Because once you have this understanding and insight, no one can take that away from you. Not now, not ever. I mentioned a moment ago that true empowerment can begin in your body. What did I mean by that? Well, it's simple: Health is the most basic need we have on this planet. We take it for granted when it's there, but when our health is threatened—as in the case of a terminal illness—it suddenly becomes our number one priority.

If people feel that their health lies outside their hands—whether the causes are genetic, environmental or anything else—then they must rely on an authority for the solution. This effectively removes their own power and places it into the hands of others. Instead, what I'm suggesting and promoting—this awareness of your body's own healing intelligence—serves to empower you in a profound way. Once you have this awareness, you don't need anyone or anything. You can never be sold a drug, a supplement or anything else that your body doesn't truly need to heal itself.

What's more, there's no substitute for the confidence that comes from knowing that you have the ability to heal yourself. You no longer have to fear the same health challenges everyone else does, and you will naturally make better choices because you fundamentally understand that you are the one who determines what happens within your own body. Everything—your weight, your appearance, your energy levels—it all comes down to your awareness and your choices. This is the root of your power, and reclaiming your health is often the best first step. You can begin reclaiming your health immediately by implementing these 9 Steps you've just learned.

Final Thoughts

I once read of a problem readers experience upon reaching the last few pages of a book. Like me, most of you have probably experienced this frustration, where although you were enlightened on the subject, confusion still exists. We're confused because despite understanding the material better, we still have questions that are not answered. This apparently is inevitable because the "unanswered questions" exist due to the author of the material having a specific fixed agenda.

It's necessary for the author to have a fixed agenda because there must be a "point" to the book. The problem, however, is that this fixed agenda is not *your* agenda. The questions in your mind may not be the same questions answered by the author. Or the author's questions may not relate to you in particular. Or new questions have arisen as you read the material. And so, you're stuck. I first became aware of this even before beginning college. When I realized this was not a unique frustration, I promised myself that when I wrote my first book, I would ensure that this problem would be solved.

I have addressed this issue with the following solution. In the members-only area of the book owners' website (www. The9Steps.com), there will be an exclusive discussion board that will give you the opportunity to ask me any question regarding the content of the book. You will also have the ability to interact with and to benefit from the support and experience of other book readers as you post questions, answers and comments on any topic relevant to the content of the book. Please understand that I cannot answer any specific medical questions due to medical liability issues. The ability to engage in these discussions also will be restricted to those who are book owners; the reason why will become clearly obvious when you first sign in.

When it comes to healing, consistency is the name of the game. Keeping in a consistently positive frame of mind as you go through these 9 Steps on a daily basis is what's going to get you to your goal. Most people see significant improvement within the first three to six weeks. Invariably, however, after a certain time, they usually feel so good that they slowly start to slip, thinking they don't need to live by the 9 Steps any longer, and they begin to revert to the choices that led to their disorder, condition or lack of health in the first place. When these problems begin to resurface and the patient comes back to me, I always ask why they stopped practicing the 9 Steps. I've been amazed at the reply I most often get back. "I stopped doing the 9 Steps because I got better."

Remember, the 9 Steps are not a "symptom management" form of medicine. In fact, the 9 Steps are not any type of medicine. They are a lifestyle! They are a philosophy that is only worth something if you *choose* to live by it. Can you do this? Of course you can. Anyone can! The question is, "Will you do this?" That's the question that only you can answer. As long as you keep on keeping on with the 9 Steps, you'll continue to enjoy the benefits of vibrant good health. And as you do, let no excuse get in your way. Put yourself first and remember the following pearls I have accumulated over the years:

1. Express your love for those you care about on a regular basis. And express it to them. It's not sufficient to tell others how much you love your children or your wife. Tell your children and your wife or other loved ones. Show them.

2. Live in a state of gratitude. If you can't think of what you have to be grateful for, think of all the people who are homeless,

hungry, missing an arm or a leg or all alone . . . and suddenly you'll have much to be grateful about.

3. Show me something you *think* you desperately need, and I'll show you hundreds of others who get along perfectly well without it.

4. Accept that some days you will be the pigeon, and on other days you'll be the statue. Remember however that regardless of whether you are the pigeon or the statue, everything that happens has a specific purpose. Nothing occurs randomly. Regardless of what you choose to believe, this is fact.

5. Remember that when you think someone else has an attitude problem, it may actually be you who has a perception problem. Look to yourself and see how you can improve. Those around you will automatically change as you do.

6. On the keyboard of life, always keep one finger on the escape key. Choose not to suffer from stress. There is nothing wrong with "healthy" conflict, like arguing which ball team is going to win the game or a spirited debate about religion or politics. But if the arguing makes you feel sick, it's no longer a healthy conflict. Do not engage. Nothing is worth getting ill about.

7. When you're worried about your own situation, find someone else to help; invariably, your source of worry will dissipate. There is empowerment in helping others.

8. Never argue with an idiot. They will always drag you down to *their* level, and then proceed to beat you with experience. Remember that the best revenge is living a good life.

9. When confronted by a difficult problem, you can always solve it easily by reducing the problem to a question, such as, "How would Spider-Man handle this?"

10. The three things that no human has a monopoly on are Love, God and stupidity. So when you encounter someone with *more* than their allotted share of stupidity, say a prayer of gratitude. Because they just left *more* Love and God for you.

11. Always do the right things in life. You know what they are. Your body will resonate to them. Use the tool you'll be given at the end of this book to always know what the right answer is when faced with any decision in life.

12. Make it a point to put a smile on someone else's face every day. It will come back to you magnified. Do this as much as possible. Keep count of how many smiles you create and try to exceed that number every day.

Everyone comes to this Earth with a purpose. Find yours and life will begin to taste sweeter. You didn't come here to suffer in order to learn. Knowledge is power, and you now have the tools to re-create the health of your youth or the health you've always dreamed you would like to have. It's all up to you now! Move forward with boldness and the universe will smile upon you. It's guaranteed.

I do not deny that medicine is a gift of God, nor do I refuse to acknowledge science in the skill of many physicians; but, take the best of them. How far are they from perfection? A sound regimen produces excellent effects. When I feel indisposed, by observing a strict diet and going to bed early, I generally manage to get round again, that is, if I can keep my mind tolerably at rest. I have no objection to the doctors acting upon certain theories, but, at the same time, they must not expect us to be the slaves of their fancies.
—MARTIN LUTHER

EPILOGUE

All I have seen teaches me to trust the Creator for all I have not seen.
—Ralph Waldo Emerson

Claim Your Power and Make the Change

Good health is among life's most noble goals, and I believe there are three things that are absolutely essential for everyone to know when setting goals and working to achieve them. It's the difference between success and failure. You need to *believe, choose* and then take *action*. No matter how difficult your situation is, remember that it could always be worse. I'm not trying to be insensitive when I ask you to consider on a daily basis what someone else might be enduring that's worse than your situation. Hunger, poverty and violent atrocities are occurring every day around us, all over the world. No matter where you are, you have blessings that you can count. Never forget that. Be *grateful* and move forward in life by *believing* in yourself, *choosing* to move forward and taking immediate *action*.

What would you say if I told you that you could overcome any obstacle and achieve anything you can imagine? I mean, *really* overcome anything! Would you laugh at me or say I was crazy? Would you change your mind if I told you that this information is far beyond the realm of "positive thinking"? It's absolute reality and scientifically supported by researchers and Nobel Prize laureates from all over the world. When you extract the emotion from your current situation (fear, doubt, uncertainty) and examine it from the objective viewpoint of quantum physics, there is nothing you cannot be, do or have. And the choice of what those things are is completely up to you.

As Henry Ford said, "Whether you think you can or can't, either way—you're right." It's all about believing you can do it. It doesn't matter if what you desire involves better relationships, finances, career options or health. If it generates such a passion inside you to the point where you will accept no other outcome than the one you desire, you *will* have it. If your resolve is 100 percent, you will see it done in your life. I am a living testimony to that, as are some of my patients who were told they were terminal and only had a few months left to live after having failed chemo and radiation with cancer-riddled bodies. But today, years later, they are still alive and living a productive and happy life. How did they do this? They simply *made a choice* and then appropriately *took immediate action*.

For those who doubt, go to either www.DrButtar.com or www.DrButtarTruth.org and watch a few of the videos. The proof has been videotaped. You can choose to believe what others with an agenda will brainwash you with, or you can trust your own eyes and ears. In either case, you're the only one who will benefit from or suffer the consequence of your own decision. Remember that you *always* have a choice. Whether it's what you put in your mouth, do with your body, the thoughts you think or the relationships you choose to cultivate, you will reap the reward or suffer the consequences. Use your own intuition as a guide and you'll always make the right choice. Intuition is the voice of God, and it resonates on a much deeper level than your intellect. Just make sure you're listening!

Once you have the belief, you next have to select the path to travel. You must choose. If you're caught in a situation and you don't know where to turn, the answer is often closer than you think. My experience has shown me that the right path is very rarely the easiest one. You can take the smooth, wide road with no challenges, but the question is, how well do you sleep at night?

The speed bumps are challenges life puts in our path to condition us, carve out our character and make us who we are. That's what makes achievement so sweet. Sometimes it may not even be the achievement itself but the simple act of taking action. It's about having the person looking back at you from the mirror each morning being pleased with how you're living your life. It's about *not* having any regrets as we prepare to transition into the next realm as our lives come to completion. It's about who you made a difference for and how you leave the world a better place.

There's a saying that goes—*If you've never had anything bad happen to you, then you can't be that interesting.* Eleanor Roosevelt also made it clear when she said, *Do one thing every day that scares you.* When you make the tough choices, you make the right choice. The universe rewards the risk-takers, and the bigger the risk, the bigger the reward. The biggest risks almost always involve doing something we think we can't do. Regardless of the obstacles you see in your way and the voice in your head that's telling you you'll never make it—do it anyway.

All decisions you will have to make in life come down to different motivations and causes. All these various motivations and causes can be distilled down to two root motivations. These two root motivations ultimately dictate every decision you make and are faced with and come into play every time you have to make any decision in life. These two root causes determine everything you do based on the choice you make. One of these root causes is love. The other is fear. Whatever you're faced with in life, you will make the choice ultimately either based on love or based on fear. You may *think* there is another root cause, but you would be wrong. Everything can be distilled down to either love or fear.

Here's the funny part, though. One of these root causes is *real!* The other is nothing more than an illusion, simply existing just in your mind, created completely by our own imagination! Love is real. It's the basis of all that is good. Fear, on the other hand, is completely an illusion. And yet, most people on this planet make decisions based on fear . . . not love! If people were to make their decisions based upon love, our planet would be in a completely different state right now. When your mind is running in ten different directions and you start to feel overwhelmed in having to make a decision, put your mental brakes on. Clear out the mental noise and ask yourself this simple question, "In this decision I'm faced with, which choice is motivated by love? And which choice is motivated by fear?" The answer will appear, clearer than if it was carved in stone. All you have to do now is make the *choice*.

Once you have belief and you have chosen your path, the only thing left to do is take action. Take *immediate action*. Whatever you fear, move into it without hesitation. The strange thing with fear is that as soon as you move into it, it dissipates and disintegrates and completely vanishes. It actually has no choice but to dissipate because fear lives *only* in your imagination. Once you've moved into it, your reality overrides and shows you that what you feared in your imagination has just been invalidated by reality. There is no other choice since you've just pushed reality into the world of the imaginary fear. Experiment with this. It's actually a lot of fun.

By the time your mind is in the middle of justifying and rationalizing the reason for allowing the fear illusion to dictate your actions, you've already moved into it. You'll find yourself scratching your head afterward trying to remember exactly why you had any fear of taking the action you just took. Remember that it was that action you took that invalidated the fear.

Whenever you ever feel helpless, lost, scared or afraid, simply stop and realize that it's the fear that you're feeling or experiencing. You now know that fear is nothing more than an illusion and that fear only gets its power from your imagination. Remember, where attention goes, energy flows. Do not allow your energy to feed your imagination. When you focus on what you want and give that your attention, your energy will begin to flow toward that upon which you are focusing. You now have all the power you need and more, in every single moment of your life. My prayer for you is that you will personally experience the limitless power that exists and lies hidden inside each and every single one of us on this planet. It's the power of God, of Source Energy. It's *your* God energy!

So now, it's all up to you. It's your *choice*. Make it a good one!

Believe nothing, no matter where you read it, or who said it, no matter if I have said it, unless it agrees with your own reason and your own common sense.

—BUDDHA

INDEX

ACKNOWLEDGMENTS

Before acknowledging all who are due appreciation, let me just say I apologize in advance for inadvertently missing anyone. I hope you will forgive me for any oversight if I forgot to mention you specifically, but remember that my appreciation for you exists even though my memory may be faltering.

First and foremost, I wish to thank my gorgeous better half and love, Debbie, my beautiful and gifted daughter, Sarah, and my incredibly talented and amazing sons, Abie and Hanni, for tolerating my continued distraction from their lives and for their unconditional love. I would also like to thank my parents for giving me birth and putting up with me (and still putting up with me), as well as my sister and both my brothers and their respective beautiful families; I am blessed to have such special nieces and nephews.

A heartfelt "thank-you" to members of my immediate team who helped with the book, including Luke Cowles, Marie-Pierre Blanchette, Melissa Lingle, Kimmy Dell, Anthony Flores, and Joshua Pettit, each of whom helped me directly or indirectly finish this book and subsequent book-related projects. I am firmly convinced Josh and Anthony, especially—the two wingless angels— were sent by God himself to help me in all my work.

To the editorial and production team at Greenleaf Publishing, which includes Lisa Woods, Sheila Parr, Linda O'Doughda, Bill Crawford, Lari Bishop, Bryan Carroll and Justin Branch, all of whom were instrumental in making everything finally come together in such a perfect way, thank you for your professionalism, talent and attention to detail.

To all my incredible patients who continually teach me, thank you for providing me with the phenomenal feedback in a constructive manner that helps us improve what we do and how we do it and for providing me with the motivation for our work to continue on a daily basis.

To my close friends who unconditionally support me and would follow me into the depths of hell just to watch my back (and some already have), I'm eternally grateful for having the privilege of calling you my friends. I'm blessed that this list is extensive and you all know who you are, but a few who I am compelled to mention specifically include Sal Bharwani, Tom Bader, Dr. John Trowbridge, Dr. Kevin Craft, Dr. Victor Marcial-Vega, Dr. Jim Smith, Greg Provenzano, Alden Butcher, Dr. Jim Hawver, Sam Abukittah, Tracey Nathan, John Malherbe, Dr. Robin Bernhoft, Dr. Dianne Farley Jones, Dr. James Holbert, Dr. Bob Marshall and Greg Adams.

"One great friend, who I especially want to thank, honored me by writing the foreword to this book. Known in the highest of circles for the extent of his vision, devoutness of his belief, magnitude of his generosity and strength of his faith, Aymen Boughanmi is a mountain among men. A constant student of learning, he is

98% heart and has become a close confidant. I am very grateful he accepted my invitation to write the foreword."

To my extremely talented, dedicated and loyal staff, without whom I would not be able to do a fraction of what I do, I thank you all for being in my life and for supplying the source of passion that allowed this book to finally come to fruition. Special thanks are due to Tasha Claridge, Jenna Bryan, Tim Reid, Nina Wall, Robin Wines, Amanda Elliott, Ilona Alvarez and Johnny Gryglewicz, as well as Amber Goode and Mark Viktora at the lab.

And to the two people instrumental in my life without whom I would be unable to function professionally (and who I never fail to remind that they are a pain in my rear), a very special thank-you that words simply won't capture to my associate Jane Garcia Grubbs, APN, and my partner Dean C. Viktora, PhD.

To my colleagues who constantly practice the true art of medicine while under the massive and real threat of being restricted, fined or even imprisoned, you are the ones who inspire me to fight. Each of you continues to do "the only right thing" for your patients even though you risk almost certain prosecution from the hierarchy that has much to lose if the world learns the truth. I appreciate each of you more than you realize.

Naturally, I also can't forget my attorneys who may have thought I was crazy in the beginning, but now tirelessly fight to defend something far greater than just me, my name or my work.

Last, and most important, I thank the Creator, the source of all energy and beauty, the all-knowing Universal Consciousness, the "Only True Healer" for His guidance and for His allowing me to be a conduit of His incomprehensible power. I am grateful to just be in His presence. May I be worthy of all the countless blessings He has bestowed upon me.

RESOURCES

The resource section of a book is often the most important because it directs the reader to further resources that the reader has an interest in or from which the reader may benefit. However, I have found that the resource section of most books tends to become outdated more often than the authors would like to admit. Sometimes, information that is of greater benefit comes to fruition only after the book has been published. Other times, the resource mentioned may change the quality of their information, product or service, and so the recommendation originally made is no longer valid. Essentially, the inability to update resources in a book prevents the resource section to be as valuable as it could be.

As a result, we have created a dynamic resource section in the "members-only area" of the "book owners' website." The purpose of this website-based resource section is to provide you with up-to-date information, resources and recommendations while, at the same time, providing "the next level" of information for those who desire it. One of the greatest components of the book owners' website resource section is the "Community Forum." Here, you can ask questions, gain insight, share experiences and advance your knowledge, all by engaging with other book owners as well as a few highly selected special doctors, my staff and myself.

In addition, you will have special discounts for many different items available only to book owners. For example, all book owners will enjoy special permanent discounts from one of the only places to have fully certified organic foods (including produce, meats, dairy, etc.) shipped directly to your front door, overnight.

There is no cost to join this members-only book owners' website. We just ask that you NOT share your password with others who are not book owners. Go to www.The9Steps.com and register. Be sure to have your book with you because the first time you log in, you will need the book in order to access the website.

To Find a Good Doctor

www.CentersForAdvancedMedicine.com—A highly select group of physicians who have distinguished themselves from their peers, hand picked by Dr. Buttar, who have trained and are well versed in Dr. Buttar's methods and protocols.

www.AMESPA.org—Doctors trained in Dr. Buttar's methods and have attended Dr. Buttar's physician training course.

www.ABCMT.org—Doctors who have received proper training and are board certified or board eligible in addressing heavy metal toxicity through the American Board of Clinical Metal Toxicology.

Recommended Books

This is only a partial list of recommended reading.

- *Beating Cancer with Nutrition* by Dr. Patrick Quillin
- *Cancer: Step Outside the Box* by Ty M. Bollinger
- *The Hidden Messages in Water* by Masaru Emoto and David A. Thayne
- *Healing Poisoned Medicine: Medicine to Heal or Medicine to Kill* by Dr. Reed Sainsbury
- *Our Toxic World: A Wake Up Call* by Dr. Doris J. Rapp
- *Politics in Healing: The Suppression & Manipulation of American Medicine* by Daniel Haley
- *Racketeering in Medicine: The Suppression of Alternatives* by Dr. James P. Carter
- *Detoxify For Life!* by Dr. John Cline

Benefits of the Book Owners' Website

The Three Foundations

Systemic Detoxification, Immune Modulation and Hormonal Optimization

You will receive access to the Advanced Health Evaluation and Assessment for Detoxification, Medical Assessment Program, or AHEAD MAP for short. This assessment program and clinical evaluation tool was compiled with over 150 years of clinical experience behind it and will assess the four areas of detoxification of your body, plus your pH status. This is a $300 assessment that you can access at no charge. You will be given a score at the end after taking the assessment, and every 30 to 45 days, you can repeat the AHEAD MAP to see how you have improved. To access the AHEAD MAP, log onto www.The9Steps.com.

Step 1—Nutrition

Details are available at www.The9Steps.com.

Step 2—Supplementation

There are only four brands of Supplements recommended by Dr. Buttar. There may be others that are good products but of all the brands Dr. Buttar has used and tested, these are the only four Dr. Buttar recommends. Of these four, "**Garden of Life**" is the only one available over the counter directly to the consumer.

Two of these brands are used by health practitioners and are only available through these professional channels. Both are used in a unique manner with direct energetic feed back from the patient/client. One is **Standard Enzyme** and the other is **Premier Research Laboratories (PRL)**.

The **Standard Enzyme** practitioners use a unique and advanced form of electro-dermal testing known as CSA (Computerized Stress Analysis) to evaluate and determine the energetic and nutritional needs unique to that individual client / patient. This technology optimizes the 5000 year ancient science of acupuncture and catapults it into the 21st Century.

The **Premier Research Laboratories (PRL)** practitioners also use a revolutionary method of analyzing the body's biofield using Quantum Reflex Analysis (QRA) to determine the hierarchy of physical requirements needed by the client / patient. This identifies precise detoxification needs and nutritional imbalances to most rapidly restore ideal health for each individual.

The last brand recommended by Dr. Buttar is **Balance Nutraceuticals**. This brand is the only medical brand available exclusively through medical professionals (DO's and MD's) and is available at select medical offices throughout the world. More details on all four brands are available at www.The9Steps.com.

Step 3—Water

Wellness Filter discounts and information on exciting advances in water technology are available at www.The9Steps.com.

Step 4—Exercise

Dr. Al Sears PACE book and program—special discount

12-Minute Fat Loss Protocol exercise program—free online

Dr. Buttar's special breathing and stretching program—free online

Access free programs at www.The9Steps.com.

Step 5—Vices

Fantastic and effective self-hypnosis program that will help program your subconscious mind. More details at www.The9Steps.com.

Step 6—Relaxation/Stress Management

Highly effective sleep-induction CDs based on the content of the DVDs. More details are available at www.The9Steps.com.

Step 7—Prayer/Meditation

Meditation CD program which is highly recommended. More details at www.The9Steps.com.

Step 8—Laughter

More details are available at www.The9Steps.com.

Step 9—Physiological Regeneration

For an exclusive offer just for book owners, visit www.The9Steps.com.

The 7 Toxicities

Watch the nine free videos at www.FactsOnToxicity.com.

Miscellaneous

These other websites may be of interest:

- www.DrButtar.com (Clinic)
- www.DrButtarTruth.org
- www.TheMedicalSeries.com
- www.IslandsOfHope.com
- www.CentersForAdvancedMedicine.com
- www.PM3A.com (for physicians only)
- www.AMESPA.com
- www.BuildASuccessfulLife.com

Recommended Newsletters

Health Optimization and Wellness Report (free weekly subscription)—www.DrButtar.com

Second Opinion Newsletter (paid subscription)—www.SecondOpinionNewsletter.com

ABOUT THE AUTHOR

Rashid A. Buttar, DO
FAAPM, FACAM, FAAIM

I first met Dr. Rashid A. Buttar at a medical conference about five years ago. We had much in common. A year later I went to one of his AMESPA physician training courses and was amazed at the effort and creativity he had put into bringing medicine into the 21st century. I have learned a lot from him since. We've written papers together, become good friends and have been close associates ever since.

A 3 palm Eagle Scout, Boy's State selectee and West Point appointee, Dr. Buttar chose to attend Washington University in St. Louis on a full military scholarship. He played varsity football, was a member of Phi Delta Theta, served on the student body and was a ROTC cadet ranger. After earning a double major in Biology and Theology, he attended medical school at the University of Osteopathic Medicine and Health Sciences, College of Medicine and Surgery, in Des Moines, Iowa, and then trained in General Surgery and Emergency Medicine.

Dr. Buttar served with and/or was attached to multiple units, including the 2nd Infantry Division, the 101st Air Assault

Division and the 5th Special Forces Group. He served as Brigade Surgeon for 3rd Brigade, 2nd ID, in the Republic of South Korea and later as Chief, Department of Emergency Medicine, at Moncrief Army Community Hospital at Ft. Jackson in Columbia, South Carolina. Dr. Buttar is board certified and a Diplomate in Clinical Metal Toxicology and Preventive Medicine and is board eligible in Emergency Medicine. He has achieved fellowship status in three separate medical societies: Fellow of the American College for Advancement in Medicine, Fellow of the American Academy of Preventive Medicine and Fellow of the American Association of Integrative Medicine.

Dr. Buttar practices in Charlotte, North Carolina, as the medical director of the Center for Advanced Medicine and Clinical Research. The center specializes in the needs and treatment of patients for whom the standard and conventional treatment approach has failed, attracting patients from forty-two states and thirty-seven different countries. With a special emphasis on the interrelationship between toxicity and the insidious disease process, the center specializes in reducing the resulting oxidative stress and helping those suffering from cancer, autism, heart disease, stroke and many other conditions too numerous to list regain their health and vitality.

Dr. Buttar also serves as Director of Clinical Research and Development for V-SAB Medical Laboratories, where he is involved in research with peptide sequencing and identification technologies as well as innovative methodologies for drug delivery systems. He has presented more than 150 lectures worldwide at scientific congresses and professional symposiums and is frequently invited to speak at medical conferences. Dr. Buttar has been featured in local, national and international media, such as the *Wall Street Journal, US News and World Report* and the *New*

York Times, as well as interviewed by such major TV programs as *20/20, PBS Frontline* and *CBS World News.*

Dr. Buttar has testified before the North Carolina Legislature as well as the United States Congress, giving special testimony before the Congressional Subcommittee on Human Rights and Wellness. He also received a bi-partisan nomination from Congresswoman Diane Watson (CA) and Congressman Dan Burton (IN) for the National Institute of Health's Director's Pioneer Award for his clinical work in metal toxicity and autism. He was in charge of the national training program leading to board certification in metal toxicology through ABCMT and was also a member of the twelve-member National Metals Task Force appointed to address the endemic nature of metal toxicity and the implications on world health. Phillips Publishing, Health Directions Inc. and Dr. Stephen Sinatra have listed Dr. Buttar among the "Top 50 Doctors in the United States" since 2003.

Dr. Buttar currently serves as the Chairman of the American Board of Clinical Metal Toxicology, is the past-President of the North Carolina Integrative Medical Society and the President of the Advanced Medical Education and Services, Physician Association and the Centers for Advanced Medicine Physician Associates. He has served on numerous boards as well as Continuing Medical Education committees for a number of medical organizations and has served as Visiting Scientist and Nutritional Scientist at North Carolina State University. Dr. Buttar continues to teach such mainstream medical courses as Advanced Trauma Life Support through the American College of Surgeons as well as Pediatric Advanced Life Support and Advanced Cardiac Life Support for other physicians, nurses and emergency response personnel.

—Robin A. Bernhoft, MD, FACS
Ojai, California

A SPECIAL GIFT FROM DR. BUTTAR

The following section provides a preview of the award-winning DVD series entitled *Know Your Options, The Medical Series*. These DVDs are available at www.Amazon.com, www.TheMedicalSeries.com and other select online retail outlets.

Each DVD retails for $89.55 and can be purchased separately or in a full set consisting of the 6 available DVDs. However, as our way of thanking you for purchasing *The 9 Steps to Keep the Doctor Away*, we are offering you any one of the 6 currently available DVDs to show you our appreciation.

Please choose any one of the 6 available DVD titles in the *Know Your Options, The Medical Series* collection and we will ship it to you within 72 hours. All you do is pay a few dollars for shipping and handling. Simply go to www.The9Steps.com/FreeDVD to place your order.

In return, all we ask is that if you found the information in *The 9 Steps to Keep the Doctor Away* to be valuable and empowering, "pay it forward" and tell others your experience with the book. Be the hero and direct them to the gift of health and longevity.

Please note that this offer applies only to the DVDs that are already available (1 through 6) and is limited to one DVD per book purchased. Simply visit the link provided to learn how you can get this real $89.55 value for just the price of the shipping and handling.

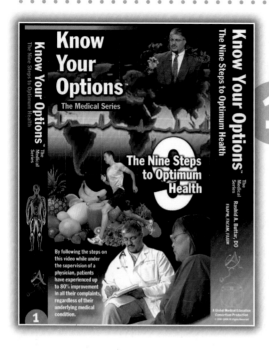

The Nine Steps to Optimum Health

By following the steps on this video while under the supervision of a physician, patients have experienced up to 80% improvement in all their complaints, regardless of their underlying medical condition.

Dr. Buttar's "Nine Steps to Optimum Health" are the foundation of his philosophy and an integral component of his basic treatment plan to optimize the outcome of his patients. These nine steps have been clinically proven over the last nine years to be highly effective. They have also provided the essential frame work in helping not only those patients considered to be "treatment failures," but have helped all category of patients seeking help from Dr. Buttar. The book "The 9 Steps to Keep the Doctor Away" is based on the principles found on this DVD.

Heavy Metal Toxicity The Hidden Killer

The prevalence, incidence and ubiquitous nature of chronic heavy metal toxicity may be the greatest undiagnosed medical condition and the most unrecognized contributory cause of death in the industrialized world.

This program contains the information from Dr. Buttar's seminar used to educate patients on heavy metal toxicity and the impact on chronic disease. 8 out of 10 deaths in the U.S. are due to cancer and/or heart disease. This is especially disturbing when considering both heart disease and cancer have been clearly associated with chronic heavy metal toxicity. Other chronic diseases associated with heavy metals include stroke, vascular disease, neurodegenerative conditions, autoimmune diseases, fibromyalgia and a host of other medical conditions.